BRITISH PORTRAIT MINIATURES

1. SAMUEL COOPER (1609–1672)

James, Duke of York, afterwards James II. $3\frac{1}{4} \times 2\frac{5}{8}$ in.

BRITISH
PORTRAIT MINIATURES

A History by

DAPHNE FOSKETT

LONDON

Methuen and Co Limited

36 ESSEX STREET · WC2

IN MEMORY OF

MY MOTHER

WHO TAUGHT ME TO APPRECIATE

BEAUTIFUL THINGS

CONTENTS

*

ILLUSTRATIONS

*

COLOUR PLATES

9

MONOCHROME PLATES

(Note: *In certain cases it has not been possible to obtain the measurements
of the miniatures illustrated.*)

16

CHRONOLOGY

*

25

Gibson, William (1644?–1703?)

Gibson, D. (d. 1659)

Rosse, Susan Penelope, née Gibson (1652?–1700)

Beale, Mary (1633–1699)

Beale, Charles (1660–1694?) (Son of Mary Beale)

Snelling, Matthew (worked 1647)

D.M. (worked 1663–1676)

CHAPTER VIII

Dixon, Nicholas (worked 1667–1708)

Cross, P. (b. 1630? worked till 1716?)

Cross(e), Lawrence (d. 1724)

Richter, Christian (1678–1732)

Arlaud, Benjamin (worked 1701–1731?)

Arlaud, Jacques Antoine (1668–1746)

Digby, Simon (d. 1720)

CHAPTER IX

Lens, Bernard (1682–1740)

Lens, Andrew Benjamin (1713–exhib. till 1779)

Lens, Peter Paul (1714?–1750?)

Carriera, Rosalba (1675–1757)

Goupy, Louis (1700?–1747)

Goupy, Joseph (d. before 1782)

Frye, Thomas (1710–1762)

CHAPTER X

Hone, Nathaniel, R.A. (1718–1784)

Spencer, Gervase (d. 1763)

Collins, Samuel (d. 1768)

Cotes, Samuel (1734–1818)

Carwardine, Penelope (1730–1801)

Sullivan, Luke (1705–1771)

Redmond, Thomas (1745?–1785)

Reily, James (d. 1780 or 1788)

Hamilton, Gustavus (1739–1775)

Jennings, J. (worked 1762)

Scouler, James (1740?–1812)

Sherlock, William (1738?–1806?)

Vispré, François Xavier (1730?–1790?)

Vispré, Victor (worked 1763–1772)

Day, Thomas (1732–1807)

CHAPTER XI

Cosway, Richard, R.A. (1742?–1821)

CHAPTER XII

Smart, John (1742/3–1811)
Smart, John Jnr. (1776–1809)
Humphry, Ozias, R.A. (1742–1810)

CHAPTER XIII

Engleheart, George (1750–1829)
Plimer, Andrew (1763–1837)
Knight, Mary Anne (1776–1851)
Plimer, Nathaniel (1757–1822)

CHAPTER XIV

Wood, William (1769–1810)
Crosse, Richard (1742–1810)
Meyer, Jeremiah, R.A. (1735–1789)
Shelley, Samuel (1750?–1808)
Edridge, Henry, A.R.A. (1769–1821)

CHAPTER XV

Grimaldi, William (1751–1830)
Bogle, John (1746?–1803)
Miles, Edward (1752–1828)
Barry, John (worked 1784–1827)
Nixon, James, A.R.A. (1741?–1812)
Hone, Horace, A.R.A. (1756–1825)
Jean, Philip (1755–1802)
Shirreff or Sheriff, Charles (1750?–exhib. till 1831)
Daniel, Abraham (d. 1806)
Daniel, Joseph (worked from 1777–d. 1803)

CHAPTER XVI

Buck, Adam (1759–1833)
Buck, Frederick (1771?–1839/40)
Ferrière, François (1752–1839)
Roch(e), Sampson Towgood (1759–1847)
Roberston, Charles (1760–1821)
Robertson, Walter (worked 1765–d. 1802)
Hazelhurst, Thomas (worked 1760–d. 1821?)
Paillou, Peter (worked 1763?–1800)
Donaldson, John (1737–1801)

Saunders, Joseph (worked 1772–1808)
Place, George (worked 1775–d. 1805)
McMor(e)land, Patrick John (b. 1741)
Downman, John, A.R.A. (1750–1824)
Arlaud, Louis Ami (1751–1829)
Naish, William (d. 1800)
Smart, Samuel Paul (exhib. 1774–1787)
Addington, Sarah (exhib. 1778)
Andrews, Samuel (1767?–1807)

CHAPTER XVII

Mee, Mrs Joseph, née Anne Foldsone (1770/5–1851)
Chinnery, George, R.H.A. (1774–1852)
Beaumont, John Thomas Barber, F.S.A., F.G.S. (1774–1841)
Comerford, John (1770?–1832)
Hargreaves, Thomas (1775–1846)
Biffin, Sarah (1784–1850)
Robertson, Andrew, M.A. (1777–1845)
Robertson, Archibald (1765–1835)
Robertson, Alexander (1772–1841)
Nash, Edward (1778–1821)
Gallaway, Alexander (worked 1794–1812)
Stewart, Anthony (1773–1846)
Dunn, Andrew (exhib. 1809–1820)
Chalon, Alfred Edward, R.A. (1780–1860)

CHAPTER XVIII

Fouquet, Jean (1420?–1480?)
Toutin, Jean (worked 1632)
Toutin, Henry (1653–?)
Petitot, Jean (1607–1691)
Bordier, Jacques (1616–1684)
Boit, Charles (bapt. 1662–1727)
Zincke, Christian Friedrich (1663/4–1767)
Prieur, Paul (b. 1620?)
Liotard, Jean Etienne (1702–1789)
Rouquet, André or Jean (1701–1759)
Moser, George Michael (1704–1783)
Prewett or Prewitt, William (worked 1735–1750)
Spicer, Henry (1743–1804)
Hurter, Johann Heinrich (1734–1799)

Bone, Henry, R.A. (1755–1834)
Bone, William, Senior (exhib. 1815–1843)
Bone, Henry Pierce (1779–1855)
Bone, William, Junior (exhib. 1827–1851)
Murphy, Denis Brownell (d. 1842)
Essex, William (1784–1869)
Lee, Joseph (1747–1859)

CHAPTER XIX

Loggan, David (1635–1692)
White, Robert (1645–1703)
Forster, Thomas (b. 1677?)
Paton, David (worked 1660–1695)
Forster, Charles (worked 1709–1717)
White, George (1671?/84?–1732)
Brounower, Sylvester (17th c.)
Faber, John (1650/60–1721)
Faithorne, William (1616–1691)
Simpson, John (exhib. 1831–1871)
Rouse or Rowse, James (1802–1888)

CHAPTER XX

Engleheart, John Cox Dillman (1784–1862)
Newton, Sir William John (1785–1869)
Ross, Sir William Charles, R.A. (1794–1860)
Linnell, John (1792–1882)
Rochard, Simon Jacques (1788–1872)
Rochard, François Théodore (1798–1858)
Egley, William (1798–1870)
Easton, Reginald (1807–1893)
Chalon, Maria (Mrs Henry Mosley) (1800?–1867)
Thorburn, Robert, A.R.A., H.R.S.A. (1818–1885)
Dixon, Miss Annie (worked 1844–d. 1901)
Tidey, Alfred (1808–1892)
Haslem, John (1808–1884)
Faed, John, R.S.A. (1819–1902)
Williams, Alyn, P.R.M.S. (b. 1865)
Way, Frances Elizabeth (Mrs Thacker) (1871–1961)
Smith, Muriel

PREFACE

✳

I have ventured to write this book because I believe that there are many people who even if they are not collectors of portrait miniatures, are at least interested in them as an art and who, given the opportunity and the knowledge, may become the connoisseurs of the future.

In the past many excellent and beautifully illustrated books have been written on the subject, but the majority of them are long since out of print, and not readily procurable. Collectors and students are therefore handicapped in their research, for recent books on the subject are few.

While we owe a great deal to those authors whose pioneer research did much to preserve such knowledge as was available in their lifetimes, additional information has come to light and as a result it has been possible to re-assess the work of certain artists and to add more precise details about their lives. I have included a fairly extensive bibliography, as many of the books contain valuable information and excellent illustrations which help the reader in identifying the painter and the sitter.

It is impossible within the compass of this book to do more than mention a limited number of the many artists who painted miniatures. I have confined myself to those who worked in Britain, but it must not be forgotten that there were many excellent miniaturists working abroad, particularly in France, Germany, Holland, Denmark, Italy and America.

I have purposely referred to a number of lesser-known artists, for in certain cases I have been fortunate in obtaining new information about them which I hope will be of interest.

I must record my thanks to the many people whose advice and encouragement have made this book possible. I am indebted particularly to Mr Gibbs-Smith of the Victoria and Albert Museum, who first suggested that the book should be written, to Mr Graham Reynolds, Keeper of the Print Room at the Victoria and Albert Museum, for continued help and advice over many years, to Mr Robert Cecil, Assistant Director of The Wallace Collection, to Mr Colin Thompson and Mr Basil Skinner of the National Galleries of Scotland, to Miss D. M. Kleinfeldt and Miss Young for their advice and assistance in the initial stages, and to Mr P. J. Williams for reading the manuscript and suggesting amendments.

Her Majesty the Queen has graciously permitted me to illustrate examples from the collection at Windsor Castle, where Miss Scott Elliot, Librarian there, has given me invaluable assistance. For permission to examine their collections and to illustrate from them I am extremely indebted to their Graces the Duke of Portland, K.G., the Duke of Buccleuch and Queensberry, K.T., the Duke of Devonshire, the Earl of Derby and the Earl of Haddington, K.T. The National Portrait Gallery, the Victoria and Albert Museum, the National Galleries of Scotland, the Syndics of the Fitzwilliam Museum, Cambridge, the Ashmolean Museum, Oxford, the Wallace Collection, London, the Derby Art Gallery, The Trustees of the Chatsworth Settlement, Mr A. G. Tite, Captain Woollett, Mr Sydney Sabin, Mr Michael Jaffé (who kindly provided me with information collected by his father the late Mr Arthur Jaffé in connection with J. Smart) and Mr A. J. B. Kiddell, and Mrs Graham of Messrs. Sotheby & Co., who have all given me the greatest help, without which this book could not have been attempted. Mrs M. Addison and Mrs J. Statham undertook the laborious task of typing my manuscript, for which I am most grateful.

2. Attributed to HANS MEMLINC (1430–1494)
The Madonna and Child. $8\frac{1}{2} \times 6\frac{1}{4}$ in.

CHAPTER I

THE ORIGIN AND METHOD OF MINIATURE PAINTING

*

Ever since the art of miniature painting came into being in the sixteenth century, there have always been a limited number of people who have formed collections of these delightful small portraits. In most cases they were of members of the owner's family, and before the days of photography they served as a family portrait album.

Many of them still remain in the possession of the descendants of those who originally commissioned the artists to paint them, and their size and the ease with which they could be packed away have allowed them to survive when large paintings have been sold or destroyed.

While the word miniature is used nowadays to describe any small object, in painting it is accepted as meaning a portrait executed in any medium, i.e. watercolour, oils, enamel or plumbago, and drawn to such a small scale that it may easily be held in the hand. Thus its size may vary from a portrait no larger than a thumb-nail to one of as much as 8–10 inches, and at least one example is known to exist which measures 27 × 37 inches, although this latter size is unusual.

Originally these small portraits were called limnings, or painting in little, and this name for them survived well into the seventeenth century when the word miniature replaced it. The word is derived from 'minium', the Latin word for red lead, or vermilion, the pigment used to paint initial letters on the illuminated manuscripts of the middle ages. The verb 'miniare' denotes the process, and the person who did this work was called a 'miniator'. From this we can see that the word miniature refers to the process and not the object.

The origin of miniature painting is not easy to establish, but a great deal of research has been done on the subject and a variety of theories have been put forward without any definite conclusion being reached. The two most likely sources would seem to be the art of illumination, and that of the portrait medals of ancient Rome. Illuminators of early manuscripts before the discovery of printing were employed in drawing and painting any form of written communication, which included official documents, books of hours, bibles and missals. The writing was executed on vellum or parchment, the former prepared from calfskin and the latter from sheepskin. The borders of the pages were decorated with foliage and flowers, and occasionally small paintings of imaginary persons or biblical incidents were embodied in the general illumination of the page.

At first no attempt was made at portraiture and it was not until the time of Henry VIII that any real effort was made to paint true likenesses on the documents which were in use in diplomatic circles, and for communication between one court and another. These portraits were used almost as a signature or proof that the document had been seen and agreed to by the sender, who was the person portrayed. They were not intended to be cut out and kept as separate paintings, but there is no doubt that in some cases this was done and the portraits placed in small frames. This has led to confusion between the art of the illuminator and that of the painter of portrait miniatures.

It has been suggested that miniatures can be divided into two classes: *ornamental miniatures*, those that are circular or oval, and were worn on the person as ornaments or jewellery; and *cabinet miniatures*, the larger ones which were often placed in oval or rectangular frames to hang on a wall.

The theory that another possible source of portrait miniatures may be the portrait medals struck in Rome during the fourth and fifth centuries and revived in Italy during the Renaissance arises from the fact that these medals, made in limited numbers, were for the recipient to wear. They were modelled with great care and in them the artist attempted to portray a real likeness. Moreover they were housed in small circular containers covered with glass, not unlike those used by the earliest painters of miniatures.

It is therefore true that both the miniatures and medals, although entirely different forms of art, had certain points in common: they were circular in form, similar in size, meticulously wrought, and both were used as articles of personal adornment.

The history of illuminating is a study in itself and its importance to the art of miniature painting lies in the similarity of technique and medium which the earliest miniaturists adopted. How closely the art of illuminating was allied to that of the goldsmith, who spent so much of his time working with precious stones and gold settings, may be seen by studying the pages of the original manuscript books which are to be seen in the Victoria and Albert Museum, the British Museum, and many other places both in London and the provinces.

One has only to examine these illuminations to see with what exquisite delicacy the artists accomplished their work. The paints they used were brilliantly clear and shone like jewels, while the whole painting was enriched by the lavish use of pure gold, showing clearly how much their work was influenced by that of the goldsmiths. In T. H. Colding's book *Aspects of Miniature Painting* there are some excellent illustrations of fifteenth- and sixteenth-century illuminations, while for coloured illustrations one cannot do better than examine Mario Salmi's *Italian Miniatures*. To the student of portrait miniatures the title is misleading, for the contents deal with illuminating, but the examples given are well worth studying, and illustrate how the small portraits were incorporated into the design of the pages on which they were drawn.

Vellum was the most usual foundation of sixteenth-century miniatures, the skin used being of the thinnest possible kind stuck on to cardboard. As the best card was that used for playing cards these were found to be the most suitable backings for the vellum. The colours used by the early miniaturists were bought in their raw state, ground down by the artists, and stored in small ivory containers until required. Before use they were mixed with a solution of powdered gum arabic, to which sugar was often added, and the mixture dissolved by hot water. This produced clear opaque colours, generally termed gouache, which retained their brilliance, as may be seen by examining the pages of illuminated manuscripts and early miniatures.

A detailed description of the art of limning is given in a book written in the seventeenth century by Henry Peacham (1576–1643) called *The Gentleman's Exercise*[1] or 'An Exquisite Practise, as well for drawing all manner of beasts in their true portraiture: as also the making of all kinds of colours, to be used in Limming, Painting, Tricking, and Blazon of Coates, and Armes, with divers other most delightfull and pleasurable observations, for all young Gentlemen and others'. A detailed description of how to prepare a picture in small follows: 'Take of the fairest and smoothest pastboord you can get, which with a sleeke stone rubbe as smooth, and as even as you can, that done, take the fine skin of an Abortive, which, you may buy in Paternoster Row, and other places, (it being the finest parchment that is) and with starch thinne laid on, and the skin well stretched and smoth pressed within some booke or the like, prepare your ground or tablet, then according to the generall complexion of the face you are to draw, lay on a weake colour, that done, trace out the eyes, nose, mouth, and eare, with lake or red Lead, and if the complexion be swarthy, adde either of Sea coale, lampe blacke to deepen and shadow it, when you have thus done, lay it by for a day, or till it be well dry, then by little and little, worke it with a curious hand with the liuely colour, till you have brought it to perfection'. One has only to examine the works of these sixteenth-century artists to know that they did indeed bring them to perfection.

The gold which was used to embellish the miniatures and manuscripts was not gold paint as we know it today, but was pure gold leaf. It was used in powder form tempered with weak gum water, and being stored in mussel shells became known as shell gold. When larger expanses of gold were required a preparation of gum

[1] 1st Edition, 1607.

water or isinglass to receive the leaf was put on to the design and dried. The gum preparation was breathed on to moisten it, the gold pressed gently down on to the desired place, and any redundant leaf brushed off, or cut carefully away.

The art of enamelling, the medium in which the earliest known miniature was painted, is lost in antiquity. In China it has been practised for centuries and the ancient Egyptians, Assyrians, Greeks and Romans all used it in a simple form.

Enamelled ornaments such as horse trappings and shields of Celtic and Saxon origin dating from the sixth and ninth century have been discovered, and at about this time the art was also known in Ireland, where many beautiful examples were produced. In Byzantine art it was employed mainly for ecclesiastical objects depicting religious scenes which were placed on triptyches, reliquaries, covers of missals, crosses and chalices. Fine examples of these objects were on view in Edinburgh and London during the Byzantine Exhibition of 1958. In these early enamels, as with illuminations, no attempt was made to portray the real likeness of a living person.

The two main methods of early enamelling were *cloisonné* and *champlevé*, the term 'painted enamels' being a later development. The substance used for enamelling is a combination of a simple flux which contains proportions of silica, nitrate of potash and powdered glass, together with different metallic oxides which, when mixed together, produce a variety of colours, and this compound has to be placed on a metal surface of copper, gold, or silver and fired at a given temperature.

The word *champlevé* is derived from the two French words *champ* – a field, and *levé* – raised. In this method the design is first traced on to the metal base, then the centre of the design hollowed out in order to leave space for the enamel preparation. Thin ridges of metal are left to form the outline and separate the colours. The spaces thus produced are filled with the powdered enamel, and the whole article fired in a kiln. In *cloisonné*, the design is scratched upon the surface of the metal base, after which strips of thin metal are soldered on to it to form *cloisons*, or cells. These are filled with enamel as before, and the complete work is then fired to melt the mixture, the components of which fuse together, and when cool the article is polished.

Enamel has one great advantage over any other medium, for once fired it is impervious to changes of temperature and can only be damaged by a blow or from being dropped, when it will crack. Nevertheless it is a difficult process and many enamels have been ruined in the kiln.

In early work only a few basic colours such as green, brown, violet and blue were used, brightened by touches of gold, the flesh colours being purplish or brown with opaque white added.

The earliest known portrait miniature is the self-portrait of Jean Fouquet

1. LUCAS HORENBOUT (d. 1544)
Henry VIII (1491–1547). $1\frac{3}{4}$ in. diam.

2. HANS HOLBEIN (1497/8–1543)
Lady Audley. $2\frac{3}{16}$ in. diam.

3. SIMON BENNINCK (1483/4–1561)
Self-portrait. Signed and dated 1558.
$3\frac{7}{32} \times 2\frac{3}{32}$ in.

4. WENCESLAUS HOLLAR (1607–77)
Margaret Roper *née* More (1505–44).
$2\frac{13}{16} \times 2\frac{3}{16}$ in.

5. HANS HOLBEIN
Henry Brandon (1535–51). 1⅞ in. diam.

6. HANS HOLBEIN attrib.
Self-portrait. 1⁷⁄₁₆ in. diam.

7. HANS HOLBEIN
Called Catherine Howard (d. 1542).
2 in. diam. (cut down).

8. HANS HOLBEIN
George Nevill,
3rd Baron Abergavenny, K.G. (1461–1535).
2⅛ in. diam.

(1420?–80?), painted in gold upon a black background and quite unlike any enamel portrait painted later. It is an isolated and exceptional work, for the history of portrait miniatures really begins in the reign of Henry VIII with the arrival in England of Hans Holbein in 1526. Prior to his coming Holbein had not, so far as is known, painted any miniatures, although he may have executed small oil portraits that have not survived.

The earliest sixteenth-century miniatures were all round, but towards the end of the century the oval upright form appeared and has retained its popularity ever since. Rectangular shapes were also introduced and are to be found in most periods. Small flat boxes with lids, similar to a seal box, and made of ivory and wood, were used to contain these portraits.

Another method of housing miniatures was to place them in frames made of wood, gold, silver or any suitable metal. These as time went on were frequently studded with jewels and enriched with enamels, the jewellers employed in the making of these lockets and frames not infrequently becoming miniaturists themselves.

Oil was another medium used in the sixteenth century, oil miniatures being executed on metal, wood, or even occasionally on slate. Many of them are beautifully painted and of great historic interest, but as they are rarely signed very little is known about the artists who painted them, and to ascribe them to any particular artist is therefore both difficult and unwise. It is to be hoped that some day fresh information will come to light which will assist us in this field of research.

The miniatures still in existence of Queen Elizabeth I and her Court provide us with a clear picture of the art of miniature painting as it had developed from its inception under Holbein to the elaborate work which was produced by Nicholas Hilliard (1547–1619).

That the Queen herself possessed a collection of miniatures is mentioned in the memoirs of Sir James Melville, emissary of Mary Queen of Scots, for in 1564 during an interview Queen Elizabeth showed him a little cabinet in which were a number of small portraits wrapped in paper, one of them being of the Earl of Leicester.

The backgrounds of sixteenth-century miniatures were predominantly blue and were often inscribed with the date and age of the sitter, to which occasionally a name or motto was added.

The miniatures painted by Hilliard and his followers continued to be executed on vellum or card and the backgrounds remained predominantly blue, but the inscriptions, which were frequently in gold, were more elaborate than in the past, as were the costumes and ornaments of the sitters. Three-quarter or full-length portraits were occasionally introduced with landscape or draped backgrounds.

By the time the art of miniature painting had fully established itself in the seventeenth century, further developments were taking place. These included greater appreciation of perspective and closer attention to the anatomical structure of the human face and figure, which resulted in better modelling and consequently in more lifelike portraits.

The artist Samuel Cooper (1609–72) was to a great extent responsible for the improvement in draughtsmanship, and his name stands out as one of the finest painters of miniatures that England has ever known. He put a layer of white paint on to his prepared background before starting his painting, a method which was adopted by other artists.

The ornate inscriptions so characteristic of Elizabethan miniatures were less in evidence, and simple block signatures, frequently dated, took their place. The backgrounds were inclined to be more subdued in colour and occasional cloud effects were introduced.

The fact that Charles I, who was a patron and connoisseur of art, had a number of his large paintings copied in miniature so that he could take them round with him on his travels did much to create a demand for portrait miniatures.

Two other developments in the seventeenth century were the introduction of plumbago miniatures and drawings and the discovery by a French goldsmith, J. Toutin, of a method of applying colours in much the same way as water-colours on to a thin ground of white enamel previously fired, the painting being then re-fired with scarcely any change of colour. Thus miniatures were painted on enamel and not in enamel as in the past, when a metal division had been necessary to keep the colours from running into each other.

Plumbago miniatures were in vogue from about 1660–1720. They were drawn with a sharp piece of graphite or black lead. The word is derived from the Latin *plumbum* or graphite, a pure mineral, unlike the lead in the pencils of today which is mixed with clay. These portraits were executed on vellum and on paper, and were not usually stuck down as was the case with those painted in watercolour.

Towards the end of the seventeenth century a form of stippling or dotting was introduced in shading the face and sometimes the backgrounds, a technique first used on the Continent. In about 1700 ivory began to be used instead of vellum as a foundation, an innovation which had originated on the Continent slightly earlier. The first artist to use it in Britain was Bernard Lens (1682–1740).

At first the artists painted in the old way, using gouache on rather thick pieces of ivory or bone and leaving only the face in transparent watercolour.

It was some time before any attempt was made to experiment with thin sheets of ivory, the surface of which had been dulled in order to hold the paint better. The discovery by Richard Cosway (1742?–1821) of the full possibilities of ivory and its luminosity revolutionized the whole technique of miniature painting. The only danger lay in the fact that changes of temperature had disastrous effects on the ivory since they were liable to warp it or produce a mildew which ruined the painting. There was also the problem of cutting it satisfactorily without damaging the whole piece, which was expensive to buy. However, in spite of this, from the eighteenth century onwards ivory has remained the most popular material on which to paint miniatures. The popularity of ivory brought about a decline in the use of vellum as a foundation and, owing to the expense and difficulty of obtaining it, many artists began to use paper as an alternative for their portraits.

Although porcelain is not usually accepted as a medium for miniature painting, Sidney Hand (1877–1952)[1] refers to one of John Milton painted on porcelain by John Haslem of the Derby Porcelain Works, who also painted in enamel. I have seen two porcelain miniatures in the Derby Art Gallery painted by J. Rouse, who was an apprentice at the Derby China Factory.

Miniatures were frequently placed in lockets of gold or silver, pinchbeck or cut steel. Decorated at the back with the sitter's hair and with initials designed in gold thread and seed pearls, they were sometimes placed on a background of coloured glass set over patterned silver foil and thus made to look like enamel.

The eighteenth century was the heyday of miniature painting and innumerable artists, including the better known ones such as Richard Cosway, John Smart, George Engleheart, and Nathaniel and Andrew Plimer, were untiring in their efforts to keep pace with the demands of their patrons.

With the introduction of photography in the early part of Queen Victoria's reign, miniatures lost their more intimate aspect. Whereas previously they had been contained in lockets and brooches, they were now to be found in rectangular frames standing on a desk competing with photographs, and this proved to be the downfall of the art of miniature painting.

It must be remembered that whether a miniature is set in a jewelled locket or in a simple frame it is the quality of the painting that matters, regardless of the period in which it was painted. In order to acquire the knowledge necessary to distinguish the good from the mediocre, or even bad, the collector must lose no opportunity to study the subject at first hand by seeing any good miniatures which are available either in museums or in private collections, and by reading about the artists who painted them.

It is not always possible to discover the name of the artist or that of the sitter, for with the passing of the years this information is frequently unobtainable. It adds to one's interest to know both these facts, but many small portraits are in themselves beautiful works of art and are satisfying treasures to possess.

[1] A leading London art dealer. See bibliography.

CHAPTER II

HANS HOLBEIN AND THE EARLY MINIATURISTS

✱

HANS HOLBEIN (1497/8–1543) may be regarded as the first painter of miniatures to practise his art in England. Even if he is not immediately associated with miniature painting, most people know him as a great artist, and the mention of his name will almost invariably bring to mind pictures of Henry VIII and his court, and more especially illustrations of Sir Thomas More and his family.

Born in Augsburg in 1497/8, Hans was the son of Hans Holbein the Elder, from whom presumably he learnt the art of painting. Although much of his finest work was executed in England, a considerable number of his early paintings were done in Germany and Switzerland, so that all three countries have a just claim to him. If proof were needed of his talent, it lies in the fact that today, over 400 years after his death, his work is admired afresh by each succeeding generation.

Unlike his father, Holbein appears to have had an urge to travel. In 1514 he and his brother Ambrosius went to Basle, where they became apprentices to Hans Herbster, a well-known painter in that city. Holbein remained in Basle for some time, drawing illustrations for books and painting murals as well as executing designs for buildings and jewellery. He was fortunate in making the acquaintance of Erasmus, who admired his work and recommended him to his friends. According to George Vertue (1684–1756),[1] a friendship grew up between these two, and it must have been due in no small measure to Erasmus's encouragement and patronage that Holbein's reputation grew steadily, until he was in great demand. Owing to political disturbances in Basle there was a falling off of commissions after a time, and Holbein was advised to go to England and seek fresh patrons. Some time prior to this he had married the widow of a master tanner who had been killed at the Battle of Marignano and, to quote the words of Vertue, 'His family and the froward temper of his wife increasing and his business declining he determined upon that journey'. In 1526, therefore, he set off, travelling to England by way of Antwerp, after giving out that he was leaving for only a short time in order to raise the value of his works which had become too numerous in Basle.

Just before his departure Holbein was employed in finishing a portrait for one of his patrons, and there is a story that, wishing to leave behind him a specimen

[1] *Anecdotes of Painting in England*, by Horace Walpole, 3rd Edition, London, 1782.

of his work that would make a good impression, he painted a fly on the forehead of the sitter. When the painting was delivered the patron was delighted with it and immediately tried to brush off the fly. This story soon spread and created considerable interest, just as the artist had hoped it would.

When Holbein reached Britain he brought with him letters of introduction from Erasmus to Sir Thomas More, who entertained him for several years at his house in Chelsea, during which time he painted many portraits of Sir Thomas and his family. This introduction proved to be of great benefit to the artist, for not only was More a great patron and critic of art but he introduced Holbein to the King and his Court.

A number of Flemish illuminators were already established in England before Holbein's arrival, the most notable of them being LUCAS, GERARD and SUZANNE HORENBOUT. Although these artists were best known for their work as illuminators, they are believed to have painted miniatures as well, and although no signed miniatures by them have so far been discovered, certain miniature portraits of Henry VIII have been attributed to Lucas, and both Hugh Paget[1] and Torben Colding[2] agree that there is every reason to believe that this attribution is correct. The family originated in Ghent, where Gerard became a member of the painters' guild in 1487 and numbered Albrecht Dürer among his acquaintances. In 1522 Gerard and his wife came to England where they remained until the wife's death in 1529, after which he returned to Ghent, where he lived until his own death in 1540. While in England he was undoubtedly employed by the King, for Vertue records an entry in an ancient office book signed monthly by the sovereign to the effect that on 'Feb Ano Reg XXIX Gerard Luke Hornebard, painter – 56 shillings and 9 pence per month'. His daughter had accompanied her parents when they came to England and she later married an Englishman and settled down in this country, where she remained until her death in 1545. Having been taught painting by her father, she continued to practise the art in England and is said to have painted miniatures. Her work was evidently good, for it was greatly admired by Dürer.

Lucas's exact relationship with the rest of the family has not been established, but it is possible that he was Suzanne's brother. He is known to have held salaried posts in Henry VIII's household and was appointed King's Painter in 1534. At an unknown date he became a naturalized Englishman and has always been given the credit for having taught Holbein the art of limning.

Another family of Flemish artists working in England at that time bore the name of Teerlinc. Livina or Levina Teerlinc was the second daughter of SIMON BENING, Benninck, or Beninc (1483/4–1561), who had the reputation of being one

[1] Burlington Magazine, Nov. 1959.
[2] Danish Miniatures, 1948, pp. 63, 64, 65.

of the leading illuminators in Europe. A self portrait in miniature, dated 1558, may be seen at the Victoria and Albert Museum, and although the style is that of the illuminator, it is a portrait and as such forms a link between the art of the illuminator and that of the painter of portrait miniatures.

Levina Teerlinc was court painter to Edward VI, Queen Mary and Queen Elizabeth and her name appears in the accounts of the Royal Household from 1545 onwards. She is supposed to have presented Queen Elizabeth with a portrait of her 'finely painted upon a card'. It is generally believed that the Horenbout and Bening families were closely connected through their work, although there is no evidence that Simon Bening ever lived in England.

It is impossible to ascertain what stage the art of limning had reached by the time Holbein arrived in England as no authenticated miniatures of the period have so far been discovered with which his work can be compared. For this reason there has always been a great deal of speculation over the correct attribution of those that do exist. Many portraits have undoubtedly perished and Holbein's immense popularity has insured that those which have survived have nearly all at one time or another been attributed to him. As a result, a number of paintings of uneven quality and even impossible dates have been assigned to his hand.

Mr Carl Winter[1] and Mr Graham Reynolds[2] who, as members of the staff of the Victoria and Albert Museum, have had the opportunity of close and prolonged study not only of the great collection of miniatures housed there but of other important collections to which they have had access, have examined the subject exhaustively and are of the opinion that from the large number of miniatures hitherto regarded as being by Holbein only some nine or twelve can be accepted with confidence. These are set out in Mr Reynolds' book *English Portrait Miniatures* and are as follows:

Mrs Pemberton } Anne of Cleves }	In the Victoria and Albert Museum
Lady Audley } Henry Brandon } Charles Brandon }	In the collection of H.M. the Queen at Windsor
Thomas Wriothesley, 1st Earl of Southampton	In the Metropolitan Museum, New York
A Youth	In the collection of H.M. the Queen of the Netherlands
A Man, aged 24 in 1543	In the Stadt Museum, Danzig

[1] Now Director of the Fitzwilliam Museum, Cambridge.
[2] Keeper of the Print Room at the Victoria and Albert Museum.

3. HANS HOLBEIN (1497/8–1543)
Mrs. Pemberton. $2\frac{1}{16}$ in. diam.

4. HANS HOLBEIN (1497/8–1543)
Anne of Cleves. $1\frac{23}{32}$ in. diam.

A Lady, possibly Catherine Howard	In the collection of the Duke of Buccleuch

These nine miniatures are unquestionably by Holbein, but Mr Winter and Mr Reynolds regard the following as being almost certainly by him as well:

Catherine Howard – a replica of the Duke of Buccleuch's miniature	In the collection of H.M. the Queen at Windsor
A Man with the Initials H.M., aged 27	National Museum, Munich
Lord Abergavenny	In the collection of the Duke of Buccleuch

There are in addition certain alleged self-portraits, including one in the Wallace Collection and another in the collection of the Duke of Buccleuch. These, however, are considered by some experts not to be by Holbein, but with so little knowledge available this must remain an open question. The fact that none but the self-portraits are signed adds to the confusion. There is always the possibility that other miniaturists of the period may have copied Holbein's work or even painted in the same manner – but of them we have no knowledge.

It is known that Holbein had executed small round paintings in oils prior to painting miniatures, and in so doing he was no doubt influenced by the round medallions and medals which were so popular in the country of his birth. All Holbein's miniatures are round with the exception of the one of Thomas Wriothesley, 1st Earl of Southampton, which is now in the Metropolitan Museum, New York. This seems to have been cut into an oval form at a later date. Sir Thomas Wriothesley (1505–50), later the first Baron Wriothesley of Titchfield and Earl of Southampton, took a leading part in affairs of State, holding office as Lord Chancellor of England, Graver to the Tower of London, Constable of Southampton Castle, and acting as executor to Henry VIII and privy councillor to Edward VI. Towards the end of his life he was deprived of his offices, owing to a dispute with his fellow councillors. He was later re-admitted to council, but after joining Warwick's opposition to Thomas Seymour was abandoned by Warwick, and struck off the list of councillors in 1550, the year of his death. His grandson, Henry, 3rd Earl of Southampton, was Shakespeare's patron, and *Venus and Adonis* and *Lucrece* were both dedicated to him.

It is said that Henry VIII first became aware of Holbein's genius in the following manner. One day when the King was visiting his Chancellor, Sir Thomas More, he saw some of Holbein's work and expressed his satisfaction with it. More then begged him to accept one of the paintings, but the King asked to see the painter and, when he was presented to him, immediately took him into his service, telling More that now he had the artist he did not want the painting.

Holbein was given accommodation in the Palace and a salary of 200 florins, as well as payment for the pictures he painted. A workshop was provided for him in one of the towers of Whitehall Palace, and in 1546 Holbein designed a gateway across the roadway from Charing Cross to Westminster which became known as the Holbein gate. It was drawn by Vertue, and painted by Canaletto. Vertue's drawing is reproduced in *Old and New London*.[1]

The gateway was removed between 1749–50 in order to widen the street, and the glazed bricks and stones from which it was made were sold to repair the high roads. The artist enjoyed his patron's confidence from the time he entered his employment until his death, and became the leading portrait painter in England. He was extremely versatile, his work covering a wide variety of subjects from designing buttons, buckles and jewellery to painting walls, ceilings and portraits, including those of the King's prospective brides.

Little is known about Holbein's private life nor do we know much about his character. The painting and drawing executed of him by his father show him to have a rather surly expression and, judging by the self-portraits, his nature does not appear to have changed much with advancing years. Of his family little is known except that he left them twice. His painting of his wife and family show her to be a woman weighed down with sorrow and unhappiness, and the faces of his two children bear a similar expression. According to Paul Ganz in his book on Holbein, this painting was done before 1529 and after his return to Basle from England.

Holbein returned to Basle two or three years after his departure, possibly to show his family and friends how successful he had been at the English Court, for by this time he had become a great favourite with Henry VIII and had been commissioned to paint not only the Royal family but most of the notable persons of the day.

Vertue tells an amusing story that one day when Holbein was privately painting some lady's picture for the King, a 'nobleman' forced himself into the room. The painter then threw him down the stairs and bolted out of the house straight to Henry, before whom he fell on his knees to beg for pardon, without saying what he had done. The King agreed to pardon him if he told the truth, but when the story came out repented of his promise, saying he could not easily overlook such insults and that Holbein must wait till he had learned more about the incident. When the nobleman arrived and started to complain about Holbein the King becoming angry rebuked him saying 'you have not to do with Holbein but with

[1] *Old and New London*, by Edward Walford, London, [1873–8], p. 354.

9.
NICHOLAS HILLIARD (1547–1619)
Sir Walter Raleigh (1522–1618).
$1\frac{7}{8} \times 1\frac{5}{8}$ in.

10. NICHOLAS HILLIARD
Mrs Hilliard *née* Brandon, aged 22.
Dated 1578. $2\frac{5}{16}$ in. diam.

11. NICHOLAS HILLIARD
Queen Elizabeth I (1533–1603).
$2 \times 1\frac{3}{4}$ in.

12. NICHOLAS HILLIARD
George Clifford,
rd Earl of Cumberland, K.G. (1558–1605).
$2\frac{3}{4} \times 2\frac{1}{4}$ in.

13. NICHOLAS HILLIARD
Called James I (1566–1625).
$1\frac{7}{8} \times 1\frac{5}{8}$ in.

14. NICHOLAS HILLIARD
Called
'Elizabeth Queen of Bohemia'.
$1\frac{7}{8} \times 1\frac{1}{2}$ in.

15. LAURENCE HILLIARD
($1581/2$–1640)
An unknown man. $1\frac{7}{8} \times 1\frac{1}{2}$ in.

16. NICHOLAS HILLIARD
An unknown lady. $2\frac{7}{8} \times 2\frac{1}{8}$ in.

17. LAURENCE HILLIARD
An unknown lady. $2\frac{7}{16} \times 1\frac{15}{16}$ in.

me; I tell you of seven peasants I can make as many Lords, but not one Holbein'.

After Jane Seymour's death Holbein was sent to Flanders to draw the picture of the Duchess of Milan, who had been recommended to Henry VIII as his fourth wife. The King changed his mind, and the Duchess is supposed to have sent him word that she had but one head, but if she had had two one of them would have been at his Majesty's service.

In 1539 Holbein was commissioned to paint Anne of Cleves, who had been suggested by Thomas Cromwell (1485?–1540), later Earl of Essex, as a suitable wife for the King. Holbein set off again for the Continent and two paintings by him exist of this lady, one a full-length portrait in oil now in the Louvre, the other the famous miniature which is at the Victoria and Albert Museum. The miniature is similar to the larger oil painting, but shows only the head and shoulders. The finished portrait must have flattered the lady, for Henry, thinking she was attractive, arranged to marry her. When later he discovered she was not as beautiful as he had supposed, his wrath descended on Cromwell, not Holbein. In 1540 Cromwell was accused of treason by the Duke of Norfolk and when he was condemned to the scaffold, Henry did not intervene. According to a seventeenth-century biography the following inscription was on his monument –

'Cromwell, surnamed the Great,
Whom Wolsey first raised from the forge to eminent good fortunes;
Whom Henry the Eighth used as his instrument
To supress the Pope's supremacy, and dissolve religious structures;
Whom he advanced to the highest pitch of honour and authority;
Whom he cast down suddenly and bereft both of life and dignities;
Lies here interred'.

Cromwell had praised Anne of Cleves' beauty and told the King that she excelled the Duchess of Milan as the golden sun did the silver moon. The fact that the King described her as a Flanders Mare and only married her under protest proved Cromwell's undoing. Whatever may have been the truth about her looks, it must be agreed that the miniature Holbein painted is superb.

Vertue says of it:

'I have since seen that picture in the cabinet of the present Mr. Barrett of Lee, and think it the most exquisitely perfect of all Holbein's works, as well as in the highest preservation. The print gives a very inadequate idea of it, and none of her Flemish freshness. It is preserved in an ivory box in which it came over, and which represents a rose so delicately carved as to be worthy of the jewel it contains'.[1]

[1] *Anecdotes of Painting*, 3rd Edition, London, 1782, p. 114.

Holbein was particularly good at painting jewellery and embroidery and this is clearly shown in the details of the headdress and jewellery in his miniature of Anne of Cleves.

Also at the Victoria and Albert Museum is his miniature of Mrs Pemberton, and these two portraits are of such high quality that if no other paintings existed by this master he would still be acclaimed one of the finest miniature painters that ever lived. The portrait of Mrs Pemberton shows a young woman clad in an unostentatious dress of black and white without embroidery or elaborate jewellery, her hands clasped in repose and a calm and serene expression on what can only be described as a plain face. The very simplicity which the artist has portrayed can only fill one with admiration. Vertue tells us that 'Holbein was equal to dignified character, he could express the piercing genious of More, or the grace of Ann Boleyn'.

Holbein seems to have been able to penetrate his sitters' character and to have painted them as he saw them, serene and unsmiling, without any attempt to flatter or caricature their features. He was a fine draughtsman, and the modelling of his sitters' faces and hands was excellent. The result was completely satisfactory, and even his attention to detail in the painting of jewellery did not detract in any way from the portrait of the sitter. No one who has seen the illustrations of the fine collection of drawings at Windsor Castle can fail to appreciate the sincerity and strength that Holbein has reproduced in these exquisite masterpieces. Fortunately these drawings escaped being burnt by the fire which destroyed the Palace of Whitehall in 1698 and they were mislaid and forgotten until Queen Caroline, wife of George II, re-discovered them in an old cupboard. The draughtsmanship is so perfect that one cannot but feel that if any of the persons portrayed were to appear suddenly they would be instantly recognisable.

In the collection at Windsor Castle are miniatures of Henry and Charles Brandon, the young sons of the Duke of Suffolk, who both died in 1551 of a sweating sickness when Henry was 17 and Charles only 13 years of age. The expression on their faces is rather sad, as is that on the face of the youth in the Queen of Holland's collection, while the miniature of Lord Abergavenny belonging to the Duke of Buccleuch gives the impression of strength of character and forcefulness, which it is known that he possessed.

The majority of Holbein's miniatures have blue backgrounds and are painted on thin parchment or card in water colour which was no doubt mixed with gum. He used opaque colours except on the face, where the paint is transparent. The cards on which he painted are not always completely true circles and the edges are jagged. The sitter is well placed within the circle, and the background relieved only by the beautiful inscriptions in clear squarish lettering of pure gold or black. Holbein did not use a great deal of shading, what he did use being confined to the part under the chin and the hands. The hair was neatly painted in clear outline, as were the features. The whole composition was in perfect harmony, everything being subservient to the details on the face of the sitter to which the eye is immediately directed.

After Holbein's death there were only a few miniaturists in Britain, and so far any attempt to discover their work has failed. The names of John Shute, Gwillim Strete, John and Thomas Bettes, A. Van Brounckhurst and Cornelius Devosse are known, but up till the present they have remained but names.

Today Holbein's work ranks as high as ever it did among the great painters of the world. It is interesting to note that in his book *The Gentleman's Exercise*,[1] published in 1607, Henry Peacham, when discussing the work of well-known artists of the day, says, 'What Apelles could excel Petro de Burgo for perspective, Albert Dürer for drapery, Michael Angelo for action, Goldzius for good standing and bold action, Hans Holbein for sense and the life'.

The city of Basle evidently appreciated his work, for in 1538 they bestowed an annuity of 50 florins on him for two years, no doubt hoping that he might be persuaded to return to his own country. But nothing would induce him to leave the country of his adoption and the opulence of the English Court, and he remained in England until the plague claimed him as one of its victims in 1543.

WENCESLAUS HOLLAR (1607–77) was born at Prague on 13th July, 1607, and was the son of a court official. He studied engraving at Frankfort under a topographical engraver by the name of M. Merian. In 1629 Hollar went to Strasbourg where he remained until 1632, when he went to Cologne. He became known to Thomas Howard, 2nd Earl of Arundel, with whom he travelled, and in 1636 came with him to London. He was captured by Parliamentarians at the siege of Basing House, but later escaped, and in 1644 was living at Antwerp. By 1652 he was back again in London, but travelling evidently appealed to him and in 1668 he accompanied an expedition to Tangier. He died in London on March 25th or 28th, 1677.

Hollar is best remembered as an engraver, and his etchings include landscapes as well as portraits, one of his best-known works being the illustration of Thoroton's *Antiquities of Nottinghamshire*, published in 1677. His work as a miniaturist is known by one example owned by H.M. the Queen at Windsor. The miniature represents Margaret Roper, daughter of Sir Thomas More, and was probably copied from a portrait by Holbein.

[1] 1634 Edition, p. 7.

CHAPTER III

NICHOLAS HILLIARD AND HIS SON LAURENCE

*

The Elizabethan miniature painter NICHOLAS HILLIARD (1547–1619) came of a Devonshire family of goldsmiths who had lived in Exeter for some years, where they were well known not only in their trade but for the part they played in the life of the community. Richard Hilliard, his father, had held office as High Sheriff of the City of Exeter in 1560. His mother was the daughter of John Wall, a London goldsmith.

The exact date of Nicholas's birth was a matter of conjecture for many years, but it has now been established that he was born in Exeter in about 1547. There is no doubt that during his childhood he had ample opportunity to watch both his father and grandfather at work, and he decided to follow the family tradition. When only thirteen years of age and before serving his apprenticeship he was already painting miniatures.

That he was considerably influenced by the goldsmith's art is apparent in the miniatures he painted. There are two self-portraits executed about this period, one belonging to the Duke of Portland, the other to the Duke of Buccleuch. Both these are dated 1550, but the second 5 in each case seems to have been painted over a previous figure. It is due to these altered figures that confusion at first arose over the date of his birth.

The Duke of Buccleuch has a miniature of Edward Seymour, Duke of Somerset, similar in style, dated 1560 and signed with a monogram N.H. This is one of the few known authentic signatures of Hilliard and the painting of this portrait is after the manner of Holbein. From then until 1616 it is possible to trace the style and development of his work from boyish inexperience to maturity.

In 1947 an exhibition was held at the Victoria and Albert Museum to commemorate the four hundredth anniversary of his birth. It was an impressive and representative display of over 100 of Hilliard's miniatures, not including a considerable number more that have been accepted as authentic and others which must exist but are at present unrecorded.

At the time of the exhibition a most interesting monograph and catalogue was written by Graham Reynolds;[1] it is still available. It makes a comparison between

[1] *Nicholas Hilliard and Isaac Oliver*, 1947.

5. Nicholas Hilliard (1547–1619)
George Clifford, 3rd Earl of Cumberland, K.G.
$1\frac{3}{4} \times 1\frac{1}{2}$ in.

6. Peter Oliver (1594–1647)
Edward, Prince of Wales (after Holbein).
$3\frac{9}{16} \times 2\frac{7}{16}$ in.

the work of Nicholas Hilliard and that of Isaac Oliver which does much to distinguish between them, for Oliver was taught the art of limning by Hilliard and the pupil was later to equal the master.

Nicholas Hilliard was the first English-born artist to leave any details of his life and work. Born in the year of Henry VIII's death, he lived through five reigns and enjoyed the patronage of Queen Elizabeth and James I, whose mother Mary Queen of Scots he was supposed to have painted in her girlhood. His skill as a goldsmith and jeweller enabled him to express in his miniature paintings all the colourful costumes and all the extravagance and splendour of the Elizabethan age. The fashion for gold embroidery and fine lace ruffs gave plenty of scope for Hilliard's talents and his use in many of these small paintings of a blue background to enhance the general effect makes them as attractive as they are interesting.

By 1570 he appears to have been well established in London and had evidently become a member of the Goldsmiths' Company, for his name appears in their records for that year.

It is not known when Hilliard was appointed Limner & Goldsmith to the Queen, but as his first dated painting of her was painted in 1572 it was presumably some time before this. The Duke of Portland possesses a portrait of the sovereign which is said to have been painted between 1569 and 1570. In the same year we find his name linked with those of Devosse and A. Van Brounckhurst, who were both Flemish limners. They had all apparently been infected with a desire to join in the gold rush which seems to have been an ever-present urge of the Elizabethans, and the three men became involved in some speculative prospecting in Scotland. No evidence has so far come to light that Hilliard ever went to Scotland, but Steven Atkinson in *The Discoverie and Historie of the Gold Mines in Scotland*, which was written in 1619, states that Queen Elizabeth had a very high opinion of these mines and was prepared to give some assistance in the working of them, provided she could profit from them herself. As a result, Cornelius Devosse persuaded Hilliard and Van Brounckhurst to join in the adventure and Hilliard is supposed to have procured a patent which granted them permission to seek gold 'without molestation'. Van Brounckhurst evidently travelled to Scotland and employed men to work the gold. After searching several moors they found 'gold in sundry places' and no doubt expected to make their fortunes. However, things did not work out that way. In spite of an application to the Earl of Morton, they were refused permission to remove the gold, and Van Brounckhurst was forced to become one of 'His Majesty's sworne servants at ordinary in Scotland to draw all the small and great pictures for His Majesty', the boy King James VI being then only six years old. There is no evidence that any of the prospectors received a recompense for their adventure.

No works of Devosse or Van Brounckhurst have so far come to light.

In 1573 there is a reference in the accounts of the Exchequer to Nicholas Hilliard receiving a grant of £100 under a warrant of the Privy Seal, and his position became assured under the patronage of the Court.

By 1576 he was evidently sufficiently well off to marry and his choice was Alice Brandon, the beautiful daughter of John Brandon, Chamberlain of the City of London, by whom he had eight children. Laurence, the fourth child, was baptised in St Vedast's, Foster Lane, on 5th March, 1582.[1] The miniatures of Hilliard and his wife painted by himself show them to have been a very good looking couple and judging by their clothes, they were in good circumstances. That he married twice is evident from the inscription which he presumably added at a later date on the margin of his wife's miniature, indicating that she was his first wife. This portrait, formerly in the collection of the Duke of Buccleuch and now in the Victoria and Albert Museum, is signed and dated 1578, when he was 22. The self-portrait is also to be seen at the Victoria and Albert Museum, together with the portrait of his father, Richard Hilliard, at the age of 58.

There is no record of his first wife's death other than the inscription, nor of his remarriage, and we do not know who the lady was. As there is no reference to her in his will it can be presumed that she died before him. Graham Reynolds states that in 1577 Hilliard took his wife Alice to Paris, where they evidently soon made friends among the literary and artistic circles. His first child, Daniel,[2] was born soon after they returned to London. Of his other seven children, Laurence was the one who later followed his father's profession.

In 1584, after he had been for some time established as Court painter, a proclamation was drafted granting him the monopoly of the Queen's paintings in 'little', George Gower having been given the office of Sergeant Painter with a monopoly at the same time. In the same year Hilliard was commissioned to design and execute the Queen's second great seal and for this the gift of certain estates was made to him, including the Manor of Poyle in Middlesex and the lease of other properties which had an annual value of over £40 in 1589. The upkeep of these possessions must have been costly and as the actual pay that Hilliard received from his royal mistress was practically nothing, by 1598 he was having considerable difficulty over finance. In 1599 he wrote to Sir Robert Cecil appealing for assistance because of the extremities to which he had been brought through lack of payment, and seeking permission to leave the country for a year or two to gain respite from his creditors. In an act of the Privy Council, there is a letter written to the Master and Wardens of the Goldsmith's Company from whom Hilliard had

[1] *Nicholas Hilliard*, by Erna Auerbach, London, 1961, p. 19. This new work, the first full-length monograph on Hilliard's life, contains much valuable information.
[2] *Nicholas Hilliard*, E. Auerbach, p. 12.

apparently been leasing a tenement in Gutter Lane at the rent of £30 per annum. This property had cost him somewhere in the region of £200 in repairs and the Queen supported his request for a renewal of the lease on favourable terms in order that he might be better able to serve her with his paintings.

In about 1600 he was commissioned by Richard Haydocks to write a *Treatise Concerning the Art of Limning*, which is of outstanding importance as a history of miniature painting. It is preserved in the library of Edinburgh University and was printed in volume I of *The Walpole Society*[1] published in 1911–12.

Although the manuscript is not in Hilliard's own handwriting but is by some copyist who was not very careful over his work, the authorship has been established after careful study. The contents are interesting not only to the student of miniatures but to anyone who is interested in Elizabethan art and history, for as well as technical details and advice on limning, the book includes conversations held with Queen Elizabeth and Sir Philip Sidney, besides Hilliard's opinion of Holbein, whose method of limning he says he 'ever imitated', and a slight criticism of the artist Albrecht Dürer.

The treatise is clear and direct in its advice on all the essential points to be observed in painting miniatures. He considered the portrait to be so precious that the utmost care should be taken of it. No dust or smoke should be allowed near the colours and the water used to blend them should be as pure as that distilled from a clear spring or other source. The portrait should not be breathed on or touched with the fingers, and particular care was to be taken in cold weather. Further advice includes an admonition to the painter not to get angry while he is working but to shut out questioners and busybodies.

Hilliard mentions a conversation with the Queen about shadows in painting and remarks that she had noted that the Italian artists used little shadowing. After discussing this point, the Queen chose to sit for her painting in 'an open alley of a goodly garden, where no tree was neere nor anye shadowe at-all'.

The author describes how best to use the various colours, how they should be stored and how the card on which the portrait was painted should be prepared. When painting his miniatures he usually placed his sitters three-quarters left, showing the slight indentation on the profile near the eye, which was drawn perfectly round with the lid a bold curve. No green or blacks were used in modelling the face and unfortunately the carmines on the cheeks have usually faded, leaving the portrait rather masklike. The hair was drawn freely in dark curls over a lighter background and in spite of his advice on drawing a hand with a good grace, his own efforts were rather unrealistic and awkward.

He frequently wrote the sitter's age and date in gold on the blue background

[1] See bibliography.

which he used, and sometimes added a motto or symbol such as a flower painted on the bodice or doublet, always different for each sitter, and their significance can sometimes be discovered. Few miniatures by him are signed and dated but they were all painted on vellum and stuck on to card, the shapes being circular, oval or rectangular. His colours were opaque, and he had complete mastery in drawing the intricate pattern of lace in the collars and ruffs which adorned the costume of the period.

His favoured position at Court enabled him to leave behind a vivid picture of the nobility of the Elizabethan age, and he will always be remembered as the only great artist that England produced at this period of her history.

LAURENCE HILLIARD (1581/2–1640) was one of the eight children born to Nicholas Hilliard, presumably in 1581, the year he was baptized. He was the only one to follow his father's profession, and according to letters written by Nicholas Hilliard to Sir Robert Cecil, later Earl of Salisbury, we know that he took a great deal of trouble to educate and train Laurence and to provide for him. In 1601 he wrote to Sir Robert saying, 'I hope you (in remembrance of your loving kindness promised) will take my son into your service, to place him with one of your secretaries or otherwise. He has the Spanish tongue and an entrance into well writing and drawing'. In a letter written in 1606 Nicholas refers to him as 'doing His Majesty good service both in limned pictures and medals of gold', from which we learn that he was trained as a goldsmith as well as a painter.

In 1608 a patent was drawn up appointing him limner to James I after his father's death, an appointment which carried with it an annuity of £40. He duly succeeded him and inherited most of his effects when he died in 1619.

He had already been working for King James and his Queen, Anne of Denmark, prior to this, apparently with success, and he held his office to the end of his life. In 1624 a warrant of the Council ordered payment of £42 for five pictures he had painted. No mention is made of his wife, but according to the 1849 Edition of *Anecdotes of Painting* by Horace Walpole, he had four children, Brandon, Thomas, Charles and a daughter called Laurence. Artistically he cannot be compared with his father, for he lacked the skill and draughtsmanship that was so apparent in the older Hilliard's work. He is thought to have been responsible for many of the stock replicas of miniatures of James I and his Queen, and of their family. He worked in the style of his father but the result was much stiffer and his inscriptions in gold were less finely drawn. Only in the drawing of the eyes can one see a real resemblance to Nicholas Hilliard. He used the same opaque colours and backgrounds of vellum as those used by his father.

18. ISAAC OLIVER (d. 1617)
A lady said to be Frances Howard, Countess of Essex and Somerset (d. 1632).
Signed. 5 in. diam.

19. CORNELIUS JOHNSON
(1593?–1661/2)
An unknown man. $2\frac{1}{16} \times 2\frac{25}{32}$ in.

20. ISAAC OLIVER
Anne of Denmark
(1574–1619),
wife of James I. Signed. $2\frac{1}{2} \times 1\frac{5}{8}$ in.

21. ISAAC OLIVER
James I & VI (1566–1625).
$2\frac{1}{8} \times 1\frac{5}{8}$ in.

22. ISAAC OLIVER
Robert Devereux,
2nd Earl of Essex, K.G. (1566–1601).
Sketch. $2\frac{1}{8} \times 1\frac{3}{4}$ in.

23. ISAAC OLIVER
Robert Devereux,
2nd Earl of Essex, K.G.
Signed. $2\frac{1}{32} \times 1\frac{5}{8}$ in.

CHAPTER IV

ISAAC AND PETER OLIVER

*

It is most unfortunate that the private lives and family affairs of ISAAC OLIVER and his son Peter are lost in obscurity. Born of Huguenot parents in Rouen, the father Pierre Ollivier, was a goldsmith and pewterer who fled with the boy and his mother to England to escape the religious persecution which was causing many people to leave France. The date of his birth is unknown, and although Vertue gives it as 1556, others think it is more probable that it was somewhere between 1565–7. In any case, Isaac was presumably quite young when he arrived in England and his father would no doubt have become known to Nicholas Hilliard as they both followed the same trade. This may be the explanation of why young Oliver was apprenticed to Hilliard. The family lived in Fleet Street and Isaac remained with them for a time.

It is not surprising to find another foreign artist working in England, for the sixteenth century was a period when artists moved from country to country, exchanging ideas and studying each other's technique.

Prior to the Hilliard centenary exhibition in 1947, a great deal of confusion had arisen over the work of Isaac Oliver and Hilliard, owing to their close association and the similarity of their technique. Because of the paucity of knowledge of Isaac Oliver's life and the close resemblance between his painting and that of his master, it was wisely decided to show the work of both, thus providing an opportunity for experts and collectors alike to study the painting of the two men side by side and assess their respective merits. As a result it was discovered that many miniatures had been hitherto wrongly attributed.

Oliver was undoubtedly influenced in his early work by Hilliard, but later his style became more 'continental' and he may even have been slightly influenced by Marcus Gheeraerts the Younger, whose sister, Sara Gheeraerts, he married as his second wife. Basil Long tells us that they were probably married in 1602 at the Dutch Church in Austin Friars. In about 1594 his first wife Elizabeth, had borne him a son, Peter, who was later to follow his father's profession. In the register of St Peter's, Cornhill, there is a record of the burial of his first wife Elizabeth on 6th September, 1599. The Duke of Portland owns a miniature of her which is a particularly fine example of his work and shows the dexterity with which he could paint embroidery and lace.

So far no record has been found of the death of Sara, his second wife, but his third wife, also called Elizabeth, by whom he had a son called Jacques, was his executrix and survived him.

In spite of the fact that he had lived in England for over forty years, Vertue's quotations from a notebook of his makes it seem likely that he made little attempt to learn the language, for his English remained elementary in the extreme while his French seemed quite satisfactory.

He is known to have studied art in Italy and was in Venice in 1596. It is known from the work he did there that he made copies of pictures by Correggio, one of which, dated 1588 and now in the collection of the Queen of Holland, is considered to be his earliest dated and fully signed miniature. It is very probable that he visited the Netherlands at this time and a number of his miniatures of this period are in collections on the Continent. It was possibly during his stay on the Continent that he acquired an interest in the landscape backgrounds that help to distinguish his work from that of Hilliard. A comparison of the two artists' work has led to the observation that while Hilliard was an Englishman under French influence Oliver was a Frenchman under English influence.

While Hilliard's miniatures will always be admired for their jewel-like appearance and brilliant colouring, the style and technique that was adopted by the Olivers was a great advance artistically. The features were better modelled and lost much of that flatness which had an affinity with the illuminated manuscript style, while more character could be discerned in the faces of the sitter and richer colours were used in the drapery and background.

It was a colourful age in which the costumes worn by the Court were embellished with rich embroidery often studded with jewels, and all these adornments were painted to perfection by both Hilliard and Oliver. The use of emblems and symbolic backgrounds of which Hilliard was so fond was less in evidence in Oliver's work, and when attempted was not so effective. Oliver's drawing of the hands, which he usually placed in front of the bosom, is somewhat unrealistic and stiff, and one is reminded of Hilliard's admonition to 'Tell not abody when you draw the hands but when you spy a good grace in their hand take it quickly or pray them to stand but still for commonly when they are told they give the hand the worse and more unnatural or affected grace'. Unfortunately Oliver does not appear to have taken any notice of these words, and the result is obvious.

It is interesting to note that even during his lifetime he was considered a great artist. Henry Peacham in *The Gentleman's Exercise*[1] says – 'nor must I be ingrate-

[1] 1634 Edition, p. 7.

fully unmindful of mine owne Countriemen, who have beene, and are able to equall the best, if occasion served, as old Mr. Hilliard, Mr. Isaac Oliver inferiour to none in Christendom for the countenance in small'.

Oliver is known to have copied a number of large paintings and in this he was no doubt influenced by having studied the works of the Italian masters. It is tantalizing that, although a large number of his portrait miniatures have survived and enhance many of the world's best collections, most of the historic and figure subject pieces have disappeared.

In Oliver's early miniatures there is a great similarity in style to the work of Hilliard, but the treatment of the hair is different and appears softer and more natural. The backgrounds of earlier works are usually blue-white, in those executed later they vary from a pinkish-grey to reddish-pink and include landscapes and draperies. These portraits were painted, like those of Hilliard, on prepared cards or grounds of different shades which were laid aside and then selected according to the complexion of the sitter. These grounds were usually of parchment or vellum stuck on to a card or panel and their shape varied from circular and oval to rectangular.

That Oliver was an exceedingly fine draughtsman is evident from the most expressive head of a boy in crayon, erroneously called 'Henry Frederick, Prince of Wales', owned by the Duke of Buccleuch; and in the Earl of Derby's collection, which is at present on loan to the Manchester Art Gallery, there is also a fine un-finished sketch for a miniature of Robert Devereux, 2nd Earl of Essex.[1] The British Museum also has a few drawings, together with some executed in pen and ink. It is quite evident from the eight large portrait miniatures by Oliver known to exist that he took a delight in combining his skill at composition on a large scale with that of expert portraiture, and the detail to be seen in the landscape back-grounds is quite superb.

He did not sign or date his miniatures as frequently as Hilliard, but often used the monogram I.O., forming it like a Greek Ph surrounded with four dots, although occasionally he signed in full, as in the two in the Victoria and Albert Museum. One, of Richard Sackville, Earl of Dorset, is signed 'Isaac Olliuierus fecit 1616' and the other, of Sir Arundell Talbot, is inscribed on the back 'adi 1ʒ Magio 1596 In Venetia Fecit m. Isacq oliuiero francese ΦV. i4 da L.8 (may 13, 1596 made by Isaac Oliver the Frenchman in Venice).'[2] This mention of his French connection rather shows how proud he was of his nationality.

In spite of the fact that Hilliard had held a favoured position at Court for so long, Oliver succeeded in obtaining a distinguished clientèle which included,

[1] The completed miniature belongs to Her Majesty the Queen and there is another copy in the Duke of Devonshire's collection at Chatsworth.
[2] *British Miniaturists*, by B. S. Long, p. 318.

among others, Queen Elizabeth and Anne of Denmark, Queen of James I, for whom he painted numerous portraits for presentation, particularly those of the two princes, Henry and Charles. This must have meant that he had become a serious rival to Hilliard, who for some time had been oppressed with anxieties and debts.

One of Oliver's finest miniatures is of Frances Howard, Countess of Essex and Somerset (d. 1632). Signed with the monogram I.O., circular and five inches in diameter, it was formerly in the collections of J. West, P.R.S., and Horace Walpole, and now belongs to the Earl of Derby. It is a truly superb miniature both in its draughtsmanship and colouring and the draperies show all the richness and elaborate embroidery of the period.

A fine example of his rectangular miniatures is the one which was said to represent Sir Philip Sidney (1554–86) which belongs to Her Majesty the Queen and is at Windsor Castle. Although it is no longer considered to portray Sir Philip, the quality of the miniature is superb and shows the landscape background that helped to distinguish his style from that of Hilliard. Another interesting pair of miniatures now attributed to Oliver are those of two girls, one aged four and holding an apple, the other aged five and holding a red carnation, which are at the Victoria and Albert Museum (Salting Bequest). These had been for many years attributed to Levina Teerlinc, but the date makes this impossible.

From the knowledge available it is not possible to discover what sort of a man Oliver was, but the two self-portraits, one owned by the Earl of Derby and the other by Her Majesty the Queen, give one the impression that he had a jaunty air and perhaps a devil-may-care disposition! He was painting without any sign of loss of power right up to the end of his life, and was somewhere between 50 and 60 years of age when he died at his house in Blackfriars, London, in 1617. He was buried in St Anne's Church, Blackfriars, on 2nd October, and according to Vertue his son erected a monument to his memory. By his will he bequeathed to his wife 'the third of his effects and the lease of his house in Blackfriars, excepting only to his eldest son Peter, all his drawings, limnings, historical or otherwise, finished or unfinished, of his own handyworks, or in the case of Peter's death, to any of his other sons that should follow his profession. All the other two parts of his effects to be sold and equally divided between his sons and daughters. His other paintings or collections to be sold, allowing his son Peter to purchase whatever he pleased thereof at 5/- per pound less than the true or genuine value of them.' Hilliard, who was at this point imprisoned for debt, survived him by two years.

PETER OLIVER (1594?–1647) was, as has already been mentioned, his son by the first wife, Elizabeth, and almost nothing is known about his private affairs except that he was married.

He was a pupil of his father and it is generally supposed that he assisted him considerably by making replicas of a number of paintings for the King, particularly towards the end of Isaac Oliver's life, when numerous copies of Prince Henry's and Prince Charles's portraits were called for. This fact makes it difficult to distinguish some of his earlier paintings from those of his father, but as time went on he developed a broader and freer style. He was a very pleasing draughtsman and the Earl of Derby has an interesting pair of drawings on card, one a self-portrait of the artist, the other of a woman, which is inscribed on the back, presumably by Oliver, 'P. Oliver, his Wife.' His usual signature was, however, P.O., conjoined and often surrounded by dots.

He certainly complied with his father's wish that he should finish any uncompleted works that remained, as far as the painting of the 'Entombment of Christ' was concerned. This was at one time in Charles I's cabinet, but like so many others is now lost and all that remains is the preliminary drawing by Isaac Oliver now in the British Museum. Like his father, Peter Oliver painted on vellum or parchment stuck on to card, the shapes being oval and rectangular, and Dr G. C. Williamson[1] states that some were even heart-shaped, with backgrounds varying from blue to grey, violet and brown, occasionally having reddish curtains at the rear of the sitter. Both father and son painted the hair in a lighter manner than had previously been seen, giving a softer, more transparent effect. His earliest portraits appear to date somewhere about the 1620's. In view of the fact that there were no artists in Europe to compare with the Olivers in miniature painting it is to be regretted that so much of Peter's life was taken up with making copies of other men's work. Whether this was by design or force of circumstances, we do not know, but a number of fine and accurate historical miniatures after Titian, Correggio and Raphael are to be found in the Royal Collection at Windsor and in the Victoria and Albert Museum, painted for his patron, Charles I. The Duke of Devonshire owns a miniature of Edward, Prince of Wales (1537–53) after Holbein, signed P.O., which is beautifully painted. In general Peter Oliver's work is considered of finer quality than that of his father, to be more life-like and to show more character in the faces of the sitters.

He died in 1647 and was buried at St Anne's, Blackfriars, on 22nd December, two years before Charles I was beheaded. Most of Charles I's collection was dispersed or lost during the long years of the Commonwealth, and when in 1660 the Restoration brought Charles II back to his country, he was unable to trace any of these paintings which he would have liked to recover for himself. However, on making enquiries he discovered through a mutual friend of the Olivers that Mrs Oliver was still alive and living at Isleworth, and furthermore that she had in her

[1] See bibliography.

possession a number of copies of the paintings that her husband had executed for Charles I. The King then went disguised to see Mrs Oliver with, so Vertue tells us, 'one, Rogers of Isleworth'. He was shown a number of these miniatures both finished and unfinished, and asked if he could buy them. The reply was that 'she had a mind that the King should see them first' and if he did not purchase them she should think of disposing of them. On discovering that her visitor was the King she then produced some more pictures to show him. Charles asked her price for those he wanted and she promised to look up her husband's books and let him know what Charles I had paid. Thereupon the King took with him the paintings he liked, and later sent her an offer of £1,000 or an annuity of £300 for life. Unwisely, as it turned out, she chose the latter, for when some years later she discovered that the majority of these paintings had been given to the King's mistresses, she expressed herself in no uncertain terms and with considerably more candour than tact, saying had she known to whom they would have been given he should never have had them. When the King heard this, he promptly stopped her annuity.

CHAPTER V

JOHN HOSKINS AND HIS CONTEMPORARIES

*

Once again we are faced with the problem of two artists of the same name who were both in all probability painters of miniatures. It would appear from the scanty information that is available about JOHN HOSKINS (d. 1665) that he must have lived during at least part of the reign of Charles I, and certainly during the Commonwealth and for five years after Charles II was restored to the throne in 1660. He is believed to have died in Bedford Street, London, on 22nd February, 1665, and as on more than one occasion there are references to 'old Hoskins', it is likely that he reached an advanced age.

His miniatures were of the highest quality and excelled any that were painted between the time of Nicholas Hilliard and Samuel Cooper.

In this case, unlike the artists who have already been discussed, insufficient evidence has come to light to make any conclusive statement, but it has been established by John Hoskins the elder's will, dated 1662, that there certainly were two of them and that the elder left his son the sum of £20 to purchase a ring or to be expended otherwise as he should think fit. The same John Hoskins, the younger, received a further legacy from Samuel Cooper after his death in 1672. It is thought probable that the wife of John Hoskins, the elder, was called Cooper, as it is known that both Alexander and Samuel Cooper were Hoskins' nephews, and that they were both 'bred up under the care and discipline of Mr. Hoskins' and when they were old enough their uncle instructed them in the art of limning. In an early biography it is stated that John Hoskins senior was 'a very eminent limner in the reign of Charles I whom he drew with his queen and most of his court, he was bred a face painter in oil but afterwards taking to miniatures he far exceeded what he did before'.[1]

Unfortunately any oil paintings he may have executed have either disappeared or remain unrecognized. Allowing for the fact that Hoskins senior would have needed training and practice before becoming accomplished at his work, it is probable that he was born somewhere about 1595 as, judging by their costume, the earliest of his miniatures date from about 1620 to 1625.

Charles I appointed Hoskins as his limner, and in 1640 granted him an annuity

[1] *The Art of Painting*, 1706. Translated from De Piles, p. 437.

of £200 a year for life 'providing that he work not for any other without His Majesty's license'. It was evident from the miniatures that he painted that Hoskins must have ignored this command of his royal patron, and the cause of this was no doubt that like many other painters employed by the Stuarts, little or no money was ever paid him. That this was so is proved by a published State paper of 1660, recording a petition from him for a payment out of some delinquent's estate of £4,150 arrears of the £200 a year pension of which he had received no benefit since 1640, so that had he not had other patrons he would have been in considerable financial difficulty.

It is frustrating that in spite of a great deal of research, so little has been discovered about Hoskins' life and family. As has already been mentioned, his wife's maiden name is thought to have been Cooper, and, according to Graham Reynolds,[1] her christian name was Sarah and she was alive when he made his will in the parish of St Paul's, Covent Garden, on 30th December, 1662, when he was 'weak in body but of good and perfect memory'. Basil Long tells us[2] that John Hoskins the younger was also married and had a daughter Mary.

It is not possible at present to distinguish between the work of father and son. It is therefore John Hoskins senior who is the artist usually referred to. In the past an attempt was made to attribute miniatures to them individually by the differences in signature, but attribution by this method is impossible owing to the fact that the dates and costumes of the sitters are inconsistent with the ages of the artists. There is a strong case for the belief that John Hoskins the younger probably painted miniatures in collaboration with his father, and there is every likelihood that the father had several assistants working for him, quite apart from his nephews, Alexander and Samuel Cooper. W. Sanderson, writing in his 'Treatise' in the *Graphic*, 1658, says, 'For Miniature of Limning in water colours, Hoskins and his son, the next modern since Hilliard's father and son', and in Pepys' Diary for 19th July, 1668, we find the entry, 'come Mr. Cooper, Hales, Harris, Mr. Butler that wrote Hudibras and Mr. Cooper's cosen Jacke'. The 'cosen Jacke' is thought to be John Hoskins junior.

Hoskins like other artists also made copies of large paintings by great masters, and these include copies of portraits by Van Dyck. Van Dyck evidently made a great impression on Hoskins, for, whereas the style of his earlier paintings had emerged from that of Hilliard and Oliver, his later portraits, painted after Van Dyck arrived in England, developed in quite a different manner.

In the miniatures painted before 1632 the background was still often blue or brown, following the style of earlier artists, but occasionally they had a red curtain

---

[1] Reynolds, *English Portrait Miniatures*, p. 46.
[2] B. S. Long, *British Miniatures*, p. 223.

24. SIR BALTHASAR GERBIER
(1592–1667)
Prince Charles, afterwards Charles I (1600–49).
$4\frac{1}{4} \times 3\frac{1}{8}$ in.

25. PETER OLIVER (1594?–1647)
Said to be a self-portrait.
Approx. $2\frac{1}{2} \times 2$ in.

26. PETER OLIVER
Mrs Peter Oliver. Signed. $3\frac{1}{4} \times 2\frac{1}{2}$ in.

27. PETER OLIVER
Self-portrait. Signed. $3\frac{1}{4} \times 2\frac{1}{2}$ in.

28. JOHN HOSKINS (d. 1665)
Called Elizabeth Vernon,
Countess of Southampton (d. after 1625).
Signed and dated 1650. $2\frac{1}{2} \times 2$ in.

29.
EDWARD NORGATE (Bapt. 1581–d. 1650)
Mrs Norgate aged 25. Dated 1617.
$2\frac{5}{32} \times 1\frac{23}{32}$ in.

30. JOHN HOSKINS
Lady Catherine Erskine,
1st wife of 2nd Earl of Haddington.
$3\frac{3}{4} \times 3$ in.

31. JOHN HOSKINS
William, 2nd Duke of Hamilton (1616–51).
Signed and dated 1647.
$3 \times 2\frac{1}{2}$ in.

behind the sitter; later, landscapes were sometimes used, and in the case of one in the Duke of Portland's collection, a portrait of the Duke of Buckingham signed I.H., he introduces a rocky background with a ship at sea against the sky. The question of signatures is one which has been considered by all the authorities on the subject, and nothing decisive has so far come to light. The earlier signatures are I.H. in monogram, the next is an H. with a dot above the first vertical line. The initials I.H. are also used separately, and the punctuation varies, a semi-colon often being placed after the initials while yet a further method is for the first stroke of the H. to be elongated into a J. A number of these signatures are also dated, at least one is known to have been signed in full, and on many the signature is in gold.

The Hoskins, like their predecessors, painted on parchment stuck on to card, and used mainly the oval upright format which, after Van Dyck's influence became felt in England, tended to become larger in size, no doubt in order to give sufficient scope for successful reproductions in miniature of that artist's work. At first the style of these copies and of the portraits painted from life remained the same, but as time went on Hoskins seemed to absorb some of Van Dyck's methods and a bolder and a freer style emerged, which remained in evidence to the end of his life.

During the reign of James I, Sir Theodore Turquet de Mayerne, the King's physician, visited Hoskins and noted that Samuel Cooper was still with his uncle. He must have had an interest in painting himself, as he described how Hoskins used to put his colours into small turned ivory dishes so that they did not dry up too quickly, and how when he was working he used a turned ivory palette about 4 inches in diameter and slightly hollow in the centre. He put his colours in small quantities one beside the other at the end of the palette, having first wetted them with gum and water, and when he wanted to use them he moistened his brush in clear water before applying the colour. When using white and blue he kept these separately in little ivory pots.

The miniatures painted by Hoskins have a charm that cannot be denied, and this remains even through the changes of style. He succeeded in making the hair look natural and finely drawn, and his method of painting the eyes was that of Hilliard's school, showing the pupils round and clear with the light reflected in them. His colouring is on the whole subdued and the general effect simple and dignified, while he had an obvious insight into the character of the sitters. In the shading of the faces he used a greenish stippling or *pointilliste* dotting, which was later used by other artists.

One of his friends was Cornelius Johnson, and according to a sale catalogue of Lady Weardale's miniatures in 1925 a portrait of George Villiers, Duke of Buckingham, was offered, which was inscribed on the back, 'Hoskins, drawn by himself and by him given to old Johnson ye painter of whose son I bought it at Utrecht 1700 F. St. J'.

Being one of the few miniature painters whose work is comparable with that of Hilliard, Hoskins bridges the gap between the Elizabethan age and its illuminated manuscript style and that of the great period of Samuel Cooper, whose work was to excel by far that of his teacher and uncle, and we may well re-echo Vertue's regret that 'for the life of this valuable master we find fewer materials than of almost any man on the list who arrived to so much excellence'.

CORNELIUS JOHNSON (1593?–1661/2) has had his name spelt in a variety of ways which include Jansen and Janssens. His family came from Cologne originally but later settled in Antwerp, and from there must have come to England, for Cornelius was baptized in London on the 14th of October, 1593. On 16th July, 1622 he married a lady called Elizabeth Beke, or Beck, and they remained in England until 1643. On 10th October of that year it is recorded in the Journals of the House of Commons that 'Cornelius Johnson, Picture Drawer, shall have Mr. Speaker's Warrant to pass beyond the seas with Emanuel Passe and George Hawkins and to carry with him such pictures and colours, bedding, household stuff, pewter and brass as belonged to himself'. Horace Walpole records that during his stay in England Johnson lived in Blackfriars in London, and on leaving the country he went to Holland where he became a member of the painters' guild at Middleburg, and from there went to Amsterdam, where he continued painting until his death somewhere between 1661–2.

Walpole admired his work which, although consisting mainly of large oil portraits, also included miniatures painted both in oil and water colour. These, Walpole says, are distinguished by their clearness, neatness and smoothness, and were generally painted on cardboard. He thought that they were true to nature and showed a serene expression on the faces of the sitters.

Not many miniatures by Johnson are known to exist, but there is a very fine one in oil of Sir Nicholas Crisp, which had probably been inherited by the sitter's grand-daughter Anne, the wife of James Sotheby, and which came into the sale rooms when the Sotheby heirlooms were disposed of in 1955. The Duke of Devonshire has one of a man in a falling ruff, and the Duke of Portland owns one in oil on copper, signed at the back, 'C. Johnson, fecit 1639'. We are told by Walpole that the Johnsons had a son, also called Cornelius, who became a painter in Holland. He was said to have been ruined by the extravagance of a second wife and died a poor man. Like John Hoskins, Cornelius Johnson the elder fell under the influence of Van Dyck and imitated his style. He is known to have signed C.J. in monogram and to have charged five broad pieces for a head; he copied in miniature a considerable number of his larger paintings.

EDWARD NORGATE (bapt. 1581, d. 1650) is mainly associated with the art of illuminating, but is closely linked with miniature painting and is known to many by his treatise entitled *Miniatura or the Art of Limning* from the manuscript in the Bodleian Library, Oxford, which was published in 1919. He was the son of Dr Robert Norgate, Master of Corpus Christi College, Cambridge, and having taken up limning and heraldry, came to London where he eventually made many friends among the leading painters of the day. He taught the sons of the Earl of Arundel, becoming Blue Mantle Pursuivant in 1616 and Windsor Herald in 1633, and he was employed to illumine royal patents and to write letters to foreign sovereigns. In 1628 he was made Clerk of the Signet, and in 1639 went with Charles I to Scotland. Norgate had not until recently been included in any history of miniature painting, but three or four authentic portraits by him have now come to light, one of them being that of his wife, Judith, née Lanyer, whom he married in 1613. This miniature is at the Victoria and Albert Museum and others have been discovered in private collections. From these discoveries, Norgate is shown to have followed unspectacularly in the style of Hilliard and Oliver. During his lifetime he established himself as an art connoisseur and was employed to negotiate the purchase of pictures for Queen Henrietta Maria. He died at the Heralds' College, London, and was buried at St Benets, Paul's Wharf, in 1650.

SIR BALTHASAR GERBIER (1592–1667) was born at Middleburg on 23rd February, 1592, the son of French Protestant parents. He seems to have been a most versatile man for he included among his accomplishments those of being an adventurer, painter, architect, musician, author, courtier and diplomat, besides being a good linguist. While visiting Rome he is supposed to have made crayon copies after Raphael. In 1615 he was employed by Prince Maurice of Orange, whose portrait miniature by him, dated 1619, is in the Queen of Holland's collection. In 1616, however, he came to England, where he practised miniature painting and was taken into the service of the Duke of Buckingham. When the Duke and Prince Charles went to Spain in 1623 he accompanied them. By 1625 Gerbier was in Paris, and it was here that he met Rubens. A friendship must have sprung up between them, as Gerbier and he corresponded after this meeting and Rubens stayed with him at his house in London. In 1628 Gerbier was knighted by Charles I, and in 1631 was sent by the King as an envoy to Brussels. In 1641 he was acting as Ambassador in Flanders. After numerous visits of varying duration to Holland and later to Surinam, he went on to Cayenne, where he was involved in mining projects which never bore fruit. He returned to England after Charles I's execution, but never again regained his position at Court, and turned his attention to architecture. He died while engaged on the task of building a house for Lord Craven in Hampstead Marshall, Berkshire, and was buried in the chancel of the church. He had eight children, one of whom was killed at Cayenne. There are only a small number of miniatures attributed to him, but among those known to be authentic is one of Charles I, dated 1616, now in the Victoria and Albert Museum. There are also several small portraits in pen and ink.

DAVID DES GRANGES (1611?–75) was the son of one Samson Des Granges of Guernsey and his wife Marie Bouvier. Although he was baptized as a Huguenot in London sometime between 1611 and 1613, he later became a Roman Catholic. He started his career as an engraver and as early as 1628 engraved the painting of 'St George and the Dragon' by Raphael which belonged to the Earl of Pembroke. He enjoyed the patronage of both Charles I and Charles II, and followed Charles II when he fled to Scotland from the Parliamentary forces. He was appointed His Majesty's limner in 1651, and is thought to have been a friend of Inigo Jones.

He painted a considerable number of miniatures, and their quality varies a great deal; at his best he was a very good artist and his work shows feeling and restraint, particularly in the colouring. I have one fairly large one in my own collection, painted on vellum stuck on to card and showing a man with a moustache and small tufted beard, and dark hair falling over a Van Dyck collar. A white shirt, edged with lace, shows in relief against the brown background and black cloak draped over one shoulder. Des Granges is known to have copied other artists' portraits, including those of Hoskins. He usually signed his work with the initials D.D.G. arranged in a triangle, or just D.G. with sometimes a date added. The earliest signed and dated miniature by him is that of Catherine Manners, 1639, which is at Windsor Castle, and in 1640 he painted a copy after Titian of the 'Marquis del Guasto with his Mistress'. This, one of his finest works, is signed in full, and if it were not for the signature Graham Reynolds considers that it might be attributed to Peter Oliver. An interesting collection of family miniatures is owned by the Earl of Haddington, among which are four by Des Granges, three signed.

Although he is usually thought of as a miniaturist, there is no doubt that he also painted a limited number of large pictures, although these are rarely seen. One called 'The Saltonstall Family', and owned by Sir Kenneth Clark, was loaned to the Exhibition of seventeenth-Century Art in Europe, held at the Royal Academy in 1938. The group consists of Sir Richard Saltonstall (d. 1650) of Chipping Warden, his wife, Elizabeth Bas, and their three children. The mother is lying in the centre on a bed draped with red curtains, and the nurse sits beside her holding the new-born baby. On the left of the picture is the father bringing in the two younger children to see the baby. The colouring of the whole painting is predominantly red. The children are well drawn, as are the features of the rest of the group, but the father is placed in rather an angular pose.

The last record we have of Des Granges is when in 1671 he petitioned Charles II

32. DAVID DES GRANGES (1611?–75)
Queen Henrietta Maria (1609–69).
$2\frac{1}{8} \times 1\frac{11}{16}$ in.

33. DAVID DES GRANGES
Inigo Jones (1573–1652). $2\frac{1}{4} \times 1\frac{13}{16}$ in.

34. DAVID DES GRANGES
An unknown man. $3\frac{5}{32} \times 2\frac{5}{8}$ in.

35. DAVID DES GRANGES
James, 1st Duke of Hamilton (1606–49).
Signed. $3\frac{1}{4} \times 2\frac{1}{4}$ in.

36. SAMUEL COOPER (1609–72)
Elizabeth Cromwell (Mrs Claypole)
(1629–58).
Signed and dated 1653. $2\frac{5}{8} \times 2\frac{1}{4}$ in.

37. SAMUEL COOPER
Sir Thomas Hanmer, 2nd Bt. (1612–78).
$2\frac{7}{8} \times 2\frac{1}{4}$ in.

38. SAMUEL COOPER
Possibly Barbara Villiers,
Duchess of Cleveland (1641–1709).
Signed. $3\frac{1}{2} \times 2\frac{7}{8}$ in.

39. SAMUEL COOPER
Called Elizabeth Vernon,
Countess of Southampton (d. after 1625).
Dated 1647. Approx. $2\frac{1}{4} \times 1\frac{7}{8}$ in.

for £72 which was still owing to him for painting thirteen portraits of him. In the petition he says he is old and infirm, with failing eyesight, quite unable to support his children and obliged to rely on charity. It would appear that once again the Royal Patrons were not good payers, and history does not relate whether poor Des Granges ever got his money, or what became of his family, for he died about four years later in 1675.

Sir James Palmer (1584–1657) was only a comparatively small link in the chain of miniaturists that extended from the time of Elizabeth I to the rise of Samuel Cooper. The third son of Sir Thomas Palmer of Wingham, Kent, who had held office as High Sheriff of Kent in 1695, he was appointed Gentleman of the Bedchamber to James I in 1622, and later became friendly with Charles I, who appointed him to the position of Gentleman Usher of the Privy Chamber. Charles I held him in such high esteem that he relied to a great extent upon his advice over the formation of his art collection.

In 1645 he was made Chancellor of the Order of the Garter, and was also appointed one of the Governors of the Royal Tapestry Works at Mortlake. He was allowed to make copies in miniature of pictures in the Royal Collection, one of them being a copy of Titian's 'Tarquin and Lucretia' which he is said to have presented to the King.

Palmer was an amateur painter whose work was executed in the style of Hilliard and Oliver. It was known, through references in Van Der Doorts' Catalogue of Charles I's collection, that he practised miniature painting, but it was not possible to ascribe any examples to him until three miniatures signed with the monogram J.P. were discovered in different collections and compared with some large portraits in the possession of various members of the family. It was at once apparent that they were the work of the same artist. Two peculiarities were discovered, namely, that he wrote the date of his miniatures horizontally across the background, and used a rather scratchy looking brush stroke to emphasize the shadows under the chin.

Palmer married a lady called Margaret Pooley, and their son Roger was created the Earl of Castlemain, his wife being the notorious Barbara Villiers, later Duchess of Cleveland. An interesting miniature by Palmer of James I, signed and dated 1623, and housed in a locket 2 inches in diameter was sold at Sotheby's on 1st May, 1958.

CHAPTER VI

SAMUEL AND ALEXANDER COOPER

*

The name of SAMUEL COOPER (1609–72) stands supreme among the miniaturists of the seventeenth century, and his reputation as a great artist was acknowledged both at home and abroad even in his own time. Little or nothing is known about his early life and parentage, but he must have been born somewhere in the year 1609, for on his tomb-stone it is stated that he was 63 years of age when he died in 1672. James I, son of Mary Queen of Scots, had already been on the throne six years, and by the time Samuel was sixteen Charles I had succeeded his father as King.

Historically, Britain was passing through troubled times and the somewhat gaudy and ostentatious age of the Elizabethans had passed, giving way to a more austere way of life. This was especially noticeable in people's attire, and the seriousness of the times was reflected in their faces. In art great changes were taking place; all the characteristics of the school of illuminators were forgotten, and a serious attempt was being made to portray true likenesses.

The artists working at this time had discovered how to achieve greater modelling on the face of the sitters, and whereas in Elizabethan miniatures the hair was painted to show every strand separately, the later miniaturists succeeded in painting it more realistically in soft flowing masses. Greater harmony of colour was achieved in the draperies and backgrounds, and whilst in the period of Hilliard and Oliver backgrounds were mainly blue, often inscribed in gold with the names and date of the sitters, it now became more popular to introduce stormy cloud effects alternating with trees, curtains, or even backgrounds of dull browns and greys. Plain monograms with occasional dates took the place of lengthy inscriptions, and the whole effect was quiet and harmonious. Even the frames in which the miniatures were placed underwent a change, and instead of the bejewelled settings of the Elizabethans, portraits were now housed in frames or lockets of plain metal or wood.

It was, therefore, into a rapidly changing world that Samuel Cooper was born, and his inspiration and experimental ability enabled him to leave behind him some of the greatest masterpieces of the seventeenth century.

According to Richard Graham, in an appendix to *The Art of Painting*, translated into, English in 1695, Cooper was 'bred up together with his eldest brother Alexander under the care and discipline of Mr. Hoskins, his uncle'. We do not know how old these boys were when their parents died, nor in what circumstances they were left. Therefore we can only assume that the orphaned boys were cared for and trained by their uncle and aunt, and when they were old enough, apprenticed to him in the art of limning. It is doubtful if John Hoskins could have foreseen when he took them under his care that in the course of time Samuel would become such an excellent painter that he would one day be described as the 'Apelles of England' and supplant him in popularity.

Samuel is said to have been a Jew, but this fact has never been established, and when he died he was certainly given a Christian burial at his own request. He was considered to be the finest miniature painter of his day, and this assessment has withstood the test of time and modern criticism; he remains the greatest English-born painter in miniature, and some would say the finest miniaturist in Europe during the seventeenth century. Contemporary biographers tell us that he was an accomplished linguist and that he did a great deal of travelling. It has been said that he spent many years abroad and that he was well known to most of the eminent men in Holland and France as well as to those in England, and that his works were 'known throughout all parts of Christendom'.

He numbered among his friends such men as John Milton, Thomas Hobbes, Samuel Butler and Samuel Pepys, and it is surprising therefore that no letters or documents have survived to add personal details to the story of his life. As far as is known, the only document that exists in Cooper's own handwriting, apart from his signatures, is the recipe for preparing lead white which was given to Sir Theodore Turquet de Mayerne (1573–1655) and which is preserved with the Mayerne manuscripts in the British Museum. Sir Theodore was a Swiss physician and in 1600 held office as Royal District Physician in Paris. In 1603 he came to England where he was appointed physician to Queen Anne, wife of James I. After a further visit to Paris he returned to England in 1611 and remained in this country for the rest of his life, and was knighted in 1624. The Duke of Portland owns two portraits of him, one by Bernard Lens, and the other an enamel of the school of Petitot; an enamel also attributed to the same school was sold in London recently among the contents of the Dyson Perrins collection. Sir Theodore was a close friend of Petitot and assisted him by his chemical knowledge in the technical process of enamelling.

Samuel Cooper's interest in music and his accomplishment on the lute did much to increase his circle of friends beyond those primarily interested in painting, and may even have accounted for the fact that the demand for his work never lessened during the period of the Commonwealth, and continued after Charles II was restored to the throne in 1660. He was evidently working for his uncle for some years, for the Mayerne manuscript tells us that he was still with Hoskins in 1634, by which time he was 25 years of age. The period 1635–42 is the time to which the least number of miniatures can be traced, and it is possible therefore that it was during those years that he was abroad. From 1642 onwards, however, a complete chain of signed and dated portraits carries us on without a break or loss of power in execution, to his death in 1672.

There are a certain number of references to his work and life by contemporary writers, and Norgate in his *Miniatura* makes reference to portraits in crayon and the excellence of their quality. The exact date on which Cooper ceased to work for his uncle is not known, but the story has been passed down that his departure was due to the fact that Hoskins, on finding that his nephew's work was surpassing his own and in such great demand, became jealous and took him into partnership, but finding that Cooper's pictures were still obtaining more patrons than his own, 'was pleased to dismiss the partnership' and Cooper then set up on his own.

Of the few crayon drawings that have survived, the most notable is that of Thomas Alcock, which is preserved in the Ashmolean Museum, Oxford. There is an inscription on the back of the drawing which reads, 'This picture was drawn for me at the Earl of Westmoreland's house at Apethorpe in Northamptonshire by the great (though little) limner the then famous Mr. Cooper of Covent Gardens when I was 18 years of age'.

Due to the fact that the majority of Cooper's portraits were head and shoulders only, and in some cases unfinished, a legend grew up that he was unable to draw other parts of the body successfully. The reason for this is not far to seek, for his uncle John Hoskins employed him mainly in painting the features, no doubt because of his great ability in obtaining excellent likenesses. It is quite evident that Cooper lavished all his care on the faces and heads of his sitters, giving special attention to the hair, for which he was particularly gifted, and not paying as much attention to the draperies and backgrounds; but his portrait of Margaret Lemon, formerly in the Pfungst collection, shows that he could have drawn limbs with as much dexterity as he achieved in the faces.

There are a number of his unfinished sketches in well-known collections, the most famous of them being his miniature of Oliver Cromwell. Two originals of this exist, one belonging to the Duke of Devonshire and the other to the family of the Duke of Buccleuch, into whose possession it passed from the Franklands who were descendants of Cromwell. When he was working on the sketch of Cromwell, Cooper decided to make a copy of it, and one day while he was drawing the Protector arrived, caught him in the act, and immediately took it away with him.

40. SAMUEL COOPER
Jane Penruddock.
Unfinished portrait. $2\frac{13}{16} \times 2\frac{5}{16}$ in.

41.
SAMUEL COOPER
Frances Stuart,
Countess of
Richmond
(1647–1702).
Unfinished
portrait.
$4\frac{7}{8} \times 3\frac{7}{8}$ in.

42. ALEXANDER COOPER (d. 1660?)
Prince Rupert (1619–82). $2\frac{5}{8} \times 2\frac{1}{8}$ in.

43. THOMAS FLATMAN (1635–88)
An unknown man. Signed and dated 1675.
$2\frac{7}{8} \times 2\frac{3}{8}$ in.

44. THOMAS FLATMAN
Charles Beale the elder (1660–94).
$3\frac{3}{8} \times 2\frac{3}{4}$ in.

45. MARY BEALE (1633–99) attrib.
Charles II (1630–85). $3\frac{3}{16} \times 2\frac{19}{32}$ in.

Graham Reynolds quotes another version of its history from Vertue, who records the fact that it was bought from Samuel Cooper for £100 by Richard Cromwell after his father's death. The face in these portraits is finished, but the rest only partly drawn. There is a further copy of it in Her Majesty the Queen's collection at Windsor, and yet another one by Bernard Lens in the Duke of Portland's collection at Welbeck. Thomas Carlyle said of the portrait, 'I do not know of any other mortal head so fine – the miniature by Cooper has got his face', and John Bailey said, 'He was not afraid to paint the wart on Cromwell's nose because he knew that he could so give the nobleness of the whole face that the wart would merely add to the truthfulness of the portrait without detracting from its nobleness', while Horace Walpole observed that 'if his portrait of Cromwell could be so enlarged I dont know but Van Dyck would appear less great by comparison'.

Numerous copies of Cooper's miniatures have been made, both in the seventeenth century and since, many of them because of the historical interest of the sitters, particularly Cromwell, and some of them have been so well painted that they have in the past confused the authorities and made it difficult to assess Cooper's work to the full. It is fortunate that we have in Britain several extremely fine collections which are especially rich in early miniatures, including the work of Cooper, the most notable being Her Majesty the Queen's collection at Windsor, the Duke of Buccleuch's, the Duke of Portland's and the Duke of Devonshire's, to mention but a few. Others are those at the Victoria and Albert Museum, the Wallace Collection in Manchester Square, the Fitzwilliam Museum, Cambridge, and the Rijksmuseum, Amsterdam, as well as those owned by museums in the provinces.

Among the fine examples at Windsor is the unfinished miniature of the Duke of Monmouth as a boy, of which the Duke of Buccleuch has a copy, and of Frances, Duchess of Richmond, and Barbara Villiers, afterwards Countess of Castlemaine. The Duke of Devonshire has a sketch in profile of Cromwell that has often been reproduced and which is of fine quality. When the Sotheby heirlooms were sold in London in 1955, a miniature, rightly described as superb, of James Duke of York, afterwards James II, signed S.C. and dated 1661, in an oval $3\frac{1}{4}$ in. × $2\frac{5}{8}$ in., which had been exhibited on several occasions and of which there is a replica in the Buccleuch Collection, was bought by the Victoria and Albert Museum for £2,300. A number of miniatures by Cooper were dispersed in this sale, as well as paintings by other early miniaturists, and among the seventy-four items were some of the choicest portraits that have come into the sale-rooms in recent years.

Cooper's paintings are endowed with a great sense of character which marks his work out from that of any other artist living at the time, and the rich yet subdued colours he used are restful and unostentatious. Unfortunately the carmine he employed has faded rather badly, but the other shades have in most cases retained their brilliance; it is mainly the flesh colours that have deteriorated by exposure to the light. Like his predecessors, Cooper painted on vellum laid on to card. As has already been mentioned, he was equally versatile in crayon and pencil, and some of his unfinished sketches are undoubtedly among his finest works. No oil miniatures by him are known. The size and shape of his portraits varied, many of them being fairly large ovals as much as 3 inches in length, while others are rectangular. He painted with a characteristic broad, strong brush stroke which had not hitherto been known, and in drawing the eyes his style differed from the work of Hoskins. Where Hoskins painted them round and clear, Cooper made them appear large and heavy, giving the impression that they were pressed down upon the lids.

No doubt much of his success was due to his method of lighting. While Hilliard cautioned his followers to paint 'in an open alley of a goodly garden where no tree was near nor any shadow at all', Cooper's method is described by Evelyn in his diary when in January 1662 he was called to His Majesty's Closet where Mr Cooper, 'the rare limner', was crayoning the King's head and he held the candle for him so that he could find the shadows. This method of holding a light high overhead and to one side allowed the shadow of the eyelids to fall on the eyeballs and bring out the modelling of the opposite corner of the eye, so drawing out the features to the full and penetrating the character by throwing emphasis on the lines and furrows of the face. His colour is invariably opaque and a ground of opaque white was laid on before the miniature was drawn, while he favoured a rather strong reddish brown for the shading of the face instead of the pinker tones previously used. This was not at first to everyone's liking, and it is recorded that Pepys thought the colour a little forced. Despite the fading of some of the pigments during the passage of years, the harmony and blending of the colours endows Cooper's work even today with a richness that is only matched by the power and depth of his draughtsmanship.

The majority of Cooper's miniatures were painted from life, but he executed a limited number of copies of other artists' work, including Van Dyck's. His usual signature was S.C., either separately or conjoined, sometimes punctuated, and often followed by a date. His portraits of men are generally considered to be better than those he painted of women, but this criticism may be partly due to the fact that he did not flatter them but presented them as living persons whose beauty could be discerned by their strength of character rather than by artificial means or exaggeration.

From about 1642 onwards Cooper was living in Henrietta Street, Covent Garden, then a fashionable part of London. He had a most distinguished clientèle, and from the miniatures available in the various collections it is obvious that there were few of the important men and women of the day who did not sit to him. His wife was Christina Turner, whose father was one William Turner of York, her sister Edith being the mother of Alexander Pope the poet. An unfinished miniature of Cooper's wife is in the collection of the Duke of Portland. It originally belonged to Lawrence Cross, and at the sale of his effects on 5th December, 1722, was acquired by Edward, Lord Harley for £26. It is inscribed on the back 'Sam Cooper's wife painted by himself', but is not Cooper's writing and was probably written by Cross.

When Charles II was restored to the throne Cooper became known to him and was soon established as the principal miniaturist. In 1663 he was appointed the King's limner at a salary of £200 a year and certain perquisites, but the payment seems to have fallen into arrears. He received only £600 and consequently had to apply for the remainder, when an order was made granting him payment of the arrears plus the £200 per annum.

Samuel Pepys' references in his diary of 1668 to the painting of his wife's portrait by Cooper are well known and make interesting reading, particularly as they throw a certain amount of light on Cooper as a man. Mrs Pepys appears to have had at least eight or nine sittings, and to many of these she was accompanied by her husband and her maid 'Deb'. Pepys evidently enjoyed Cooper's company and admired his accomplishments, and though at first he did not consider Cooper's portrait of his wife to be as good as he expected, when it was completed he appeared highly satisfied and paid him at once to be 'out of his debt'.

The high esteem in which Cooper was held never lessened, and he was painting with as great a skill as ever up to the last few days before his death, when he was busy with commissions for the King and other of his patrons. A miniature of Lady Exeter was referred to by Charles Manners in a letter to Lord Roos, in which he says that Cooper had fallen dangerously ill and was not expected to live three days, and in the diary of Charles Beale, the painter, there is an entry, 'Sunday, May 5th, 1672, Mr. Samuel Cooper, the most famous limner for a face, died'.

In his will Cooper left 'his dearly loved wife' sole executrix, and made various bequests to John Hoskins, the younger, and to the Hayles family. His wife inherited certain lands near Coventry. He was buried in Old St Pancras Church when it was still situated among green fields, and a monument was erected to his memory on the east wall of the nave. His widow was granted an annuity of £200 by Charles II in return for several paintings, but she did not seem to have fared any better than did others before her, and in 1676 she was petitioning for her money. She died in 1693 at the age of seventy and was buried with her husband.

ALEXANDER COOPER (died 1660?) was Samuel Cooper's elder brother and, as has already been mentioned, was apprenticed to his uncle John Hoskins who is presumed to have brought him up.

It has been said that he had instruction in painting from Peter Oliver as well as from his uncle, but there is no real proof of this, due mainly to the fact that whereas many artists from the Continent were coming to England to work, Alexander Cooper did the opposite and went abroad, obtaining employment notably in Holland and Sweden. The extent of his travels is not really known and it is to be hoped that some day it may be possible to ascertain more clearly many more of the relevant details of his life and work. He gained his initial experience in England and was already an expert miniaturist when he left the country. His work, although excellent, was never so widely recognized as that of his brother, and due to the fact that accurate information about his life and painting is difficult to obtain, a true assessment of his portraiture has never been possible. There is only a small number of his miniatures in Britain accepted as authentic, and of this number two are in the Victoria and Albert Museum. For the rest it is necessary to visit Amsterdam, The Hague, Stockholm and Göthenburg, and it is possible that there are miniatures in Copenhagen as well as in private collections.

Alexander Cooper must have been working in Holland somewhere about 1631, and evidence for this is to be found in inscriptions on the backs of miniatures owned by the Countess of Craven and depicting the King and Queen of Bohemia with William Lord Craven, who fought for their cause. The Kaiser Friedrich Museum, Berlin, has nine miniatures by Cooper of the Bohemian Royal Family, painted between the years 1632 and 1633, three of which are signed. Cooper resided at The Hague from 1644–6 and it has been said that in 1645 he was paid a hundred florins for a picture by Prince Frederick Henry of Orange. There is evidence that he was in contact with Sandrart, a Dutch painter, sometime before 1642 when the latter left Amsterdam, and Cooper is supposed to have shown him some miniatures he had painted of persons at the English Court. In about 1647 Cooper travelled to Sweden to work at the court at the invitation of Queen Christina, and he is also known to have painted for Charles X when he succeeded to the throne. From 1647–57 his name is mentioned in Swedish documents, and Dr Williamson states that in one of these documents he is referred to as the Jew Portrait Painter, but this fact has never been established.

When he was sick and bedridden towards the end of his life he was in financial straits, having apparently received no salary for some time, and in 1652 he was obliged to petition for 18 months' arrears. There appears to have been no response to this appeal, and in 1654 he approached Prince Charles Gustavus for assistance. History does not relate whether he ever received any help, but he is thought to have died in his rooms in Copenhagen in the year 1660.

Alexander's painting does not show the same force as that of his brother, but his draughtsmanship was good. He tended to show separate strokes on the brush-work of the face, and his backgrounds were sometimes a purplish colour. His signature was executed in neat initials painted either in black or gold.

CHAPTER VII

MINIATURISTS IN THE LATTER PART
OF THE SEVENTEENTH CENTURY

*

THOMAS FLATMAN (1635–88) was born in London and received his education at Winchester and at New College, Oxford, where he became a fellow in 1656. He was admitted to the Inner Temple in 1655 and called to the Bar in 1662, but it is not known if he ever practised. He seems to have been a man of parts, for he not only qualified in law but was reasonably successful as an author, and a number of his works were published, including a volume called *Poems and Songs* in 1674, and from his writings it is possible to discover a great deal about his temperament and vision of life. He was evidently moody, varying between elation and depression. He must have had an interest in art at an early age, and in spite of his numerous other interests soon acquired great skill as a miniature painter. Although there is no evidence of his having been taught limning by Samuel Cooper, his painting has a close affinity to that artist's work, and as Cooper was still at the height of his power when Flatman's earliest known miniature was painted in 1661, he would no doubt have had ample opportunity to study Cooper's style and technique.

Flatman has not always been appreciated as he deserves, but Vertue at least considered him to be in the first rank, for he said of him that 'Flatman may well deserve the title of master in the art of limning and indeed equal to Hoskins senior or junior and next in imitation of Samuel Cooper'. Vertue also quotes an amusing epigram by Mr Oldys –

> *Should Flatman for his client strain the laws,*
> *The painter gives some colour to the cause,*
> *Should critics censure what the poet writ*
> *The pleader quits him at the Bar of wit.*

Although he owned an estate at Tishton near Diss in Norfolk, he lived for the greater part of his life in Three Leg Alley, St Bride's, London. He numbered among his friends the portrait painters Charles and Mary Beale, and Dr Woodford, with whom he shared rooms for a time and as a result of which a lasting friendship grew up. Dr Woodford became a Canon of Chichester in 1676 and of Winchester in 1680 and was himself a writer, publishing poetical paraphrases of the psalms and canticles. A signed portrait of him by Flatman is in the Fitzwilliam Museum, Cambridge. As well as Woodford and the Beale family, Flatman was also friendly with the musicians Blow and Purcell among others, and the circle of their friends was predominantly artistic. In Charles Beale's diary for 1661 there is a reference to Flatman painting the portraits of Charles and Mary Beale and their children, two of whom, Charles and Bartholomew, on starting their careers, were sent to Flatman to study the art of limning. Flatman introduced Samuel Woodford to the Beales, and as a result he fell in love with their niece Alice whom he married.

Flatman was earnestly religious and wrote a poem dedicated to William Sancroft, then Dean of St Paul's, who was evidently a relation. A certain amount of correspondence took place between Sancroft and Flatman, in which Flatman refers to himself as 'meanest kinsman' or 'poor kinsman'.

According to some letters recently discovered, written by him to Charles Beale, he at one time contemplated committing suicide as a means of escaping his anxieties, which numbered, among other things, a small debt to Charles Beale. When he was young he was evidently very much opposed to marriage, and in 1672 he even wrote a *Bachelor's Song* against it, but when he was thirty-seven he evidently changed his mind, for Anthony à Wood, the antiquary and historian, says he was 'smitten with a fair virgin and more with her fortune', and they presumably married. What became of her was not recorded, but Graham Reynolds mentions that they had a son who apparently died before his father and that both were buried in St Brides.

His miniatures are well painted, and even if his earlier work lacks much of the power and depth of the later, the likenesses are nevertheless good, and show promise of later greatness. Although he imitated Cooper in many respects, he used a rather brown flesh colour, favoured sky backgrounds and used a rather harsh blue, all totally unlike anything used by Cooper. His painting was done on the same card or vellum as his predecessors used, and the shape of his miniatures was mainly oval. As Flatman's style developed it became broader and freer, and as a result many of his portraits have been thought to be by Cooper. Signatures were added to some of his portraits which were passed off as Cooper's, and caused a certain amount of confusion.

There is, among others, a self-portrait in the Victoria and Albert Museum that is particularly fine and, as has already been mentioned, the Fitzwilliam Museum, Cambridge, owns a portrait by him of Samuel Woodford, 1661. Besides these, there are examples of his work in Her Majesty the Queen's Collection at Windsor, the collections of the Duke of Buccleuch, the Duke of Portland and Earl Beauchamp, as well as some in smaller collections. He died in 1688 when he was fifty-three, and from Anthony à Wood's description that 'he gave way to his fate' it is generally believed he committed suicide.

Working at the same time as Thomas Flatman were several artists by the name of Gibson, about whom little is known. This has caused a great deal of confusion and made it difficult to attribute miniatures to any one of these artists with any degree of certainty. The first whose life and work can be traced to any great extent is RICHARD GIBSON (1615–90), commonly called 'the dwarf'. According to Basil Long he was possibly born in Cumberland.

His early life was spent as a page to a lady in Mortlake, and while there he evidently showed a certain aptitude for drawing and was taught painting by F. Cleyn who was director of the Mortlake Tapestry Factory. The works of Sir Peter Lely made a great impression on him and had a considerable influence on his painting. There is reason to suppose some degree of friendship between the two, and that Lely soon after his arrival in England gave Gibson some instruction. He is known to have painted more than one portrait of Gibson and his wife. Having been introduced into the Court of Charles I, it was not long before Queen Henrietta Maria noticed him, and a bride of his own size was found called Ann Shepherd, both of them being three feet ten inches in height. Their marriage is supposed to have taken place at Court, and must naturally have attracted considerable attention which resulted in the poet Waller writing a delightful poem published in 1640:

> *Design or chance make other wives,*
> *But Nature did this match contrive,*
> *Eve might as well have Adam fled*
> *As she denied her little bed,*
> *To him for whom Heaven seemed to frame*
> *And measure out this only dame. . . .*

Richard and Ann Gibson had nine children and it is interesting to note that those about whom anything is known grew to a normal size. One of them, Susan Penelope, became a painter of miniatures.

Gibson is supposed to have painted portraits of Cromwell, but if so they have not been traced. His popularity at Court is evident from the fact that he became drawing master to both Princess Mary and Princess Anne, the daughters of James II by his first wife, Lady Anne Hyde. Princess Mary became the unwilling wife of William of Orange in 1677, at the tender age of fifteen, and Princess Anne was later married to Prince George of Denmark. Richard Gibson, we are told, accompanied Princess Mary to Holland, where he remained on and off from 1677, living at first with a silversmith called J. Nieulant, and in 1679 renting a house on the east

46. CHARLES BEALE (1660–94?)
Sir Peter Lely (1618–80), after Lely.
Signed and dated 1679. $7\frac{1}{8} \times 6\frac{5}{8}$ in.

47. CHARLES BEALE
Antoine Triest,
Bishop of Ghent (1576–1657),
after Van Dyck. Signed and dated 1679.
$3\frac{1}{16} \times 2\frac{1}{2}$ in.

48. SUSAN PENELOPE ROSSE *née* GIBSO
(1652?–1700)
A member of her family. $3\frac{1}{4} \times 2\frac{3}{4}$ in.

49. SUSAN PENELOPE ROSSE
Mary of Modena (1658–1718),
wife of James II. $2\frac{1}{8} \times 1\frac{11}{16}$ in.

50. SCHOOL OF GIBSON
An unknown man. $2\frac{1}{2} \times 2\frac{1}{16}$ in.

51. Front of case to Gibson portrai

side of the Boekhorstratt at The Hague for 290 florins a year, only returning to England to live when William and Mary came to the throne in 1688.

In assessing Gibson's work one has constantly to bear in mind the other artists who bore the same name, worked at the same period and about whom very little is known. WILLIAM GIBSON (1644?–1703?) was said to be a nephew of R. Gibson, and was a pupil of his and of Lely, whose work he copied. He is supposed to have painted miniatures, but none can at present be attributed to him. He was employed by Henry Cavendish, Earl of Ogle, son of the second Duke of Newcastle, and there is evidence of this in proceedings taken in Chancery over some debts the Earl incurred in employing Gibson to paint some portraits for him.

Edward Gibson, another relative, was a painter in oils and pastel, although no miniatures by him have so far come to light. During the last twenty years the existence of a D. GIBSON (d. 1659) has been established. Nothing is known of his life and parentage or whether he was in any way related to the other artists of the same name, but three miniatures exist, signed either in monogram D.G. or D. Gibson in full, and dated 1656, 1657 and 1658 respectively. It is to be hoped that more of this artist's work will be discovered as his miniatures are well painted and very similar in technique to the work of R. Gibson; so much so, that a number of unsigned miniatures of this period can only be described as of the school of Gibson.

SUSAN PENELOPE ROSSE, née Gibson (1652?–1700), to whom reference has already been made, was taught painting by her father. The exact date of her birth is not known, but since all her known miniatures belong to the period after her marriage to a jeweller called Rose or Rosse, she is better known by her married name. She was an admirer of the work of Samuel Cooper, and both studied his technique and copied a number of his miniatures. Vertue tells us that in 1682 she painted a half-length miniature of an ambassador from Morocco, who was at the time sitting for Sir Godfrey Kneller, but the painting has unfortunately since been lost.

An interesting set of fourteen miniatures in the Victoria and Albert Museum were for some years thought to be the work of Samuel Cooper but have now been identified as the work of Mrs Rosse. Many of these are unfinished but are of particular interest as they include two self-portraits of the artist and various members of her family. A few of them are copies of works by Cooper. Some of her miniatures were comparatively small, and although they do not possess the quality of those of the greater seventeenth-century artists they have an attractiveness of their own. Her brush stroke was thinner and more minute than the broad brush work of Cooper, and she seems to give her sitters a slightly pouting lower lip. Her signatures were either S.R. or S.P.R., and occasionally the letters were sloping. She appears to have copied Cooper's method of putting a layer of white on the vellum before beginning the drawing. She died at the age of 48 in 1700 while living in Covent

Garden, and was buried in the church there. Her husband survived her for many years and was still living in 1735, and it was from him that Vertue obtained much of this information. Rosse evidently allowed Vertue to see his collection of paintings, which included among others a portrait of Lely by Gibson.

Another woman artist of this period is MARY BEALE (1633–99) who was the daughter of the Reverend John Cradock, Rector of Barrow in Suffolk, where Mary was baptized on 23rd March, 1633.

The family had many connections in Suffolk, and one branch settled at Wickhambrook near Bury St Edmunds.

Mary Beale is said to have been a pupil of Robert Walker, and it has always been believed that she was also taught by Sir Peter Lely, whose work she copied as well as that of Van Dyck. It would appear that both these men were friends of the family. On 8th March, 1651 she married Charles Beale, Lord of the Manor of Walton-on-Thames, an officer of the Board of Green Cloth, an amateur painter, and a maker of artists' colours. They had two sons, and it was Charles' cousin Alice who, as has already been mentioned, married Dr Samuel Woodford. The sons, Charles and Bartholomew, were both painters, although the latter gave up painting to study medicine. CHARLES BEALE, junior (1660?–94), continued painting miniatures, and dated ones exist up to 1688. He is known to have suffered from bad eyesight which necessitated his giving up miniature painting, but he continued to paint in oils as well as in water colour, often assisting his mother with the backgrounds and draperies. He was taught painting by Thomas Flatman who, it will be remembered, was a friend of the Beale family. He died at the house of a Mr Wilson who lived near St Clement's Church in the Strand, and as he was in his debt many of his pictures were retained by Wilson in token payment.

Mary Beale is better known as a painter of oil portraits but she also worked in crayon and painted a small number of miniatures, including one of Henry Somerset, Duke of Beaufort, which is in Earl Beauchamp's collection, and one of Charles II in my own collection. She had a distinguished clientèle, was considered to be of an amiable disposition, was well liked by all who knew her, and mingled happily in both the learned and artistic circles of the day, as well as in those of the nobility. She also made at least one literary attempt when she wrote a discourse on Friendship, in which she states that 'Friendship is the nearest union which distinct souls are capable of'.

As there are so few known miniatures by Mary Beale it is impossible to assess her work. After a full and what must have been a strenuous life, she died in Pall Mall, London, on 8th October, 1699[1] (not on 28th December, 1697 as stated by Walpole) and was buried in St James's Church, Piccadilly.

[1] *The Connoisseur*, March 1953 (article by Elizabeth Walsh).

MATHEW SNELLING (worked 1647–1670?) was another painter who worked in the reign of Charles II. Charles Beale senior purchased colours from him from time to time. Little of his work has survived, and the miniatures that do exist do not place him among the first rank of painters. His style was often in the manner of Hoskins but much inferior. His signature on the miniatures that are known is either M.S. or M:S:, the initials being cursive.

One artist who signed himself D.M. remains a mystery. Several miniatures signed in this way exist, and he appears to have worked from about 1663 to 1676. His fondness for full-length portraits merely served to emphasize his weak draughtsmanship. There is an example of this in the Duke of Buccleuch's collection called 'Henry Fitzroy, Duke of Grafton, K.G.', signed and dated 1675–6.

CHAPTER VIII

MINIATURE PAINTERS WORKING AFTER THE RESTORATION

*

Nicholas Dixon (worked 1667–1708), who has sometimes been wrongly called Nathaniel Dixon, is another artist about whom very little is known. No facts about his parentage or early life have so far been discovered, nor yet the year in which he was born, but he lived for some time in the parish of St Martins-in-the-Fields, and from his paintings we know that he was evidently well-liked at Court and had a distinguished clientèle.

In 1673 he succeeded Cooper as limner to Charles II and this in itself shows in what esteem he was held at Court. On appointment as Keeper of the King's Picture Closet he was granted an annuity of £200 which was not, however, paid with any degree of regularity, and it is doubtful if the position carried with it more than the privilege of the title and a considerable amount of work.

The style in which some of his earlier miniatures are painted gives reason for thinking that he may have been a pupil of Hoskins. He must have been painting during the latter part of the Commonwealth, but the earliest known miniatures that have come to light so far date from 1667. He was working at about the same time as several of the artists already mentioned, Thomas Flatman, the Beale family and Mrs Rosse, for example, but while Flatman had fallen completely under the influence of Samuel Cooper, Dixon on the other hand developed a style of his own which became more marked as time went on.

The characteristics of his miniatures are the brownish red colour he used in painting the flesh, and the expression of the eyes. Where Cooper relied on the particular lighting effect from above to produce the shadows which assisted him in the modelling of the eyes and face, Dixon's treatment was the complete opposite. It showed more the influence of Hoskins' work and the effect was softer. The eyes were drawn to an elongated oval, giving the appearance of an exceptionally full lower lid, and making them appear half closed. The backgrounds to his sitters were usually plain, with an occasional cloud effect, and the painting was on vellum or card. He succeeded in portraying the character of his clients without being in any way dramatic.

His signatures were often in monogram, with the last stroke of the N following

52. NICHOLAS DIXON
(worked 1667–1708)
An unknown lady.

53. NICHOLAS DIXON
Possibly Anne Palmer,
Countess of Sussex (1660/1–1722).
Signed.

54. LAWRENCE CROSS(E) (d. 1724)
rah Jennings, Duchess of Marlborough (1660–1722).
Signed. Approx. $3\frac{1}{2} \times 3$ in.

55. LAWRENCE CROSS(E)
William Cavendish,
1st Duke of Devonshire (1640–1707).
Signed. $3\frac{1}{2} \times 2\frac{3}{4}$ in.

56. LAWRENCE CROSS(E)
Prince James Francis Edward Stuart
(1688–1766).
Signed. $3 \times 2\frac{7}{16}$ in.

57. JACQUES ANTOINE ARLAUD
(1668–1746)
Prince James Francis Edward Stuart.
$3\frac{1}{4} \times 2\frac{3}{8}$ in.

58. PETER CROSS (b. 1630? worked–1716?)
An unknown lady. $2\frac{1}{8} \times 1\frac{13}{16}$ in.

59. PETER CROSS
T. Carter. Signed and dated 1716. $3 \times 2\frac{13}{32}$ in.

the first of the D, and were frequently painted in gold. In his later miniatures there was a noticeable deterioration in his work and his draughtsmanship was not as careful. This may have been due to financial embarrassment and the necessity of speed, or to too much copying of larger paintings, or even to advancing years.

In 1698 he became involved in a lottery called 'The Hopeful Adventure', of which he was possibly instigator, for he is described as Mr Dixon, Painter, in St Martin's Lane, principal contriver. The total sum was considerable, £40,000 in all, which was to be divided into 1,214 prizes ranging from £3,000 to £20, together with a collection of pictures in limning which were to be seen at Dixon's house.

In spite of the participation of Princess Anne as an Adventurer, the lottery could not lay claim to having been more than hopeful, for it certainly did not meet with success. By 1700 Dixon was evidently in further trouble, and, presumably in order to meet his obligations, had to mortgage 70 miniatures, probably the collection mentioned in the lottery, and 30 of which are now in the Duke of Portland's collection at Welbeck.

In the catalogue of the Welbeck Abbey miniatures published by the Walpole Society in 1916,[1] Mr Goulding says that there are particulars in a recorded deed of bargain and sale, preserved at Welbeck Abbey, from which it appears that on 23rd November, 1700 Nicholas Dixon of the Parish of St Martins-in-the-Fields in the County of Middlesex, Gentleman, mortgaged his limnings, 70 in number, and that on the 14th February, 1707–8, they were transferred to John Holles, Duke of Newcastle for the sum of £430. This deed is signed by Dixon and has a schedule accompanying it also in his handwriting. These limnings, which consist of large (miniature) copies of old masters executed on vellum, were inherited on the Duke of Newcastle's death by his daughter Henrietta, Countess of Oxford, and from her they descended to her daughter Margaret, Duchess of Portland. What became of the remaining forty miniatures no one knows; they may have been dispersed or destroyed, or even yet be lying hidden away in some forgotten corner. Their titles are known and, with those at Welbeck, cover a wide field which, besides reproducing copies of the works of great masters such as Correggio and Guido Reni, include both religious and mythological subjects. It would be interesting to know for whom this large number of miniatures was originally intended.

Vertue says that Dixon died in the King's Bench Walk, where he was then living in hopes of avoiding prosecution, presumably for the debts that he incurred in connection with the unsuccessful lottery.

The next two artists who merit our consideration are two of the same name: P. CROSS (1630?–1716?) and L. Cross(e). For many years the existence of an artist who signed P.C. had been known, and the miniatures with this signature had

[1] Vol. IV, p. 25.

been attributed without any accurate information either to Penelope Cleyn, one of the six children of Franz Cleyn, all of whom were supposed to have painted miniatures, or to Paolo Carandini of Modena, a law student in Rome who was known to be a miniaturist. J. J. Foster quotes a legendary story that Carandini accompanied Mary of Modena when she came to England in 1673 to marry James II, but there is no evidence to support this, and Graham Reynolds says that a contemporary writer speaks of him as dead in 1662. Be that as it may, the whole position over the mysterious P.C. was clarified in 1935 when a portrait miniature of a Mr William Gore came into the sale room and was bought by the Victoria and Albert Museum. It was inscribed on the back, P. Cross fecit 1670, and its appearance enabled experts to compare the work with the hitherto wrongly attributed miniatures and to reassess them. Of the miniatures at present known, which are signed P.C., nine are dated between 1661 and 1691, from which we may deduce that he was in all probability born somewhere about 1630.

Reynolds makes the suggestion that P. Cross may have been a son or relative of Miguel de la Cruz, a Spanish painter, which, if in fact the case, might help to account for the seemingly foreign style Cross initiated.

One of the characteristics of Cross's work is a particular greenish blue stippling used in shading the flesh, and very thin brush strokes in the modelling. Hoskins alone of earlier painters used a greenish tint in this way. I was fortunate enough to obtain a very attractive miniature of a girl, attributed to Cross, and this shows his style to perfection. How well he was able to portray expression may be seen by looking at the distinctly saucy face of the young lady, which is framed in a perfectly painted lace wimple tied with a black ribbon under the chin. Under this she is wearing a red dress edged by a green collar. In the treatment of the hair, in which each strand is drawn separately, a glossy sheen is visible, while tiny downward brush strokes can be discerned round the edge of the face. The whole effect is very attractive as well as exceptionally well painted, and works of this quality place him high among the miniaturists of the seventeenth century. I have recently purchased a miniature signed on the front in gold lettering P.C., and on the back of the card is written in what appears to be a contemporary hand, T. Carter 1716. P. Cross fec. This is puzzling for two reasons. Firstly, no miniature by this artist and dated as late as this has so far been discovered, and if, as is likely, this portrait is by him and the inscription can be assumed to give the date of its painting, it means that he was working twenty-five years later than had hitherto been supposed. Secondly, the style of painting is much more that associated with L. Crosse, and were it not for the signature would undoubtedly have been attributed to him.

LAWRENCE CROSS(E) (d. 1724) is known to have spelt his name with and without an 'e', but the generally accepted spelling is Crosse. If Graham Reynolds is correct in his surmise that L. Cross was the son of P. Cross, it would appear that only the son used the alternative spelling. The date of his birth is unknown, though Basil Long considered that he must have been born prior to 1654, and Graham Reynolds considers 1653 most likely. He was a collector as well as a painter of miniatures, and his cabinet included works by Hoskins and Cooper. The collection was sold at his house, 'Blue Anchor' in Henrietta Street, Covent Garden, on 5th December, 1722, two years before his death. Once again, it has so far been impossible to discover any details about the artist's life or origins, and we do not know by whom he was taught or even in what country. His style is somewhat like that of P. Cross, and has more affinity to the method adopted on the Continent rather than to that employed by the English school of miniaturists, but in view of the fact that there was a precedent for this in the works of P. Cross and J. Hoskins, it may have been merely an adaptation of these artists' styles.

Whether his early training and work was done abroad or not, it would appear probable that he was working in England by 1678, as a chalk drawing of the Duke of Monmouth signed by him is in the collection of Her Majesty the Queen at Windsor, and judging by the costume of some of the sitters his miniatures may even have been painted about 1675. He must have executed a considerable number of portraits, for he is well represented in both museums and private collections. The Duke of Buccleuch and the Duke of Portland have a number of his works, and the persons portrayed show him to have had an aristocratic and extensive clientèle. His signatures are usually a cursive monogram L.C. with the C attached to the stalk of the L. LC. in monogram followed by f. for fecit is known, while there is one at Welbeck signed on the reverse, with the name of the sitter.

The material on which he painted was vellum or parchment stuck on to card, the back of which was painted over with a white gesso-like composition, and the shape he normally used was oval, although a rectangular one is known to exist. His colouring was perhaps slightly on the sombre side, and the backgrounds were often plain brown or reddish, with an occasional addition of curtaining draped to one side. He seems to have taken a great delight in painting the elaborate wigs which were still the height of fashion, while in modelling and shading the face he continued the method adopted by P. Cross of using a minute stippling which he applied in varying shades of red, blue and a greenish hue. The style closely resembles that of the *pointillistes* and was one that was to be practised on a much wider scale in the following century. His habit of leaving much of the miniature unpainted gave a slightly luminous effect which the adoption of ivory as a base was to develop to perfection.

One of the miniatures often associated with Crosse is that of Mary Queen of Scots, which belonged to the Duke of Hamilton and which, having been damaged, the Duke sent to Crosse to repair, asking him to make it as beautiful as he could. It is not known what the miniature originally looked like, but after its restoration the shape of the face appeared round. It was later discovered that the Queen did not look like this. The result of this deception was that it was copied by Bernard Lens and others in the eighteenth century when it became popular to possess her portrait.

Examples of his work may be found at the Victoria and Albert Museum, the Wallace Collection, the National Portrait Gallery, the Ashmolean Museum, Oxford, the Liverpool Museum, and elsewhere.

The larger paintings of this period were greatly influenced by the work of Sir Peter Lely, particularly before the arrival of Sir Godfrey Kneller in 1676. Although the manner and style of these masters' work was bound to have some effect on portrait miniatures, it never at any time dominated the work of the miniaturists. A change had come over the nation, and, freed from the domination of the Puritan way of life, a nonchalance and gaiety was apparent in the mode of living and the people's attire, and showed itself also in miniature painting in the rather self-confident and assured expression on the faces of the sitters.

Crosse's miniatures are full of character and he has an assured place among the artists of the seventeenth century. He was also a link with the eighteenth century, as, according to Vertue, he was still working and active in 1723 when seventy years of age. He died in October 1724 and left behind him a considerable quantity of excellent miniatures which now enrich many collections.

The artist CHRISTIAN RICHTER (1678–1732) was of Swedish extraction and was born in Stockholm in 1678. He was the son of Hans Davidson Richter, an Assessor to the Goldsmiths' Corporation, and his mother's maiden name was Briter Snelling. Apprenticed as a goldsmith from 1695 to 1698, he studied medal engraving and is known to have modelled a wax portrait of Augustus II when visiting Berlin and Dresden. In 1702 he came to London where a number of his fellow countrymen were already established, including Hysing, Dahl and Boit. He and Boit were already acquainted, having been boyhood friends in Stockholm.

Richter (who according to B. Long had a brother and cousin, both called David, miniaturists about whom nothing is known) soon became accepted as a leading painter of miniatures. He is also supposed to have executed enamels, but so far the only miniatures that have come to light have been those painted in water colour.

Much of his work consisted in copying oil paintings by Lely, Kneller and Dahl, and miniature paintings by Samuel Cooper, the most famous being those of Cromwell, which, while they are faithful replicas of the original, are nevertheless painted in his own style and therefore earn him his own place as a first-rate miniaturist. Examples of this copy are in H.M. the Queen's Collection at Windsor, in the

60. BENJAMIN ARLAUD (worked 1701–31)
An unknown man. $2\frac{3}{4} \times 2\frac{9}{32}$ in.

61. BENJAMIN ARLAUD
An unknown lady.
$3\frac{1}{2} \times 3$ in.

62. SIMON DIGBY,
BISHOP OF ELPHIN (d. 1720)
nn Hough, Bishop of Worcester (1651–1743).
$3\frac{1}{8} \times 2\frac{1}{2}$ in.

63. CHRISTIAN RICHTER (1678–1732)
Oliver Cromwell (1599–1658), after Cooper.
$4\frac{1}{8} \times 3\frac{5}{16}$ in.

64. BERNARD LENS (1682–1740)
Self-portrait. Signed and dated 1724. $5 \times 3\frac{7}{8}$ in.

65. BERNARD LENS
A. B. Lens (1713–?). Signed and dated 1723.
$4\frac{1}{16} \times 3\frac{1}{32}$ in.

66. BERNARD LENS
Called Mary Queen of Scots (1542–87),
after L. Cross(e).
Signed and dated 1720. $2\frac{21}{32} \times 2\frac{1}{8}$ in.

67. BERNARD LENS
An unknown lady. $3\frac{1}{2} \times 3$ in.

Wallace Collection in London and the Devonshire Collection at Chatsworth. The Wallace Collection also possesses a miniature by him of Charles II after Cooper, and there are other works in the collections of the Duke of Buccleuch, the Duke of Portland and the Duke of Devonshire.

The reason that his miniature painting was mainly confined to copies of other men's work was apparently due to an unpleasant illness that disfigured his face and made it embarrassing for people to look at him. Vertue says 'his nose fallen by some accident in ye Gardens of Venus made him looked on with a suspicious eye and did much to prevent his public appearance'.

In view of the fact that Vertue considered his paintings from life to be better than any of those of his contemporaries, it is unfortunate that he was unable to produce more of them.

His technique was rather different from that of previous artists in that he used a minute stippling on the face, combined with a number of nearly perpendicular small brush strokes which, with a lens, can be seen even on the eyeballs. He favoured a shading that was a mixture of reddish colour and grey, and he painted on a thin parchment laid on card which had been previously prepared. His miniatures are colourful and in every way excellent works of art. He normally signed on the back of the card with a cursive monogram C.R. in pencil, with the date below it. Occasionally the surname is written in full, and only very rarely is the signature on the front.

The illness which had so much hampered his career is said to have been the cause of his death in Brewer Street, Golden Square, and he was buried on the 18th of November, 1732, in St James's, Piccadilly.

BENJAMIN and JACQUES ANTOINE ARLAUD are believed to have been brothers and natives of Switzerland; they were the great uncles of Louis Ami Arlaud who worked in the latter part of the eighteenth century and the beginning of the nineteenth, and are thought to have lived in Geneva and to have been the sons of a watchmaker who came from Auvergne. Little is known about Benjamin's life but it is thought that he worked for a time in Amsterdam before coming to England. The exact date of his arrival is not known, nor do we know the year in which he died, but it is believed that he continued to work until about 1731. Miniatures by him are scarce; one is at the Victoria and Albert Museum and another in the Wallace Collection, while the National Museum at Munich possesses several, and a limited number are in private collections. I have a fine example depicting a man in a full bottomed wig, which shows excellent modelling and draughtsmanship of the face. The unknown gentleman portrayed is wearing an attractive cherry red coat which looks well against the blue background characteristic of earlier miniaturists. A pinkish brown shading can be seen on the curls of the wig, and the face is shaded with a greenish grey and red brush stroke; a red line delineates the contours of the face, nose and eyelids, and a slightly amused expression on the face of the sitter almost suggests that he and the artist were sharing a joke. A letter written by Basil Long in May 1927, and now in my possession, attributes this miniature to Arlaud, an opinion since confirmed by Graham Reynolds. His works are not always signed but those that are generally have the signature on the back, followed by the date.

The elder brother, Jacques Antoine Arlaud (1668–1746) was a very successful miniaturist and his work was well drawn. Started on a career of classical studies in which he showed considerable brilliance, he decided to take up miniature painting and was employed by a firm of jewellers at Dijon. His work met with such success that in 1688, when he was only about 20 years old, he went to Paris where he was soon accepted and given employment. Here he became friendly with the two eminent French painters, Largillière and Rigaud. Largillière has been called the Van Dyck of France, and Jacques Arlaud appears to have studied his technique. He was provided with rooms in the Château of St Cloud by the Duc d'Orléans who, on the death of his uncle Louis XIV (1638–1715), acted as Regent, and favours were showered upon him. In 1721 he came to England with a letter of introduction to the Princess of Wales, afterwards Queen Caroline. He brought with him a copy in miniature of 'Leda and the Swan' after Michael Angelo or Correggio, and is supposed to have sold it in London for £600, but there is no record so far of any miniatures painted by him during his visit to England. After returning to Paris he finally settled in Geneva, the place of his birth, and having apparently amassed an ample fortune, lived there until his death in 1746. Largillière painted a portrait of him which is in the gallery at Geneva, and examples of his work are in H.M. the Queen's Collection at Windsor, the Victoria and Albert Museum, the Wallace Collection and the Louvre. He is also known to have painted religious and mythological subjects. He tended to use a red and grey shading on the faces of his sitters.

His signatures are usually in full, and Basil Long mentions one signed in a sprawling hand 'Jacobus | Antonius | Arlaud | Genevensis | pingabat | ad vivum | in Ædibus Regiis |'.

SIMON DIGBY (d. 1720) a son of Essex Digby, Bishop of Dromore, Ireland, was educated at Trinity College, Dublin, and, following in his father's profession, became Rector of Dunshaughlin and Chaplain to the Earl of Ossory in 1668, Bishop of Limerick in 1678 and Bishop of Elphin in 1691.

He was evidently an accomplished miniaturist and painted many of the leading men of the day. The National Museum, Dublin, has three examples: portraits of Bishop Tillotson, Lord Capel and Henry, Lord Sidney; while the National

Portrait Gallery has a miniature, $3\frac{1}{2}$ in. $\times$ $2\frac{1}{2}$ in., of John Hough, Bishop of Worcester, and other portraits are known to exist.

He died at Lacken, County Roscommon, on 7th April, 1720, and was buried on the 20th 'in the church of Tosara, (Mount Talbot), in the said county, together with his Lady, who died a few days after him.'[1]

[1] Works of Sir James Ware. Revised 1739.

CHAPTER IX

BERNARD LENS AND THE
TRANSITION PERIOD

*

Much has been written in recent years about the life and customs of the British people in the eighteenth century. From the biographies and historical novels that are available it is possible to build up a very clear mental picture of the country in this period of its history.

The period has sometimes been called the Age of Reason and it is certainly true that much interchange of ideas and discussion prevailed among the more leisured classes. The Arts were well patronized, and the numerous artists painting in England had no difficulty in obtaining work. The Grand Tour had become for the more wealthy an accepted part of eighteenth-century education, and resulted in a greater appreciation of art in all its forms. New vistas were opened to those who travelled, and many valuable possessions changed hands and countries.

In 1717 Horace Walpole was born, and proved to be one of the greatest connoisseurs and patrons of art that England can boast. His *Anecdotes of Painting in England*, in which he edited the material collected by George Vertue, was first published in 1762 and has been a standard book of reference ever since. In the preface to this book he says of the eighteenth century, 'but whatever has been the complaint formerly, we have ground to hope that a new era is receiving its date. Genius is countenanced and emulation will follow'. And again, later: 'At this epoch of common sense one may reasonably expect to see the arts flourish to as proud a height as they attained at Athens, Rome or Florence.' This prophecy was very largely fulfilled, and in every aspect of life, in art, music, the theatre, science and literature these are names remembered today: Samuel Johnson, James Boswell, David Garrick, Thomas Gainsborough, Sir Joshua Reynolds and many more.

It was during this period of new experiments and fresh ideas that the miniaturist BERNARD LENS (1682–1740) came to the fore. He was born in London of a family which had had connections with art for three or four generations. His father, also called Bernard, was a mezzotint engraver and drawing master who, with Sturt, was responsible for opening a drawing school in St Paul's Church Yard, London, and it was no doubt here that Bernard Lens, junior, had his early training. The school was evidently successful and had a good reputation, as Mr Goulding mentions a letter written on 7th June, 1707 to Robert Harley (1661–1724) who had been making enquiries about the best man to teach the art of drawing to his son Edward. In this letter the writer says 'I have sent for Mr. Lens a very able and the best master we have in London, a sober, diligent man and very careful'. It is not certain whether this refers to the father or son, but it is more probable that it was Bernard Lens the younger who was being spoken of, as he was responsible for a number of miniatures which are still at Welbeck.

Edward Harley, afterwards second Earl of Oxford, married Lady Henrietta Cavendish Holles, and their daughter Margaret married William Bentinck, second Duke of Portland, in 1734. Fortunately the Duchess possessed her father's and grandfather's love of art, and when on the death of her mother she inherited the family treasures, including the miniatures, she in turn added her own collection, and this still remains at Welbeck Abbey. The second Earl kept a careful note of any of his purchases and bills, and among them are those relating to the miniature frames made by Lens. The majority of his notes are preserved in the British Museum, and are described as the 'Harleian Manuscripts'.

Bernard Lens the younger must have begun his career soon after 1700, at a time when a number of foreign artists were arriving in England. It was fortunate that at this crucial point in the history of miniature painting we had an artist who was able to grasp the opportunities that presented themselves and develop a fresh technique that was to have far-reaching results. Walpole refers to him as an admirable painter and there is no doubt that his work justifies this statement. A story is told that illustrates his interest in obtaining true likenesses: while Lens was painting a lady's picture in a dress similar to that worn by Mary Queen of Scots, the lady said: 'But Mr. Lens, you have not made me like the Queen of Scots.' 'No, madam,' he replied. 'If God Almighty had made your ladyship like her, I would.'

Lens soon became one of the leading miniaturists of the day. He was in great demand as a teacher and had many interesting pupils, amongst them George I and George II, the Duke of Cumberland, the Princesses Mary and Louise, the Duchess of Portland and Horace Walpole. He was also drawing master at Christ's Hospital, and in 1735 published some etchings, while a volume entitled *New and Complete Drawing Book* was written by him but not published until after his death. He painted from life as well as executing copies of other artists' work in miniature, many of the copies being taken from paintings by Kneller, Rubens, Van Dyck, and miniatures by Cooper, Hilliard and Petitot. Besides this, he was proficient in making topographical and archaeological drawings.

In 1723 he copied Cooper's unfinished portrait of Oliver Cromwell, and this miniature is in the Duke of Portland's collection at Welbeck. It is in a rectangular pearwood frame of the type he was employed to make for Lord Oxford, and records of which are at Welbeck. Frames similar to these are frequently referred to as 'Lens frames'.

The earliest known miniature by Lens is dated 1707, when he was twenty-five years of age. He will always be remembered as the first English artist to paint on ivory, although he continued to use vellum for some portraits. The use of ivory in miniature painting was a complete innovation in England, although it had been used as early as 1696 on the Continent by Rosalba Carriera, an Italian artist. The exact date when Lens began to use this material is not known, but miniatures by him painted on ivory are to be found from 1708 onwards. It has been suggested that Lens copied Rosalba Carriera's technique as there appears to be a similarity of style, but as there is no evidence that he ever went abroad the assumption is that he may have seen some of her work which was brought to England by those who admired it in Venice. The changeover from vellum to ivory did not at first make a great difference, as Lens continued to paint in opaque body colour and only used transparent water colour on the face and any exposed parts of the flesh. The real advantage that the luminosity of ivory had over vellum was not fully realized until later in the century when Richard Cosway brought this method to perfection.

Lens married Katherine Woods on 30th November, 1706, at Gray's Inn Chapel; they had three sons, of whom A. B. Lens and P. P. Lens both followed their father's profession, the eldest, Bernard, obtaining a clerkship in the Exchequer Office through the assistance of Horace Walpole. A large circular miniature of Lens' wife aged fifty-two, formerly in the Dyson Perrins collection, was sold recently for £220. It is signed and dated 1733 and an oval copy of it is in the Ward Usher Museum, Lincoln. Several self-portraits of the artist exist in private collections and there is one at the National Portrait Gallery and a very good one at the Ashmolean Museum, Oxford.

Lens was responsible for several copies of the Duke of Hamilton's miniature of Mary Queen of Scots, which, as has already been mentioned, was restored by Lawrence Crosse. I have a Lens copy of this in my collection, which is signed in monogram on the front, and has the words 'Maria Regina Scotorum' in gold at the top, while on the paper which is stuck on to the back of the ivory is a further signature, 'Bernard Lens jun. fecit et Londini, 1720'. He was one of the last miniaturists to copy classical and mythological subjects and to make copies of miniatures of historic interest.

From the portraits he painted of himself and his wife it could not be said, as it was of Mr and Mrs Hilliard, that they were a handsome couple, for their features were coarse, and, as Graham Reynolds puts it, 'rather John Bullish'. His portraits from life show Kneller's influence, particularly in the shape of the face and the flesh colouring. This was less natural than that previously painted, and Lens favoured a greenish brown shading which was not suited to ivory. At his best he was a fine artist, and in his miniature of his wife the treatment of the corsage and lace and brocade trimmings on her dress are painted to perfection. The blue background of this miniature is stippled, and the signature B.L. in monogram is painted in gold together with the date. On the back is written, 'Bernard Lens, fecit, 1733, July 2th'. He used a variety of shapes for his miniatures, oval, rectangular and circular.

He held office as unpaid miniature painter to both George I and George II, and his work served as a link during the transition period between the great artists of the seventeenth century whose tradition had sprung from that of the medieval illuminator, and the birth of the more flattering charm and elusiveness shown by the painters of the eighteenth century and made possible by the introduction of ivory for which Lens must be given the credit. He died at Knightsbridge on 30th December, 1740.

His two sons ANDREW BENJAMIN and Peter Paul, believed to have been born in 1713 and 1714 respectively, both took up miniature painting and were very successful. Both would no doubt have had a good grounding in the art by their father. Andrew painted portrait miniatures as well as mythological subjects, and exhibited at the Free Society of Artists from 1764 to 1779. The first public exhibition of English artists' work took place in 1760 and the Free Society was founded in 1761 and continued until 1783, when, due to lack of interest, the exhibitions they had sponsored came to an end. The Society of Arts, which had already been formed in 1754 to promote the arts, manufactures and commerce in Great Britain, established itself and obtained a royal charter in 1765. After various differences and difficulties the Royal Academy was formed in 1768 with Sir Joshua Reynolds as its president. The first exhibition of this new venture was held in 1769 and the Academy has enjoyed continued success up to the present day. According to Algernon Graves, A. B. Lens exhibited at the Society of Artists from 1765 to 1770, and at the Free Society from 1764–79. His address at this time was given as at 'Mr. Mitchell's a peruke maker, Jermyn Street, St. James'.

A collection of miniatures belonging to A. B. Lens and his father was sold in 1777 and the advertisement read as follows: 'To be sold by auction by Messrs. Langford at their house in the Great Piazza, Covent Garden, on Wednesday, the 16th inst. at 12 o'clock The Collection of miniatures and other pictures of Mr. Andrew Benjamin Lens the chief of which are the works of that ingenious artist and his father'. His early work, usually signed with a cursive monogram A.B.L., although not as good, resembled that of his father to whom some of his paintings have at times been attributed. No information is available so far about the latter part of his life or the date of his death, which must have taken place well towards the end of the eighteenth century.

PETER PAUL LENS (1714?–1750?) is thought to have been born in 1714 in view of the fact that there is a miniature of his mother painted in 1729 when, according to the inscription on the back, he was a lad of fifteen years of age. The Victoria and Albert Museum possesses a miniature in profile of his father, painted when he was nineteen, and his other known works lie mainly between the years 1729–1750, from which we conclude that he may have died young. The little information that is available about his life seems mainly confined to stories of his wild and irresponsible behaviour. In Dublin in 1737 and 1738 he took a leading part in a 'hell-fire' club which was called the 'Blasters', in the company of what were rightly termed loose and disorderly persons. He made no secret of the fact that he was a votary of the devil, and drank to him publicly. This behaviour was censured by the Irish House of Lords and as a result he had to leave the country speedily and return to England, where he once more took up the art of miniature painting.

Like Andrew, his work had an affinity to that of his father, but both brothers differed from it in one respect. In the stippling of the background they tended to shade it in such a way as to leave an area of light reflected on the right side of the head. Peter Paul Lens usually drew the portrait in such a way as to occupy the main portion of the oval with the sitter's head. He was good at portraying character, and there was a naïveté about his work that had a charm of its own.

His miniatures are more frequently met with than those of his brother and he seemed particularly happy at drawing children. The miniature at the Victoria and Albert Museum of the 'Ragged Little Boy' is tremendously appealing and shows that he had a sympathetic side to his character in spite of his loose way of living. He generally drew his faces almost round. His signature varied from P.L. in a cursive monogram in front, to P. Lens in full or even 'P. P. Lens pinxt' at the back.

Although ROSALBA CARRIERA (1675–1757) never, so far as is known, came to England her work had such an influence on the art of the eighteenth-century miniaturists that I feel it worth while to include her in this survey. She was born in Venice of a family of artists and her father held office under the government. Both her father and her grandfather were painters so that her love of art was in no small measure inherited from them. When young she was taught how to make *point de Venise* lace, and unlike most children spent the major part of her time in drawing instead of in amusement. Her father gave her every encouragement and she copied many of his designs, whereupon, realizing her talent, he gave his consent to her taking lessons from Antonio Nazari, a well-known pastel painter. Later she studied under Antonio Balestra, and was finally taught miniature painting by Antonio Pellegrini.

68. PETER PAUL LENS
(1714?–50?)
An unknown man.
$1\frac{5}{8} \times 1\frac{3}{8}$ in.

69. PETER PAUL LENS
An unknown man.
$1\frac{19}{32} \times 1\frac{5}{16}$ in.

70. ROSALBA CARRIERA (1675–1757)
Called Lady Mary Wortley Montagu
(1689–1762).
$3\frac{1}{32} \times 2\frac{1}{4}$ in.

71. ROSALBA CARRIERA
The Duchess of Berwick. Approx. $3 \times 2\frac{1}{4}$ in.

72. NATHANIEL HONE, R.A.
(1718–84)
Horace Walpole (1717–97). $1\frac{1}{2} \times 1\frac{1}{4}$ in.

73. SAMUEL COTES (1734–1818)
An unknown man.
Signed and dated 1775. $1\frac{13}{16} \times 1\frac{1}{2}$ in.

74. JAMES SCOULER (1740?–1812)
Robert Scouler, brother of the artist.
Dated 1768. $3\frac{1}{2} \times 2\frac{3}{4}$ in.

75. THOMAS DAY (1732–1807)
Mr J. (or I.) Mckerral. Dated 1794.
$2\frac{13}{32} \times 2$ in.

Unfortunately from childhood she suffered from bad eyesight, and although she enjoyed painting miniatures she was reluctantly forced to give it up and change to painting pastels on a larger scale.

Her greatest claim to fame was the introduction of ivory as a background to miniatures, and her *fondelli*, as she called them, or small boxes with these attractive portraits incorporated in them became all the rage. Their popularity soon spread from the Continent to Britain. The earliest date when ivory is known to have been used by her is 1698, and it was not until the turn of the century that Bernard Lens followed her example, although there is no evidence that these two artists ever met, in spite of the similarity of their work.

As a pastel painter she was in great demand and painted at the Courts of Poland, Denmark, France, Tuscany as well as Austria, besides painting the reigning family in Modena. She was a woman of great ability, and in addition to being a great artist was an accomplished musician; yet in spite of the honours and admiration that were showered upon her she remained unspoilt. In 1720, when she was at the height of her power, she went to France, where her work was particularly popular and where she remained for a year, during which time she was elected a member of the Academy and patronized by the King and his Court. Her works are not numerous in Britain but she is well represented on the Continent.

A miniature in my collection, said to be of Lady Mary Wortley Montagu, is an interesting one both from the point of view of the artist and the subject. It is painted on vellum stuck on the back of a playing card on which is written, 'Lady Wortley Montague by Rosalba.' Professor Robert Halsband, who has been engaged in careful research on the life of Lady Mary, has not so far discovered any reference to her sitting to Rosalba, but a letter of 5th September, 1758, to her daughter Lady Bute contains the following passage – 'I believe I owe his (Antonio Mocenigo, head of the famous Venetian family) favour to having shown him her (his wife) miniature by Rosalba, which I bought in London: perhaps you remember it in my little collection . . .'. Without any corroborative evidence it is impossible to be certain which if either of these two ladies is the subject of my miniature. In it the sitter is wearing a Turkish dress which was characteristic of Lady Mary and which not unnaturally caused some comment. Lady Mary will of course be remembered as having introduced to England the cure for small-pox. Rosalba's work was well painted and she employed soft colouring which showed the influence of pastel drawing. Her eyesight deteriorated considerably by the time she reached fifty, and she eventually became totally blind. She lingered on into old age, dying in 1757 in Venice.

Two artists called Goupy practised miniature painting at this period: LOUIS GOUPY (1700?–1747) who is said to have been the nephew of Bernard Lens, and

JOSEPH GOUPY, a nephew of Louis. Louis, about whose work very little is known, was born in France some time before 1700, and died in 1747. Joseph Goupy was born at Nevers and came to England when quite young. In 1711 he went to Kneller's Academy to study art, and became a fashionable drawing master. He received the patronage of the royal family and had as a pupil Frederick Prince of Wales and George III. There is a miniature by him at the National Portrait Gallery. His collection was sold by auction in 1765.

THOMAS FRYE (1710–62) was born near Dublin, and after studying painting went to London in about 1729, where he became acquainted with Sir Joshua Reynolds. He painted portraits in oil and was an accomplished miniaturist, counting among his patrons Frederick Prince of Wales, whose portrait he painted in 1734. By 1738 he had established himself in London as a painter and engraver, besides being an able draughtsman and painting on enamel.

His miniatures are good and may occasionally be obtained in the sale rooms. Basil Long mentions one signed in gold, the signature being parallel to the edge of the oval. The Victoria and Albert Museum possesses a good oil miniature painted in 1737, and two miniatures in water colour of the years 1761 and 1762 respectively.

CHAPTER X

LESSER MINIATURISTS OF THE EARLY EIGHTEENTH CENTURY

*

The middle of the eighteenth century was a period of no great merit so far as miniature painting was concerned. The men whose work was to be the means of a revival towards the end of the century were only just starting on the rungs of the ladder that was to carry them to fame. In the meantime, the considerable number of miniature painters working at the time produced adequate but unpretentious portraits which had a certain charm about them, without being in any way great works. Even the size of the portraits had shrunk from the $3\frac{1}{2}$ in. ovals of the earlier part of the century to small paintings measuring as little as $1\frac{1}{4}$ in. and $1\frac{1}{2}$ in. in height, almost as if the artists were apologizing for the modesty of their efforts. Nevertheless many very pleasing and attractive miniatures were produced, and the art was kept alive until the great masters blossomed at the end of the century.

NATHANIEL HONE, R.A. (1718–84) was born in Dublin where his father was a merchant. It is not recorded who taught him to paint, but as Dublin was one of the centres where miniature painting flourished, he would have had no difficulty in obtaining a teacher. For reasons that are not known he left Ireland and practised as an itinerant portrait painter in England for some years. In February 1742 he married in York Minster a young woman called Mary Earl(e) of whom nothing is known except that she was in receipt of an annuity from an unknown member of the nobility to whom Hone wrote on her death. The tenor of this letter makes it clear that Mary Earl(e) had some personal claim on the unknown nobleman for the payments she had received, and Sylas Neville in his diary edited by B. Cozens Hardy in 1950 says, speaking of Hone, that 'he married some lord's cast-off mistress for £200 a year'. After his marriage Hone and his wife settled in London, and after her death he apparently married a second time. His last wife evidently survived him and a notice of her death at Hendon appeared in the *Dublin Chronicle* on 15th February, 1791.

Hone had ten children, five boys and five girls. Of these, three girls, Lydia, Sophia and Floreth, and two boys, Samuel and Apelles, died young. John Camillus Hone and Horace Hone both followed their father's profession and attained good positions as miniature painters. In 1750 Hone went to Rome, where he stayed for

95

two years, and in 1752 he travelled to Florence, where he was made a member of the Academy. Returning to London in the same year, he lived in Henrietta Street, Covent Garden, but evidently had no desire to settle, for he went to Dublin in July 1752, and in August 1753 visited Paris, after which his address was Frith Street, London.

During his travels in Italy he met Sir Joshua Reynolds, and it has been suggested that a feud sprang up between them there. In one of Sir Joshua Reynolds' notebooks of this period there is a caricature of Hone, and it is probable that their dislike of each other was mutual. This ultimately found expression in the unfortunate episode over Hone's painting, commonly called 'The Conjurer' or 'The Pictorial Conjurer displaying the whole art of optical deception', which he sent to the Academy. In it the painter portrayed Reynolds as an old man holding a wand; a child is leaning on his knee and he is performing incantations while various prints and designs, from which the artist was supposed to have taken ideas, float round in the air. The real reason for the trouble that ensued was not so much this attack on Reynolds as that a nude figure was to be seen on one of the sketches closely resembling Angelica Kauffmann, whose name had been linked with that of Sir Joshua Reynolds for some time. Hone protested strongly that he had not intended this to represent the lady, and offered to make amends by altering it, but the Council of the Academy finally decided that the picture must be withdrawn and refused to allow Hone to contribute any further pictures that year. As a result of this he immediately arranged a separate exhibition of his own works, placing the much discussed picture in the centre, having first clothed the nude figures, but copying the faces from well-known portraits by Reynolds.

Hone evidently enjoyed the good things of life and spent a considerable amount on his attire and personal pleasures. He painted a number of large oil portraits as well as miniatures on ivory and in enamel, and practised etching and mezzotinting. His miniatures are usually small and very well painted, and bracelets were one of his favourite settings for them. Evidence of opaque white may be found in the lace-work on his portraits of ladies, while in some of those of men a soft diagonal hatching can be seen on the face. His portraits in enamel are more frequently found than those on ivory, and as far as is known he painted no miniatures for the last fifteen years of his life. His usual signature appears to be N.H. in monogram, with the letters conjoined and the signature generally followed by a date. Examples of his work are to be seen in a great number of museums both in London and in the provinces.

GERVASE SPENCER (d. 1763) was an interesting artist, for although information about his origin is scanty it has been established that he was a gentleman's servant and, according to Vertue, worked for a Doctor W. Who taught him to paint

76. GERVASE SPENCER
(d. 1763)
An unknown man.
Signed and dated 1759.
$1\frac{1}{8} \times 1$ in.

77. LUKE SULLIVAN
(1705–71)
An unknown lady.
Signed and dated 1760.
$1\frac{3}{4} \times 1\frac{1}{2}$ in.

78.
PENELOPE CARWARDINE
(1730–1801)
Maria Gunning,
Countess of Coventry
(1733–60).
Dated 1757. $1\frac{3}{4} \times 1\frac{7}{16}$ in.

79. J. JENNINGS
(worked 1762?)
An unknown man.
Signed and dated 1766.
$1\frac{5}{32} \times \frac{27}{32}$ in.

80. SAMUEL COLLINS
(d. 1768)
An unknown man.
$1\frac{5}{16} \times 1\frac{1}{8}$ in.

81.
GUSTAVUS HAMILTON
(1739–75)
An unknown lady.
Signed and dated 1758.
$1\frac{9}{16} \times 1\frac{9}{32}$ in.

82. RICHARD COSWAY, R.A.
(1742?–1821)
Self-portrait. 4 × 3 in.

83. RICHARD COSWAY, R.A.
Mrs Fitzherbert (1756–1837).
$2\frac{13}{16} \times 2\frac{3}{8}$ in.

84.
RICHARD COSWAY, R.A.
Sir Edward Astley,
afterwards Earl of Hastings
(1729–1802). $2\frac{1}{8} \times 1\frac{3}{4}$ in.

85. RICHARD COSWAY, R.A.
An unknown lady. Signed and dated 1794.
$3\frac{3}{8} \times 2\frac{13}{16}$ in.
86. Reverse of No. 85.

remains a mystery, for although it is conceivable that he might have been self-taught in water colour it is unlikely that this would have sufficed for his painted enamels, which were good. The portrait of Lady Mary Wortley Montagu in the Ward Usher Museum at Lincoln is a good example of his work. The majority of his miniatures were small and his signature varied. The simple letters G.S. are found in black and gold with or without a date, while G.S. f and G. Spencer also occur, and some miniatures are signed on the back. The initials on the early miniatures are usually cursive while the later ones were often slightly irregular Roman capitals.

Two other artists who cause a certain amount of confusion are Samuel Collins and Samuel Cotes. SAMUEL COLLINS (d. 1768), the son of a clergyman, was born at Bristol and began his career as an attorney, but evidently abandoned this in favour of painting. For a time he practised at Bath, but went to Ireland about 1762 to escape his creditors, and settled in Dublin where he remained until his death in 1768. He was succeeded at Bath by his pupil Ozias Humphry[1] who was then only a young man. It is not possible to attribute miniatures to Collins with any degree of certainty, as few signed works exist. The Victoria and Albert Museum possesses one signed 'Collins' in full and dated 1763, and all the authentic ones fall between the years 1760 and 1768.

SAMUEL COTES (1734–1818), whose initials were identical to those of Collins, was born in London and was the youngest son of an ex-mayor of Galway who worked as an apothecary in Cork Street, London. He was trained to this work but no doubt having watched his younger brother Francis painting, became interested himself and decided to train as a miniature painter, taking lessons from his brother. There is at present insufficient evidence to make it possible to distinguish between the work of Samuel Collins and Samuel Cotes, and until more information is available any portraits after 1768 should be assigned to Cotes, with the proviso that an unknown Sarah Coote (who worked from 1777–84) also shared the same initials, and it is also probable that Cotes worked as early as 1757. He exhibited at the Society of Artists from 1760–68 and at the Royal Academy from 1769–89 and his last dated miniature at present known was painted in the year 1786. A characteristic of his was to use opaque colours to touch up the hair and any lace or cravats worn by his sitters. In the later miniatures there was a noticeable increase in the size of format from the smaller ones that he used in the initial stages. A portrait in my own collection, signed S.C. and dated 1775, has the background painted in a brownish grey opaque paint, while the shading on the face is a bluish grey.

He was married twice and his only child died in infancy. His second wife was Sara Shepherd or Sheppard, an amateur painter who died in 1814. Cotes survived her by four years, and died in Paradise Row, Chelsea, in 1818.

[1] Ozias Humphry, R.A., 1742–1810. (See Chapter XII.)

As if there had not been sufficient confusion between the artists who shared the initials S.C., further complications arose over those signed P.C. For many years miniatures painted between 1750 and 1765 and signed P.C. have been attributed alternatively to Penelope Cotes, the supposed sister of Francis and Samuel Cotes, or to Penelope Carwardine (1730–1801). There is no documentary evidence available to establish the existence of P. Cotes, and no mention is made of her in Francis Cotes' will of 1770. She appears first in Doctor Williamson's book, *The History of Portrait Miniatures*, published in 1904. PENELOPE CARWARDINE, on the other hand, was the eldest of six daughters of John Carwardine of Thing-hills Court, Withington, Herefordshire, by his wife Annie Bullock of Preston Wynn. Carwardine was evidently reckless and extravagant, and as a result the family were ruined and Penelope took up miniature painting to earn her living. By the age of twenty-four she had established herself as a miniaturist, and about 1772 married a Mr Butler who was organist at Ranelagh, St Margaret's and St Anne's, Westminster. No miniatures painted after her marriage have so far come to light. They had no children and her husband evidently died first, as she is known to have been a widow before her death.

If the theory is accepted that there has been some mistake and that P. Cotes never existed, then all the miniatures hitherto attributed to her must be regarded as the work of P. Carwardine, and the statement that this artist was taught by Ozias Humphry must be incorrect in view of the fact that Humphry was born in 1742 and starting his career in 1762, whereas P. Carwardine had been working since 1754. It is conceivable, however, that when Humphry was painting her portrait in 1767 (and incidentally there is reference to her having painted him) she may have asked him to assist her in improving her technique which had hitherto shown the influence of Lens together with that of the more modern approach.

LUKE SULLIVAN (1705–71) was another artist who had Irish connections. Born in County Louth, he was the son of humble parents and went to England when quite young with his father, who was groom to the Duke of Beaufort. The Duke assisted him to obtain lessons in engraving from an engraver called Le Bas. Later he became an assistant to Hogarth and was evidently a person with many gifts, for not only was he an engraver but he also painted water colours, landscapes, architectural views and miniatures. He belonged to a club of amateurs and artists that met in Leicester Square, and from all accounts led a rather dissipated life, frequenting the taverns and less desirable parts of the city, and his paintings depicted mostly young girls who were to be found there.

He exhibited at the Society of Artists from 1764–70, giving his address firstly as at Mr Mackenzie in Norris Street, Haymarket, and later at The Golden Lion, St Albans Street. A miniature exhibited in 1770 was said by Walpole in Graves

Dictionary of Artists to be exceedingly fine, and J. T. Smith refers to him as 'the most extraordinary of all miniature painters'. The general opinion of those who have seen his work is that it is colourful and attractive. Occasionally his flesh colours have a yellowish tinge. He signed with a monogram L.S., the S clinging to the stalk of the L. and protruding below it, and his miniatures were often dated.

THOMAS REDMOND (1745?–85) is thought to have been born about 1745 or possibly earlier, and was supposed to have been the son of a clergyman from Brecon.

He was apprenticed to a housepainter at Bristol, but later went to London and studied painting at the Academy in St Martin's Lane. He exhibited at the Free Society from 1762 to 1766 and at the Society of Artists from 1767 to 1770, giving as his address such varying places as Brecknock, South Wales and The Grove, Bath. His work, which included crayons as well as miniatures, was not outstanding and his colouring rather varied. He signed with his initials T.R., often using a light colour on a darker background. He was married and had three sons.

Two more miniaturists who worked in Dublin were JAMES REILY (d. 1780/88) and Gustavus Hamilton. Reily studied at the Blue-Coat School, Oxmantown, Ireland, from 1745–48, and was trained as an artist at Robert West's Drawing School in Dublin. The Victoria and Albert Museum have a signed miniature of a man by him.

GUSTAVUS HAMILTON (1739–75) was born in Ireland and was the son of a clergyman who could boast of both Irish and Scottish antecedents. He studied painting under Robert West, and established himself as a miniaturist with a fashionable clientèle. His works appear from time to time and are signed in various ways, with his initials, with the abbreviated signature Ham., followed by a date, and occasionally Gus. Hamilton, with or without a date. I have a good miniature of a lady in a blue dress with a lace collar, which is signed in the right-hand bottom corner G.H. 1758. P. in block letters in lines one above the other. In the top left corner is the inscription in cursive lettering, Etat 70. His draughtsmanship was not always good and the shading of the face inclined to be bluish.

An artist signing himself J.J. is thought to be one J. JENNINGS, about whom nothing is known. I have a small miniature of a man in a blue coat signed J.J. and dated 1766, in which the flesh colouring is rather pale and the shading on the face and round the eyes inclined to be blue, while the background is dark brown with little or no sign of stippling.

JAMES SCOULER (1740?–1812) was born in London, his father having been a native of Edinburgh, where he worked as an organ builder and kept a music shop. Scouler was trained in the art of painting at the Duke of Richmond's Gallery and the St Martin's Lane Academy, and was given a premium by the Society of Arts in 1755. He was a regular exhibitor at the Society of Artists and the Free Society as well as the Royal Academy, and his work was considered to be good. He painted both crayon portraits and miniatures with a certain resemblance to John Smart, though without the smooth finish achieved by that artist. His signatures, the surname in full followed by a date, were often scratched in on the paint on the edge of the miniature. He is also known to have signed with his initials J.S. and J. Scouler, again with the date.

WILLIAM SHERLOCK (1738?–1806?) was another Irish artist who was born in Dublin about 1738, the son of a fencing master. Like many of his contemporaries he went to London and studied at St Martin's Lane Academy where he was awarded a premium by the Society of Arts in 1759 and 1760, and like Sullivan studied under Le Bas, the engraver. He painted in oil and water colour as well as executing miniatures, and was a picture cleaner in addition to being responsible for engraving heads for Smollett's *History of England*.

FRANÇOIS XAVIER VISPRE (1730?–90?) is thought to have been born in Paris although it has also been suggested that either he or his brother Victor came from Besançon. François was working in Paris in 1750 but must later have come to London, for he exhibited at the Society of Artists from 1760 to 1783 from various London addresses. His brother VICTOR (w. 1763–72), whose work was mainly confined to painting on glass, was also an exhibitor. Both are supposed to have gone to Dublin in 1776 and to have exhibited there in 1777, François becoming a member of the Dublin Society of Antiquaries. They both returned to London in 1780. François, in addition to painting miniatures and figure subjects, executed portraits in oils and in crayon, and also painted on glass. He practised too as an engraver, and executed mezzotints after Liotard; there is an engraving of his wife Mary in the British Museum. I have seen a well-painted miniature of a lady, signed Xavier. The year of his death is uncertain but it is usually given as 1790.

THOMAS DAY (1732–1807) was a native of Devonshire, who at the outset of his career is reputed to have had ample private means. He was a pupil of Ozias Humphry in 1766 and of Daniel Dodd in 1768, from which year he exhibited at the Society of Artists and the Free Society, continuing to do so until 1783. From 1773 to 1788 he also exhibited at the Royal Academy and in 1774 was living at Brentwood.

If, as it is supposed, he is identical with the Day who spent twelve years in Rome and became known as Macgilp Day, a painter and restorer, his income must have been spent liberally, for during the last three years of his life he was supported by the Duke of Bedford and Sir Henry Mildmay, and on his death in December 1807 he left a widow and at least two daughters in reduced circumstances.

His works are superficially like those of Smart, and show his influence, particularly in the face colouring and backgrounds, the shading on the face often being a reddish grey. His signatures varied, but the most common were T.D. in cursive initials and T. Day, followed by a date and inscribed near the edge of the portrait.

CHAPTER XI

RICHARD COSWAY AND THE GREAT REVIVAL

*

The name of RICHARD COSWAY, R.A. (1742?–1821) is probably more widely known than that of any other miniaturist of the eighteenth century, and needs little or no introduction. Even those who do not profess to be knowledgeable on the subject of art usually know that he was intimately connected with portrait miniatures, and associate him with the frivolous, gay period of the Regency and the extravagance of Georgian England.

He is thought to have been born sometime during the year 1742 in Devonshire, for according to an entry in the Parish Register at Okeford near Bampton he was baptized there on 5th November, 1742. His parents' names were given as Richard and Mary Cosway, and as far as is known he was their only son. The Cosways were of Flemish descent, an ancestor having emigrated from Flanders during the reign of Elizabeth I. They evidently settled in Tiverton where they established a very prosperous and successful woollen business and became the owners of a considerable amount of property in the area.

Richard Cosway's father was a schoolmaster and was headmaster of Blundell's School, Tiverton, when his son was born. The family were said to have been great lovers of pictures and to have had in their possession some very fine ones which Cosway as a boy spent a great deal of his spare time copying. At the early age of twelve years he had already shown unusual talent as an artist, and Graham Reynolds refers to a miniature signed and dated 1753, when he was only eleven years old – his earliest recorded work. His uncle, sometime Mayor of Tiverton and a very wealthy man, together with his godfather and a friend called Oliver Peard, a local trader, recognized his gifts and were instrumental in persuading his father to allow him to go to London for training, on the understanding that they would guarantee his upkeep. Richard Cosway was grateful for this and said that Oliver Peard's generosity was 'passing great'. Although he left Tiverton when he was young it always held many happy memories for him, and, as is so often the case, the home of his childhood remained in his affections throughout his life. Many years later, in 1784 he presented a picture to the parish of Tiverton, entitled 'The Angel delivering St. Peter from Prison', to be placed in St Peter's Church.

In London he was first taught art under Thomas Hudson, who was also tutor to

Sir Joshua Reynolds, a choice no doubt influenced by the fact that Hudson had connections with Devonshire, and had acquired a great reputation in the area. Cosway did not, however, settle very well with him, and refers to having to perform 'menial offices'. It may have been that the young boy was over anxious to get on, and resented the small jobs required of an apprentice. Be that as it may, after a few months he left Hudson and took lodgings where he could attend a drawing school run by William Shipley (1714–1803) in the Strand, and it was here that he really began what was to be a brilliant career.

Cosway soon made great progress and worked hard, often going without food and luxuries. When in 1754 the Society of Arts was founded and a prize offered for the best drawings executed by boys and girls under the age of fourteen, Cosway entered a drawing of a head, representing compassion, and was rewarded by obtaining the first prize of £5 5s., the first awarded by the Society.

This was the first of many prizes that Cosway was to win in his determination to become a leading painter. He gained several for design between the years 1757–59, and in 1760, when still only eighteen years old, he obtained the first prize of £30 for a drawing from life in a competition open to young men under the age of twenty-four. In the same year he exhibited his pictures for the first time at the Society of Artists, entering a portrait of his drawing master, Mr Shipley.

He soon began to take on his own engagements, and obtained commissions from jewellers who wanted fancy miniatures and from shop-keepers who wanted drawings of heads. He did not enter any paintings at the Society of Arts in 1761, but exhibited instead at the Free Society until 1764 and again in 1766. In 1767 his name reappears in the Society of Artists' List, and continues to do so until 1769. It was in the same year that he entered the Royal Academy Schools, and exhibited at their exhibitions from 1770 to 1787, with occasional entries between 1798 to 1803. Elected A.R.A. in 1770, he became a full member of the Royal Academy in 1771.

He intended originally to become a full-scale portrait painter, and in fact worked mainly in this manner for some years, describing himself in *Mortimer's Universal Director*, 1763, as a painter but not as a miniaturist. He was not outstandingly successful as a painter in oils, and in the *Royal Academy Review* in 1787 is the following comment: 'Mr. Cosway's pictures in large are much inferior to his miniatures. It is so arduous a matter to succeed in both walks that we are by no means surprized at his failure in the attempt'. In 1762 his address was c/o Mr Clark's, nr. Beaufort Buildings, in the Strand, and in the same year he entered an enamel portrait at the Free Society's Exhibition. There is no record of where he learnt the art of enamelling, but he was evidently a very apt pupil. In 1768 he was living at 4 Berkeley Street, Berkeley Square, but for some time prior to this he was known to have been living in a house in Orchard Street, Portman Square.

Cosway had not been endowed with good looks, but he had a great love of clothes, and from a small, rather insignificant boy he grew up to take his place among the Beaux and Dandies of the day adopting extravagant and ostentatious modes of dress. He carried this to such an extreme that Mat Darley, the famous caricaturist, produced an etching calling him 'The Macaroni Miniature Painter', and this name stuck to him. The self-styled Macaronis were the younger members of Almacks Club which was formed about 1765. Before this, White's Club, which had originated as a chocolate house, and did not become a club until 1736, had absorbed the élite young men of the day. By 1764 it had divided itself into the Old and New Club, and both were frowning upon the reckless gaming which was so popular among both young and old alike. Almacks was started to cater for those who wished for these facilities, and the younger members formed themselves into a brotherhood which they called the Macaronis. The name was taken from the macaroni which Almacks had been the first to introduce into England from Italy.

The young men were noted for their dress, elegance and manners. One of the conditions of entry was that the nominee should have travelled. They numbered among their members many distinguished persons, and the name Macaroni was applied to almost any Beau who wore absurdly extravagant dress. The craze of wearing a wig of enormous proportions was taken to an extreme by this society, who wore them as high as two feet above their heads. It is easy to see how Cosway was dubbed the Macaroni Miniature Painter. His foppish attire and extravagant taste, and in particular his habit of wearing a sword, laid him wide open to ridicule, and the wits and satirists of the day were not slow to take advantage of it. Owing in no small part to jealousy at his success, his fellow artists were only too glad of a chance to make fun of his monkey-like face and rather stupid behaviour. His sword was on one occasion literally the cause of his downfall. Whilst deputizing for the President, who was ill, he had to receive the Prince of Wales at the Academy. After seeing the Prince to his carriage, he backed, making a deep obeisance, the sword got between his legs, and he was precipitated into the mud. In spite of all the ridicule that he received, he was kind and generous to many people, and was liked by his pupils and gave them much encouragement.

He fell in love with a Miss Woolls to whom he evidently proposed, but was rejected. By 1771 he was well established and his popularity was increasing rapidly; the brilliance and dash of his style and technique were blossoming into what was to be the fulfilment of the early promise.

On 18th January, 1781, at St George's, Hanover Square, he married Maria Louisa Catherine Cecilia Hadfield, on whom he settled a sum of £2,800 as a marriage gift. She had been born in Florence in 1759, and was herself an artist, having gained a medal for drawing and been elected a member of the Florentine Academy of Fine Arts. Her father was a native of Manchester where his family were wealthy merchants, and after his death in 1778 or 1779, and at the suggestion of Angelica Kauffmann, the widow and family travelled to England where they were met by Angelica and taken to her home. Maria's hopes of becoming another Angelica Kauffmann were not fulfilled, and by the time she married Cosway, in spite of the fact that she had obtained work, the family were in considerably reduced circumstances. After her marriage she continued painting on and off throughout her life, and is said to have copied quite a number of her husband's works.

Cosway had his house in Berkeley Street redecorated before taking his bride there. They remained in the house until 1784 when he decided to move into more palatial premises, and they obtained part of Schomberg House, Pall Mall. This marked a new phase in their lives, and in their new and splendid surroundings they became the centre of attraction, holding musical parties and receptions that were attended by the Prince of Wales, Horace Walpole, the beautiful Duchess of Devonshire, the Marchioness Townshend, and many other notable persons. The exact date on which Cosway met the Prince of Wales is not recorded, but it must have been about the time of the move to Schomberg House, although according to Allan Cunningham the Prince had been known to visit them at their home in Berkeley Street.

The Royal Patronage made Cosway at once acceptable to those who formed the somewhat gay circle of Royal admirers. It is generally believed that the start of his patronage was due to a miniature he painted of Mrs Fitzherbert, which remained one of the Prince's most treasured possessions throughout his life. There is a story that the Prince had given Mrs Fitzherbert a large diamond which she had had cut into two, and her miniature and also one of the Prince by Cosway had been set into two small lockets, each covered with one half of the large diamond and encircled with smaller stones. The Prince and Mrs Fitzherbert each retained the portrait of the other, vowing that they would wear it always, and he promising that on his death her picture should be interred with him. The Prince later became George IV, and after his death William IV sent back to Mrs Fitzherbert various jewels and trinkets, but not the miniature. Anxious to know if the promise had been fulfilled, Mrs Fitzherbert wrote to enquire, and was assured by the King that it had not been removed from George IV's neck. A further story related to the Duke of Wellington, who was George IV's executor. Strict injunctions had been given to the Duke by the late King to see that nothing was taken from his body after his death. The Duke promised that this should be seen to, without knowing to what the King referred. Being left alone with the body, he noticed something suspended from the King's neck, and, being curious, could not resist lifting the collar to see what it was. The Duke then realized that the article was the small locket which contained Mrs Fitzherbert's picture. This he duly covered up again, and it was buried as the King had always promised, next to his heart.

The fact that Schomberg House was so near to Carlton House where Cosway was painting a ceiling, led to the suggestion that he had secret access to the Prince. Cosway's house had an interesting past, having been occupied in turn by John Jervis, John Astley the painter, and Nathaniel Hone who had caused some comment by having a black woman there as a model. It was here that Dr Graham had his notorious Temple of Health, and in the Cosways' time Thomas Gainsborough lived in the west wing. During the seven years that Cosway lived in Pall Mall his work went from strength to strength, and in about 1786 his success was crowned by the much coveted title of Miniaturist to the Prince of Wales. This appointment resulted in the artist becoming more pompous than ever, and he began to sign his work with a flowing and rather elaborate inscription. 'R dus Cosway, R.A., Primarius Pictor Serenissimi Walliae Principis pinxit', an affectation not unnaturally resulting in more skits on the man and his work.

In 1789 their only child was born and was called Louisa Paolina Angelica, this last after Angelica Kauffmann, to whom Mrs Cosway owed so much. General Pasquale de Paoli was her godfather, and the Princess D'Albany her godmother. Shortly after the child's birth Maria Cosway went abroad for reasons of health to Paris and Flanders and thence on to Italy. The child was left to the care of her father and friends, and it has been said that in an effort to begin her education as soon as possible, she was taught Hebrew at the age of six in order that she might be able to read in that tongue as easily as she could in English. While still abroad Mrs Cosway had news of her husband's sudden illness, and in spite of the difficulties involved in travelling at that time, she returned to London to find Cosway recovered and her small daughter, who was now about four years old, well and happy. In 1796, however, when the child was only six years old she was taken ill suddenly and, to the great grief of her father and mother, died. There were at one time several attractive portraits painted by her father; these have since been lost.

For reasons unknown, Cosway left his splendid apartments in Pall Mall in 1791, and moved to Stratford Place, to a house which he decorated and furnished in his usual lavish style. It boasted of a carved stone lion standing on a pediment to one side of the door, which gave Peter Pindar an opportunity to ridicule Cosway once more. He wrote the following lines which some wag pinned on the door:

7. GEORGE ENGLEHEART (1750–1829). A member of Lord Gerard's family. Circ. 1791. 2¼ × 1¾ in.
8. RICHARD COSWAY, R.A. (1742?–1821). Mary Anne, sister to Francis Jackson. 1⅘ × 1½ in.
9. JOHN SMART (1742/3–1811). Mr. Charles Brooke. Signed and dated 1796. 3 × 2¼ in.
10. JOHN SMART (1742/3–1811). An unknown lady. Signed and dated 1786 I. 2⅜ × 1¾ in.

When a man to a fair for a show brings a lion,
'Tis usual a monkey the signpost to tie on,
But here the old custom reversed is seen,
For the lion's without and the monkey's within.

This was too much for poor Cosway who, as soon as he could find other accommodation, moved two doors away to what was later No. 2 Stratford Place, and lived here for most of the remainder of his life.

While in Pall Mall Cosway had done a certain amount of buying and selling both of pictures and antiques, and before he left he sold quite a large collection. After the move to Stratford Place, Mrs Cosway's health again deteriorated, and between 1790 and 1791 they went abroad, apparently well-equipped with a carriage and servants. Later they returned to London, and Mrs Cosway, who had been exhibiting at the Academy on and off since 1783, continued to paint. But the improvement in her health was not maintained, and eventually she went back to Italy where she remained for some years. It was about this time that Cosway, who had always been slightly eccentric, began to show this side of his character more clearly, and after his wife's departure he became attracted to a form of religious fanaticism in vogue during the latter part of the eighteenth century, particularly among the members of the artistic and literary fraternity. Carried away by these beliefs, he imagined that the Virgin Mary had sat for him and that Charles I had appeared and they had discussed art.

When the Prince of Wales became Regent in 1811 he gradually dropped Cosway and became more selective of his immediate circle. There is no doubt that Cosway felt the loss of his patronage keenly, although he made no attempt to regain his position, but by this time his wife had returned from Italy and she devoted herself to looking after him.

He continued painting until about 1821, in which year he had two strokes and became partially paralysed, and in April, in order to be in a quieter neighbourhood, he and his wife moved to 31 Edgware Road. In July of the same year (when he was eighty years of age) he had a further sudden attack whilst out for a drive, and died before he could be got home. He was buried in Marylebone New Church, on the north wall of which was erected a monument with an inscription written by Mrs Cosway's brother-in-law, William Coombe, the author of *Dr Syntax*. He bequeathed all his possessions to his wife, who was sole executrix.

After her husband's death Mrs Cosway returned to Lodi where she had established a college some years before, and which on her return she turned into a convent, a project which had the wholehearted support of the Emperor of Austria,

Francis I, who, in recognition of her work, created her a Baroness in 1834. She died in Lodi in 1838.

The miniatures that Cosway painted at the start of his career were excellent, and even then revealed the delicacy and fine modelling that was so characteristic of his work. They were painted on a smaller scale and more modestly conceived than those that were to follow, the ivory on which they were painted being often not more than $1\frac{1}{2}$–2 in. in height. The backgrounds were frequently plain, as he had not then discovered that transparent colours permitted the luminosity that only ivory was capable of producing. I have a miniature of this earlier period, of Sir Edward Astley. The sitter is placed against a beigy-grey background, and the oval is two inches in height. The painting is so excellent that at a distance it could be mistaken for an enamel, although it does not possess the elegant elusiveness of his later works.

As time went on and the use of larger ivories became popular, so Cosway's style developed. A looser and softer line was apparent in the drawing of the hair and dress, and his method of enlarging the pupil of the eye was noticeable. By about 1785, when the size of his ivories was often as much as three inches in height, his real powers began to emerge. He began to use transparent pigments, which he discovered could be floated on to the ivory, leaving the material itself to suggest the lights in the portrait, and his finest work as well as some of the most brilliant miniatures of the eighteenth century were produced between 1785–1805. He was the first to introduce the use of what has since been described as the 'Cosway' background of blue clouds, and his use of a clear Antwerp blue is another sign of his work. The features were modelled with short grey brush strokes which are visible round the eyes and contours of the cheek, whilst in the treatment of the hair he adopted a method of painting it in soft masses rather than in definite lines. On the background, particularly near the edge of the cheek away from the spectator, long parallel strokes may be discerned, often punctuated by numerous dots or small transverse strokes, while occasionally on parts of the background away from the face may be seen groups of soft short strokes running in various directions, each one ending in a small blob of colour. There is almost always some of the clear blue paint of which he was so fond in some part of the miniature.

Cosway had a way, often copied by other artists, of giving his sitters rather elongated necks in an effort to produce more elegant portraits. The criticism that he flattered his sitters may have been true, but the portraits drew out whatever beauty could be discerned, and those he painted of men were not without character and firmness. A prolific artist, he prided himself on the rapidity with which he could produce his miniatures, and in spite of this speed his works possessed great merit and his powers of execution continued until he died.

He painted mainly on ivory, but miniatures on vellum and paper also exist, apart from the very rare enamels. Pencil drawings and tinted sketches can also be numbered among his accomplishments, as well as oil paintings and full-length portrait drawings. His miniatures are not by any means always signed. A miniature signed on the front RC-y. 1760 in gold, and sold recently may conceivably have been genuine, but any signed on the face should be viewed with suspicion unless the workmanship is unmistakable. His signatures vary at different stages in his life, most of them being as pompous as the one he used in his heyday, 'Rdus Cosway, Primarius Pictor, Serenissimi, Principis Walliae'; but R. Cosway, Rdus Cosway and even Rdus de Cosway have been found. The majority of them had Latin inscriptions, and R.A. and R.S.A. were added after his name. On his drawings the signatures differed from those on miniatures; these were signed on the front, usually with a small R in the centre of a large capital C in monogram.

Cosway's miniatures have been copied in large numbers, and reproductions are frequently to be met with in both private collections and for sale in shops, but the collector will not find it difficult to study his work as the Victoria and Albert Museum, and many other museums own fine examples. He painted almost all the members of the Royal Family as well as most of the leading members of society, and his miniatures include many lovely portraits of children.

Although the eighteenth century produced many fine miniaturists, the works of Richard Cosway have left us a picture of English society which is unparalleled by any of his contemporaries.

CHAPTER XII

JOHN SMART, JOHN SMART JNR AND OZIAS HUMPHRY

*

The reputation of JOHN SMART (1742/3–1811) has never stood higher than it does at the present time. For many years now his work has been admired by collectors and connoisseurs alike, but it is only comparatively recently that his miniatures have obtained such outstanding prices in the sale rooms and have become sought after by many more people. One of the main reasons for this is probably the fact that during the last few years a number of fine collections have been sold in London, and consequently there has been ample opportunity to examine and compare some very good examples of the artist's work, which has led to an even greater appreciation of his merit. Basil Long considered him to be one of the greatest miniaturists of the English School, and Dr G. C. Williamson referred to him as the noblest and most dignified miniaturist of the eighteenth century. It has always been stated that Smart was born near Norwich on 1st May, 1740 or 1741, but Graham Reynolds considers his birth may have been some time between May and August of that year, and Arthur Jaffé in his article in *The Art Quarterly*, 1954, considers 1742 or 1743 the most probable, as according to his tombstone he was 69 years of age at his death on 1st May, 1811.

The first fact about his life to be established is that in the first competition held in London by the Society of Arts in 1755, he won second prize and Richard Cosway first prize, Cosway aged 12 and Smart aged 11. Smart won several prizes in the following years, and in 1758 succeeded in beating Cosway and gaining first prize. Some of the drawings executed by Smart for these competitions have been discovered in recent years and show him to have had more than average ability for a boy. From the beginning of his career Smart, unlike many other artists, adopted the practice of signing his miniatures, and since his earliest known portraits are dated 1760, it is possible to trace his work chronologically from then until the end of his life. A representative collection of his miniatures painted between 1765 and 1797 may be studied at the Victoria and Albert Museum. He was apprenticed in 1755 to William Shipley, and in 1762 Smart exhibited at the Society of Artists of which he became a fellow in 1765, the year the Society was granted a charter. From 1775–83 he lived in Berners Street and became a Director of the Society of

Artists in 1771, Vice President in 1777, and President in 1778. He continued to exhibit with the Society right up to 1783, and no doubt would have done so for longer but there was no exhibition in 1784. Instead, Smart is stated to have entered some works at the Royal Academy for the first time. These entries are in fact under the name of J. Smart Jnr, from an address in Davies St, not Berners St, which was Smart's home, and were in all probability by another artist.[1] When the Society of Artists ceased to exist, Smart became an exhibitor at the Royal Academy from 1797, after his return from Madras, till his death in 1811.

In the past it has been said that Smart was a member of a strictly religious sect of Sandemanians, but Mr Jaffé was unable to trace his name among the list of members, and he certainly did not adhere to their rule of no second marriage. As a result of Mr Jaffé's research, certain new facts have come to light which have clarified to some extent the hitherto rather obscure details about his private life. The name of his first wife is still unknown, but she is known to have eloped with one William Pars (1742–82), who took her with him to Italy in October 1775, and in the *Memoirs of Thomas Jones*[2] a description is given of Mrs. Pars' death from consumption, and of her burial outside the walls of Rome. Smart had three children by this wife, John, b. 1762 (who died young), Anna Maria, 1766–1813, and Sophia, 1770–93. After his wife left him he formed a connection with a woman named Sarah Midgley, by whom he had a son, John Smart Junior, 1776–1809, and a daughter Sarah, 1781–1853.

In 1799 he married Edith (Vere?) when living at Russell Place, Fitzroy Square. The date of her death is not known, but it was presumably sometime before 1805, when he married for the third time, Mary Morton, at St Marylebone Church, she being then twenty-two years old. They had a son, John James Smart, born on 7th October, 1805, who died on 26th September, 1870, and therefore could not have been the Smart referred to by Redgrave and Long as having committed suicide in 1856. On 28th July, 1784, Smart was granted permission to leave England and sail for India, and to take a daughter with him. This he did, and sailed on the *Dutton*, arriving at Madras on 6th September, 1785. The daughter in question was Anna Maria, who was married in Madras on 11th July, 1786, to Robert Woolf of the Madras Civil Service. Her husband retired in 1803, but was still alive in 1836. The date of Anna Maria's death was 1813, so she survived her father and is mentioned in his will as residing at Leigh House, near Bradford, Wilts. A miniature of their eldest son Robert (1786–1825) at the age of 10 years was sold recently. It was fully inscribed with details of the boy, and signed and dated 1796 in his grandfather's writing.

[1] John Smart Jnr was then only seven years old.
[2] *Walpole Soc.*, Vol. XXXII.

Sir William Foster, in his article on 'British Artists in India' published by the *Walpole Society*,[1] says that after the marriage of Anna to Robert Woolf, his daughter Sophia was granted permission on 3rd December, 1788, to go to her friends in Madras, and that she duly arrived to join her father. She also seems to have become engaged within a short time, for on 8th February, 1790, she married Lieutenant (afterwards Lieutenant General) John Dighton, and died on the birth of their son in 1793. A christening is recorded as having taken place in Madras on 20th May, 1794, of the boy John Dighton and his cousin Maria. John Dighton Jnr died in London in March 1810 when he was only sixteen years old.

It has always been held that Smart was a pupil of Daniel Dodd, whose work is not very well known. While this is not impossible, there is a likelihood that some confusion may have arisen from the fact that John Smart Jnr was probably taught by him, but could not have exhibited in 1770. The suggestion that Smart was taught by Cosway is also most unlikely in view of the fact that both men were about the same age and exhibiting at the same time, and there is no resemblance between their work.

In his decision to go to India, where his arrival caused Ozias Humphry, already in Calcutta, considerable apprehension, Smart was following the example of many other portrait painters and miniaturists who had found themselves able to earn substantial sums of money by painting for wealthy English residents and native Princes, although the latter did not always pay readily. Throughout the whole of his time in India he obtained employment with the Nawab of Arcot as miniature painter to his family, as well as painting portraits for a distinguished clientèle who resided there. He was, however, owed money by the Nawab of Arcot, which had not been received before that potentate's death and of which mention is made in Smart's will.

The miniatures he painted during his stay in India can easily be distinguished, as not only did he adopt the method of placing a capital I under the date, but the dates themselves run from 1786–95, in which year he returned to England. His work was in great demand, and according to a contemporary newspaper he was expected to visit Calcutta and Lucknow where many patrons awaited him. However, after having spent ten years in Madras, Smart returned home, sailing on 26th April, 1795, in the *Melville Castle*, and arriving in England towards the end of November. He took up residence at 20 Grafton Street, Fitzroy Square, London, removing in 1799 to No. 2 Russell Place, Fitzroy Square.

Nollekens told Farington on 11th February, 1810, that Smart had settled £100 per annum on his daughter (Sarah) who had evidently been keeping house for him, in order that he could live with his young third wife 'who seems to be a well-

[1] Vol. XIX.

87. JOHN SMART
(1742/3–1811)
Self-portrait.
Signed and dated 1783.
$1\frac{1}{2} \times 1\frac{1}{8}$ in.

88. JOHN SMART
An unknown man
(sketch for a miniature).

89. JOHN SMART
Dr Parkhurst (1728–97).
Dated 1765. $1\frac{1}{4} \times 1\frac{3}{32}$ in.

90. JOHN SMART
Called Mrs Abernethy.
Signed and dated 1800. Depth $4\frac{1}{4}$ in.

91. JOHN SMART
Called Mr Holland. Signed and dated 1806.
Depth $3\frac{3}{4}$ in.

92. JOHN SMART
The Hon. John St John. Dated 1770.
$6\frac{5}{16} \times 5\frac{1}{16}$ in.

93. JOHN SMART
An unknown man. $3\frac{3}{16} \times 2\frac{3}{8}$ in.

disposed woman and has brought him to habits of regularity in attending divine service'. He had earned a reputation as a quiet and restrained man but in the *Memoirs of Thomas Jones* he is described as 'a man of most vulgar manners, grossly sensual and greedy of money to all extreme'. This was thought by Arthur Jaffé to be untrue, and he contended that Smart was a 'good husband, father and grandfather'.

After an illness of only nine days, Smart died on 1st May, 1811, having only made his will on 28th April, appointing as his executors Dr William Ruddiman and Joseph Nollekens, the sculptor, and out of what was evidently a fairly large estate he left an annuity of £60 to his sister, Mrs Deborah Wright, and bequests to his servant, his daughter Anna and her daughter Sophia,[1] as well as to his son John James Smart by his third wife, for whom he made ample provision. His residuary estate passed to this boy on his widow's death in 1854; she in the meantime had married one John Sidey Caley.

Unlike many miniaturists Smart's style and technique were fully developed at the beginning of his career, and he endowed his miniatures with a finesse that only great powers of draughtsmanship in the modelling could achieve.

He did not flatter his sitters in the way that Cosway or other artists often did, but executed what appear to be perfect character studies. His colours have not faded and the flat body colour with which he painted the costume has retained its brilliance. He usually favoured a background uniform in colour, which was often of a greyish buff, but occasionally he used a 'sky background'. A study of Smart's miniatures reveals several characteristics by which his work may be readily identified. He used a brick red colour for the complexion, and left a small 'island' of naked ivory to accentuate the highlights on the cheek. He also used shading to gain the effect of roundness to the cheek bone and a fullness to the face. Another mannerism peculiar to Smart is the way in which he drew the lines under the eyes, and even crow's feet if he saw them. The eyelashes were put in with minute care, and if a portrait was painted in profile they were painted in clearly defined lines, particularly on the lid nearest to the background. He often placed a dab of opaque white on the tip of the nose. All his miniatures are attractive and full of vigour. He usually painted on ivory, in sizes varying in different periods from $1\frac{1}{2}$ in., until about 1775, to 2 in. and, after 1790, to 3 in.

It was his practice to make portrait sketches on paper, of the same size as the miniature he was about to paint, and these water colours are often signed and named, affording an excellent guide to his work, and helping to identify some of his miniatures. He is known to have painted also on card and in enamel, and seems to have been equally successful whatever medium he chose to use. His signature,

---

[1] I have since inspected the will and find these bequests were contingent upon John James not surviving the age of 21 years.

J.S. in cursive initials is almost invariably followed by the date, and as has already been mentioned those painted in India have a Roman I painted after the date Occasionally he signed in full, 'J. Smart Pinxit', but such signatures are rare. An unusual miniature portrait of a young man, a Mr Holland, was sold in December 1958 from the Dyson Perrins collection. It was of a young man sitting gazing to the left, with his back to the spectator, painted against a draped lilac curtain, and signed and dated 1806 on $3\frac{3}{4}$ in. ivory. Basil Long has suggested that it might have been copied from a large painting. It was among several other fine examples of his work that were sold at the same time. Smart is one of the few first-rate eighteenth century miniaturists whose biography has not yet been written, and it is to be hoped that this omission will some day be rectified.[1]

There were several artists whose work slightly resembled Smart's, including Samuel Andrews, but the one whose work bore the closest resemblance was his son, JOHN SMART JUNIOR. John was too young to accompany his father to India but must later have had instruction in miniature painting, for he exhibited at the Royal Academy in 1800, 1802, 1803 and 1808. In May 1808 his father applied for permission for his son to go to India as a miniature painter. This permission was granted on 15th June of that year, but he did not arrive in Madras until 11th February, 1809, and died on 1st June.

Apart from the fact that he was a pupil of Daniel Dodd,[2] little is known of the young man's life. His work was mainly in crayon and blacklead. His painting was weaker than his father's, and inclined to be larger. He signed with his name or initials, and added the word Junior or an abbreviation of it.

OZIAS HUMPHRY, R.A. (1742–1810), like Richard Cosway, was a native of Devonshire. Both were born in 1742, Humphry at Honiton and Cosway at Tiverton, and both men attained prominence as miniaturists. Humphry, whose father was a peruke maker and mercer and whose mother had started a lace business, was educated at the local grammar school, and in spite of the fact that late in life he became almost obsessed with stories of the nobility of his ancestry, the family had evidently fallen on bad times. While still at school he showed an aptitude and love for drawing, and in 1757 he was sent to London to study at the school in St Martin's Lane and in the Duke of Richmond's gallery. This lasted only a year, for in 1758 he returned to Devon, and in February 1759 his father died, leaving the mother in sole and capable charge of the lace business. Humphry was grateful for the assistance given him by his parents and always spoke of his mother with great affection. There is no doubt that she had great hopes that he might return to help her in the family business and assist in the drawing of patterns, and although at first Humphry

[1] Valuable information regarding the life of John Smart and his family has been put at my disposal and as result of further research a monograph is now being written.

[2] The John Smart referred to may have been another artist.

did appear interested in this career, and even designed some lace patterns, it was soon apparent that his aptitude and real interest lay in painting portraits. He was much influenced by the painting of Sir Joshua Reynolds, whose work he greatly admired, and had all but persuaded his mother to allow him to study under him when a chance meeting of some kind brought him in touch with Samuel Collins who had a practice in Bath. It was decided that he should go to Collins for three years' training, and in October 1760 he began his tuition, although the contract was in fact annulled in 1762 after Collins' departure to Dublin.

Humphry was from an early age painstaking and particular in retaining documents and letters relating to his life and affairs, and owing to this we are able to get a clear picture of the man and his progress. It is not known exactly how long Humphry studied under Collins, for although Collins was a successful miniaturist his reputation as a man did not stand very high, and he evidently got himself 'entangled with his eccentric gallantries' to such an extent that he had to flee the country in the hopes of avoiding his creditors. Humphry was in an embarrassing situation; he was still a young man, legally bound to Collins, and his desire to continue painting was as strong as ever. His immediate concern was to take advice as to the best course to pursue. His mother on hearing of Collins' desertion again hoped that her son would give up his ideas of painting and return to the business, and Dr Williamson tells us that she told him, 'Your prospect is very discouraging but whatever is the issue of your choice you have only yourself to blame.' To which he replied, 'To pursue the profession of painting was my own choice and nothing can discourage me from the prosecution of it. If you will furnish me with a guinea to go to Exeter, I will never trouble you for any further assistance, but will either succeed or perish in the attempt'. Seeing that she could do nothing to persuade him against this course his mother gave him the guinea, and with this small sum in his purse he went to Exeter where he obtained some patrons and paid his way for about two months. Still somewhat concerned about his obligations to the missing Collins, he took legal advice and as a result publicly announced that owing to Collins' departure he intended to dissolve the contract. No objections being raised, Humphry then opened his own practice in Bath, and in 1762 was given rooms at the house of Mr Thomas Linley, the musician, whose daughter Elizabeth Anne later became the first Mrs Sheridan.

Humphry spent a very pleasant time with the Linleys, who appear to have been a very happy family in spite of the fact that they were not very well off and had to live frugally. They became very attached to him and named one of their sons Ozias after him.

During his stay in Bath he became acquainted with Gainsborough, who constantly urged him to go to London. This he did in June 1763, armed with an introduction to Sir Joshua Reynolds, whom he had always admired. He was allowed to copy some of the master's work, and the results were so good that Sir Joshua was filled with admiration and insisted that Humphry should leave Bath at once and establish himself in the capital. Humphry remained in London for a few weeks, no doubt trying to make up his mind what to do, for he had not intended leaving Bath so soon; but in 1764 he made the decision, and settled finally in London. On arrival he at once called on Sir Joshua, who suggested that he move near him, and for a time he lived in Leicester Square, moving later to 21 King Street, Covent Garden, where he remained until 1771.

At first Reynolds gave him help and encouragement but soon left him to stand on his own feet, much to Humphry's distress. However, he succeeded in establishing himself and obtaining patrons, and was an exhibitor at the Society of Artists from 1765–71. A miniature, exhibited in 1766, but since lost, of John Mealing, a well-known artists' model, was purchased by the King for 100 guineas, and this did much to enhance his reputation.

Humphry's character was somewhat spoiled by conceit and a quick temper, particularly if there was any suggestion of a slight; added to which he was restless and did not settle anywhere for very long. He had an only brother William, born in 1743, with whom he remained constantly in touch. William took Holy Orders and became vicar of 'Kemsing-cum-Seale and later Rector of Birling'[1] both in the County of Kent, and to both of which benefices he was presented by the Duke of Dorset. When in 1773 Ozias Humphry and George Romney set off on a trip to Italy, they stayed en route to the coast at Knole Park, the beautiful house of the Duke of Dorset. Both painted portraits of the family, and according to Dr Williamson documents remain in the possession of the Sackville family, giving several items of information about the two artists.

The tour of Italy, undertaken because of a severe fall that Humphry had had from his horse in 1772, was prolonged for four years, during which time he visited among other places Rome, Florence, Venice and Naples. His health improved and he was able to make copies of well-known paintings, but the injuries he had received eventually led to his having to give up miniature painting. In 1777 he returned to London and for a time turned his attention to painting life-size portraits in oil, and in 1779 he became an Associate of the Royal Academy where he was a frequent exhibitor.

He evidently found he was not earning as much money as he would have wished, and on hearing of the good fortune that artists such as Tilly Kettle and others were having in India, decided in 1784 to go there himself. A very full description of his

[1] Kemsing and Seale are now separate parishes.

94.
OZIAS HUMPHRY, R.A.
(1742–1810)
An unknown man. Signed.

95.
OZIAS HUMPHRY, R.A.
An unknown lady. Signed.

96. OZIAS HUMPHRY, R.A.
Sahib Zada. Signed and dated 1786.
Depth $3\frac{1}{2}$ in.

97.
GEORGE ENGLEHEART
(1750–1829)
An unknown lady.
$1\frac{11}{16} \times 1\frac{5}{16}$ in.

98.
GEORGE ENGLEHEART
An unknown child.
Signed. $1\frac{9}{32} \times 1$ in.

99.
GEORGE ENGLEHEART
An unknown man.
$1\frac{9}{16} \times 1\frac{9}{32}$ in.

100. GEORGE ENGLEHEART
The Princess Royal,
Charlotte Augusta (1766–1828).
$3\frac{3}{8} \times 2\frac{3}{4}$ in.

101. GEORGE ENGLEHEART
An unknown boy.

102. NATHANIEL PLIMER (1757–1822)
H.R.H. The Prince of Wales.
$2\frac{27}{32} \times 2\frac{9}{32}$ in.

103. GEORGE ENGLEHEART
Miss McKenzie. Signed and dated 1804.
$2\frac{9}{16} \times 2\frac{3}{16}$ in.

life in India is given by Sir William Foster, C.I.E. in the *Walpole Society Journal* for 1930–31. He arrived in Calcutta in August 1795, and letters written to his brother show that he was full of apprehension at the news of the arrival of other artists, including John Smart.

Before his departure Humphry was practically engaged to Miss Mary Boydell, whose portrait he painted. She was the niece of Alderman Boydell and it is thought that Humphry was as much attracted to her money as to the lady herself. Some years previously he had sought unsuccessfully for the hand of a Miss Paine. A correspondence was carried on between Humphry and Miss Boydell, starting when he was on board ship. The letters were singularly devoid of sentiment and full of the ladies he had met on board, all going to India in the hopes of obtaining husbands. Finally, however, the lady decided to break off the correspondence, and returned the presents he had given her to his brother to keep.

He visited Calcutta, Benares and Lucknow, painting a great many miniatures and meeting many native Princes, but the climate of India did not really suit him and this, coupled with his failure to obtain payment for many of his works, made him decide to return to England. His chief debtor was the Nawab of Oudh who had commissioned him to paint portraits of himself and of his family and ministers. Only part of the money due to Humphry was ever paid, and this so embittered him that he never forgot and he returned to England a disappointed man. By this time his health and his eyesight were deteriorating. He arrived in England in March 1787, taking up residence in London where he was made a full member of the Royal Academy in 1791. He took up portrait painting in crayons, and was given an appointment as such to the King.

Humphry copied a number of family portraits in miniature for the Duke of Dorset, but his eyesight became worse and by 1792 he was unable to paint miniatures and had to rely on commissions for large crayon portraits. In 1793 he was on the hanging committee of the Royal Academy, and in 1797 the Prince and Princess of Orange commissioned him to execute their portraits in crayon. These were the last portraits he was able to produce, and were his last exhibits at the Royal Academy of 1797.

In 1799 a young woman called Dolly Wickers, whose father William Wickers was a general dealer and shopkeeper in Oxford, bore him a son who was called William Upcott, a family name. The boy had a varied education but was obviously intelligent and made the most of his opportunities, learning among other subjects Hebrew, Greek and Latin. He chose the career of a bookseller, and for this purpose went to London and was placed with Mr R. H. Evans of Pall Mall, then with Mr J. Wright of Piccadilly, where he worked for three and a half years, during which time he learnt French from an émigré priest.

Largely owing to his father's influence he obtained the post of sub-librarian at the London Institute. Here he began collecting items that appealed to him. These included coins and tokens, of which he formed a large collection, and later, owing to the gift of some prints from a customer, he turned his interest to prints and engravings and later still to autographs and letters. This pursuit led him to the discovery of John Evelyn's diary among the Evelyn family papers. After Upcott's death in 1845 his collection of books, manuscripts, prints and drawings realized over four thousand pounds at Sotheby's. Many of them were purchased by the British Museum and the Bodleian, Oxford, and from them much information was obtained about Humphry and his life. Upcott always referred to Humphry as his godfather.

With regard to his work as a miniaturist one cannot do better than quote Basil Long's words in *British Miniaturists*: 'Humphry was one of the best English miniaturists. He was an excellent draughtsman, and he imparted to his portraits an air of elegance, grace and distinction'. He had a distinguished clientèle which included members of the Royal Family, and his portraits of Queen Charlotte and H.R.H. Princess Charlotte Augusta as a child are particularly good. Both H. Bone and H. Spicer the enamelists were his pupils, copying some of his works in enamel, and so were R. Collins and T. Day. He was a prolific artist and able to produce likenesses with amazing rapidity. His style had more affinity to that of the large-scale paintings of Sir Joshua Reynolds, and showed a tendency to produce oil paintings on a small scale, though the rich colouring he favoured was harmonious and effective. In his earlier works he often drew the eyebrows with a number of fine almost parallel lines, and particularly in men's portraits the eyes, nose and mouth are sharply delineated. A broader and freer style can be seen in Humphry's later works, and this may be studied in the miniature of Warren Hastings at the Victoria and Albert Museum. No doubt his failing eyesight had something to do with this change, as he would have found close work more difficult. Also there was a tendency during the latter part of the eighteenth century to use larger ivories and a freer technique in painting. Unlike some of his contemporaries Humphry did not enlarge the eyes of his sitters, but rather drew them slightly slanting like those of an oriental, and with an almost sleepy look about them. His signatures are usually O.H. in monogram on the front of the miniature, the H within the O and not conjoined. Another method he adopted was to sign it in ink on the back, with his initials in full, followed by a date. He painted on paper as well as on ivory and as well as drawings in crayons drew small portraits in water colour slightly reminiscent of J. Downman. Their size varied from $1\frac{1}{2}$ in.–$4\frac{1}{2}$ in. at least. Many of his works were engraved.

Humphry lived in various parts of London: in Knightsbridge, Coventry Street and Sloane Street, finally taking apartments at 39 Thornhaugh Street, a house kept by the widow of Spicer the enamel painter, with whom he had been great friends. It was here on 9th March, 1810, that he died. He was buried in St James burial ground, Hampstead Road.

CHAPTER XIII

GREAT GEORGIAN MINIATURISTS

*

GEORGE ENGLEHEART (1750–1829) can justly be described as one of the great miniature painters of the eighteenth century and was therefore understandably a rival of Richard Cosway. It has been said that in England the fashionable world was divided in its patronage between these two artists; the gay and frivolous persons of the day going to Cosway, and those of a more staid and steady disposition preferring Engleheart. The fact that the characters of the two men bore some resemblance to the preferences of their patrons may have had something to do with this choice, and their finished works certainly reflected the dispositions of the masters who painted them, Cosway's being brilliantly executed with the luminosity and dash that only he could command, and Engleheart's being painted with a simplicity and dignity that gives an impression of solidity and strength.

Engleheart came from an artistic family, all of whom made their mark in some form of art, modelling, sculpture or painting. His father, Francis Engleheart, was a German plaster modeller who had been responsible for embellishing many of the beautiful ceilings at Hampton Court Palace. He had come over to England as a boy, and when only twenty-one married Ann Dawney, daughter of the Vicar of Kew. He was evidently a prudent man and invested his money in purchasing land at Kew and elsewhere around London. During his lifetime he spelt his name in the German way, 'Engelheart', but after his death in 1773 the spelling was changed to Engleheart, and on his mother's death George was admitted as heir to the estate under that name. Francis and Anne Engleheart had eight sons, five of whom died in infancy. Of the sons who survived, Thomas became a sculptor and was responsible for some beautiful portrait waxes, and John Dillman, the third son, for a time followed his father's profession, but on inheriting a considerable fortune from an uncle, one John Dillman, retired from business and became a gentleman of leisure.

George, the youngest of the family, was born at Kew in October 1750, and on leaving school, his family sent him to study art under George Barret, R.A., who taught him to paint landscapes and cattle. After what is believed to be a comparatively short time he left Barret to become a pupil of Sir Joshua Reynolds. In 1769 he was a student at the Royal Academy Schools, and from 1773 until 1822 he was an exhibitor at the Academy.

After his father's death in 1773 he moved from Kew to an address in Shepherd Street, Hanover Square, and in 1776 to Princess Street, Hanover Square, in which year he married the daughter of a city merchant. Their married life proved to be of short duration however, for in April 1779 she died suddenly, to Engleheart's great sorrow. In 1783 he moved to a house in Hertford Street, and it was to this home that he brought his second wife in 1785. She was Ursula Sarah Browne, a half sister of Jane, the wife of his brother John Dillman Engleheart. They had a family of three sons: George, Nathaniel and Harry, and a daughter Emma, none of whom followed their father's profession.

It was in 1775 that he began to keep a fee book, and from this time onward he entered with great care the names of all his sitters and the fees paid to him, a practice he continued until his retirement. These books have remained in the possession of the Engleheart family, and parts of them were reproduced in a volume on the artist published by Dr Williamson and H. L. D. Engleheart. Engleheart was a prolific worker and painted 4,853 miniatures during the thirty-nine years covered by his fee book. The amount of time he spent on his art left little opportunity for recreation, and he does not appear to have made a wide circle of friends although he was of a bright, happy disposition and deeply religious. One of his closest friends was William Hayley, who lived at an attractive spot called Felpham in Sussex. Engleheart used to stay there when he needed periods of relaxation from his studio, and on one of these visits he met Flaxman, Cowper, Romney, Blake and Meyer. Hayley frequently composed appropriate verses for Engleheart on special occasions. Engleheart and Meyer had more than one interest in common, for, apart from painting miniatures, they were both of foreign descent and both had studied under Sir Joshua Reynolds.

Engleheart owned a country house in the village of Bedfont near Hounslow, said to have taken its name from a well which dated back to the time of the Venerable Bede, and the artist divided his time between this establishment and his house in Hertford Street, London. He had purchased the estate in 1783 and built the house upon it, decorating the interior in Adam style. It was surrounded by attractive grounds and several sketches and water colour paintings of this home are illustrated in Dr Williamson's book.

When in 1813 he decided to give up active painting, it was to Bedfont that he and his wife retired, having given up their residence in London. He was encouraged to make this decision by Hayley who, in a verse composed for the occasion, says:

Toil not too eagerly,
Toil not too long,
But in yourself prepare maturely sage,
The dignity that decks a green old age.

Although Engleheart made no further entries in his fee book after this time, he is known to have continued to paint a few miniatures and water colours until his death in 1829.

In October 1817 his wife died and was buried in the family tomb at Kew, and thereafter he and his daughter Emma lived on at Bedfont for several years. But the difficulty of keeping up what must have been a comparatively large establishment, and the fact that his daughter's health was not good, made him decide to let the house and go to live with his son Nathaniel at Blackheath. He was very attached to all his children, and their happiness and welfare were his major concern.

In May 1827, when writing to his son George, he describes a new chaise that he had bought, and enclosed a sketch of it with the letter. Later in the year he had an accident in it at Blackheath, and he and Emma were thrown out and badly bruised. This must have given him a severe shock and one from which he never fully recovered, for on 21st March, 1829, he died and was buried at Kew, the service being conducted by his son Henry, who was in Holy Orders.

There is no doubt at all that Engleheart was a very fine painter. His portraits show him to have been a good draughtsman, and the finished miniatures are pleasing and colourful to look at. As with so many eighteenth-century artists, he has not avoided the criticism that he made his sitters look somewhat alike, and one sometimes wonders whether they were as attractive as the brush painted them. Engleheart was particularly fond of painting his woman sitters wearing the large, popular picture hats perched at a saucy angle. So expert was he at painting the ribbons by which these hats were kept in place, and the frills on the costumes, that one almost feels the material can be touched. The colours he used were rich, and the portraits drawn with great care. Every effort seems to have been made to discover the good points of his sitters and to bring out their character to the full, while imparting to the portraits a sense of truth and accuracy. Even the costumes of the men were colourful whenever possible, and I shall always remember a miniature of a gentleman in a bright green coat that I had the pleasure of handling and which was in as perfect a condition as the day it had been painted, having been preserved in a fitted leather case. It is unfortunate that in many portraits which have been exposed to the light both the greens and carmines have faded.

Engleheart's method of painting miniatures can be divided into three phases. In the earliest works, painted sometime before 1780, his draughtsmanship was not always accurate, his full powers had not yet developed, and the strong colours which he later adopted were not so much in evidence. During this phase the size of the miniatures was usually small, and occasionally, as in the case of one of a child in my collection, had a darkish buff-coloured background. The shading of the background was often achieved by fine vertical or slightly slanting strokes, and lead white was applied to indicate the highlights on the nose and dress. They show the natural diffidence of an artist's early work. From 1780, and for more than ten years afterwards, his powers developed, the draughtsmanship improved, and colouring became stronger. He continued to paint on comparatively small ivories, and in spite of the number of portraits that he was able to produce, the quality was excellent.

Characteristics of the second period of his work may be found in the large deep-blue eyes set under rather heavy eyebrows, the hair drawn in lines rather than in masses, with each strand showing separately, and diagonal grey lines at the corners of the mouth. Drapery is picked out with opaque white which may be seen also in ribbons on the hair or on the hats.

The third and last phase of Engleheart's painting dates from about 1795. The size of the ivory increased to 3 and 3½ in., and in common with the practice of some other artists at the turn of the century he painted rectangular portraits. He was one of the artists who painted eye miniatures which were sometimes set in small lockets and rings, or even in tie pins. At this time costumes were fast losing the colourful and frivolous look of the Regency, and were becoming more drab. Inevitably the change showed itself in miniature painting, and Engleheart, who had always striven after truth, now painted his sitters as he saw them, without any flattery. I have seen several miniatures of this period, where the hair is executed in thicker paint more heavily put on, the brush strokes on the face are sometimes more hairy, and the flesh colouring tends to yellowish brown.

The signatures vary, his early ones being G.E. on the front, sometimes in cursive letters but occasionally in block capitals. In his next period a cursive E may be found on the front, followed by an inscription at the back, which included his full name, address and the date, while in his third and last phase he often signed G.E. on the front with a date, the letters often ending with a flourish.

Engleheart is known to have copied miniatures by Cosway and to have executed careful copies in miniature of works by Sir Joshua Reynolds.

Although he altered his style slightly as time went on, the quality of his portraits never deteriorated, and even those miniatures painted after his retirement and up to the time of his death show him to be the great artist that he was.

ANDREW PLIMER (1763–1837) and his elder brother Nathaniel were two miniature painters who, in spite of the overwhelming popularity of the great Cosway, Smart and Engleheart, succeeded in obtaining a very distinguished clientèle.

Unfortunately, as is the case with so many other men, details of their lives and work have not been preserved, and only scraps of information are available with which to piece together their story. Dr G. C. Williamson's book on the lives of the two brothers[1] records all that is known. Andrew Plimer was born at Wellington in Shropshire, where he was baptized on 29th December, 1763. His parents were Nathaniel and Eliza Plimer, his father and uncle being partners in a clockmaking business in the town. The two brothers were apprenticed to this trade but neither of them liked it and they are said to have run away and joined some gypsies with whom they wandered about for over two years, touring through Wales and the West of England, their ambition being to reach London and to take up painting. In addition to their caravans, the gypsies owned a menagerie, and the two boys assisted in decorating the vans, and designed scenery for village plays. This delighted the gypsies who would have liked them to remain with them indefinitely. During this time they adapted themselves to the life, making their own brushes and paints as they went along, and colouring their faces with walnut juice so that they might appear genuine Romanies. In spite of the gypsies' entreaties and promises of such favours as the most attractive girls among them to be their wives, Andrew and Nathaniel had no intention of remaining with them for ever, and when the caravans arrived at Buckingham they decided that the time had come to take their leave. With their few possessions tied up in a shawl they walked on to London, where in 1781 Andrew obtained a position as personal servant to Richard Cosway. According to Dr Williamson the boy was so anxious to be near Cosway that he applied for a situation in his house, and when Mrs Cosway interviewed him she was so impressed by his eagerness and good manners that she at once engaged him as studio boy. His duties included cleaning the studio, grinding and mixing the colours, announcing any callers, and generally assisting in any way that he was needed.

After a while Richard Cosway discovered Andrew copying one of his miniatures, and the result was so successful that he at once realized the boy's artistic ability and assisted him in obtaining further knowledge by letting him take lessons in drawing. The name of his teacher has never been established but is thought to have been Hallé or Hayle. After a period of training Plimer continued to work for Cosway, who by this time was evidently attached to him, and Plimer held Cosway in high esteem, describing him as 'my beloved master'.

In 1785 he began to practise on his own account at 32 Great Maddox Street, Hanover Square, remaining at that address for a year, after which he returned to 3 Golden Square, which was considered a fashionable part of London and was inhabited by other artists including Angelica Kauffmann. After living for eleven

[1] *Andrew and Nathaniel Plimer*, 1903.

104. ANDREW PLIMER (1763–1837)
Miss Rushout, daughter of Lord Northwick.
$3 \times 2\frac{1}{2}$ in.

105. Reverse of eighteenth-century miniature
case.

106. MARY ANNE KNIGHT (1776–1851)
R. Owen of Lanark. $11 \times 8\frac{1}{2}$ in.

107. ANDREW PLIMER
Louisa Plimer (Mrs Scott),
daughter of the artist. $3\frac{3}{8} \times 2\frac{5}{8}$ in.

108. WILLIAM WOOD (1769–1810)
An unknown man. Signed and dated 1809.
$3\frac{13}{32} \times 2\frac{25}{32}$ in.

109. WILLIAM WOOD
The artist's sister.

110. JEREMIAH MEYER, R.A. (1735–89)
Edward, Duke of Kent (1767–1820).
$2\frac{3}{8} \times 2$ in.

111. HENRY EDRIDGE, A.R.A.
(1769–1821)
An unknown man. $2\frac{11}{16} \times 2\frac{1}{8}$ in.

years in No. 3 he moved, in 1796, to No. 8 in the same square. On 21st February, 1801 he married Joanna Louisa Knight at Wicken in Northamptonshire, and among the guests at the wedding were Richard Cosway and his wife and Jeremiah Meyer. Plimer's wife came of an old family well known in Northamptonshire, and one whose history could be traced back to 1573. Her parents were merchants and the family consisted of ten children of whom one, MARY ANN KNIGHT (born 1776, died 1851), was a miniaturist and took lessons from Andrew Plimer, and it was this acquaintanceship with the Knight family which led to Plimer meeting Joanna. Mary Knight had quite a considerable clientèle and was an exhibitor at the Royal Academy from 1803–31. An interesting sketch book of hers, containing numerous first sketches of interesting people, was sold at Christie's on 9th February, 1960, together with several other of her works.

Andrew Plimer and his wife lived at first in London, but in August 1801 they set off on a tour which took them through Devon and Cornwall before returning finally to Golden Square. They had five children: four daughters and a son who died when he was young. The eldest daughter, Louisa, was the only one to marry, her husband being John Scott, M.D. of Edinburgh, and the wedding took place on 8th May, 1830. She was the only one of the children to survive her mother, and it was at her house in Hawick, Scotland, that Mrs Plimer died in 1861 and was buried in St Cuthbert's Church Yard.

In about 1815 Andrew Plimer was working in Exeter, but little is known of this period of his life. The family was reputed to have been quiet and reserved, and the daughters, who were attractive and cultured girls, were strictly brought up and not allowed to mix much in Society. After a stay of three years, the Plimers returned to London and lived in Upper York Street, Montagu Square, and in about 1820 Andrew set off alone on another tour of the West of England, finally arriving in Scotland, where he was very successful in obtaining patrons and is said to have lived with families whose portraits he was painting, consequently saving quite a sum of money.

In 1835 he took his family to Brighton where they settled, but the stay was again short lived, for in 1837 Plimer died, aged seventy-four, and was buried at Hove. His estate, which was in the region of five thousand pounds, he bequeathed to his family, subject to a life interest to his wife, together with all his possessions.

Although Plimer succeeded in obtaining plenty of clients and produced some most attractive portraits, his work is not as good as that of Cosway, Smart or Engleheart. The portraits of ladies all look rather alike, with elongated noses and large appealing eyes, and the style he adopted seems to have been one that appealed to copyists, for numerous 'faked' copies of his miniatures are always appearing, to confuse the unwary or unknowledgeable collector.

His draughtsmanship was not good, but his grouping, especially where several persons were included in the picture, was effective and charming. Nevertheless, one cannot help but feel that the ladies were often idealized and not true likenesses of the sitters. His portraits of men were often better than those of women; they show more vigorous draughtsmanship and stronger colouring. His portraits of children are attractive, but even here there is a tendency to exaggerate the size of the eyes, which often seem too large for the children's faces.

Thin cross-hatching in the background to the left and right of the sitter, the long nose, and the treatment of the eyes, are all characteristics of Plimer's work, together with thin cross strokes of shading in the hair. His work falls into two phases, the earlier examples, up to about 1789, being attractive and more natural than those executed later. They are often signed A.P. in Roman capitals, followed by a date.

In his second phase he did not sign his work and it was marked by elongated necks, long noses and sameness of appearance. His palette was restricted and the flesh colour inclined to fade, leaving the features looking rather cold and with a dull brownish colour in the shading, due to the fugitive nature of his paints. The size of his ivories varied from comparatively small ones to those measuring up to $3\frac{1}{2}$ in. He painted also on vellum, paper and card, and executed portraits in oil as well as miniatures in water colour. Many fine examples of his work exist and are to be found in both public and private collections.

NATHANIEL PLIMER (1757–1822), also born at Wellington, was six years older than Andrew. When the two boys arrived in London, Nathaniel obtained a position as servant to H. Bone the enameller, but after a short time left him and joined Andrew as a pupil of Richard Cosway. Little is known about Nathaniel, but he was an exhibitor at the Royal Academy from 1787–1815 and at the Society of Arts from 1790–91, and as far as is known he lived all his life in London, where he is believed to have died in 1822. He married and had four children, Georgina, Mary, Louisa and Adela. This last daughter married Andrew Geddes, a native of Edinburgh, where he was acknowledged as a portrait painter of the first rank. A portrait by him of Andrew Plimer is in the National Gallery, Edinburgh.

Nathaniel Plimer was a good artist, and although his miniatures do not possess the dash and brilliance of those by his brother, they are softer and more realistic. As with his brother, only his works painted before about 1789 are signed and dated with small Roman capitals. He used more stippling in the shading than Andrew; eyelashes are often to be found dotted in on the lower lid, and his treatment of the hair is slightly more woolly. His works are not always easily identified when they appear in the sale rooms, and are not met with as frequently as those of many other artists. Examples may be seen at the Victoria and Albert Museum, London, and the Fitzwilliam Museum, Cambridge.

CHAPTER XIV

MORE NOTABLE GEORGIAN ARTISTS

*

Throughout the whole of the eighteenth century there was a growing demand for portrait miniatures and one has only to glance through the pages of Basil Long's *British Miniaturists* to realize that there was an increasing number of artists all working hard to produce the vast number of portraits required to satisfy their patrons. Owing to the great growth of the population and the increase in wealth, many who had hitherto been quite unable to afford articles of artistic merit now found themselves in a position to move into more spacious surroundings and to become collectors in one field or another. The fact that miniatures are so personal, being painted primarily to be worn, or to be carried about by their owners, meant that they had a great appeal to all classes of society and the many artists who sought patrons had no difficulty in obtaining them. These artists were to be found not only in London and the provinces but also in Scotland and Ireland.

A great number of these men, like Engleheart and Cosway, were prolific workers and Engleheart is known to have painted as many as 228 pictures in a year. The majority of those who painted miniatures must have succeeded in earning a living and one can only regret the fact that so little has been recorded about their lives and sitters.

WILLIAM WOOD (1769–1810) is one who has not always had the recognition he deserves. His works are well executed and of a very high quality and he must have been a popular artist for he is known to have painted at least 1,200 miniatures. He is reputed to have been born in 1769 in or near the town of Ipswich in Suffolk, but details about his early training in art have never been discovered. He appears to have been a careful man who gave attention to detail, and an interesting manuscript list of his sitters together with notes and comments about the actual paintings and pigments used is now in the possession of the Victoria and Albert Museum. From it we learn that he not infrequently adapted or altered his miniatures as and when the occasion demanded, either to touch them up or because of some change in the social position of the sitter. From his ledgers it is evident that he took a delight in painting his own portrait but these efforts never entirely satisfied him and were frequently destroyed.

Most of his working life was spent in London at addresses in Knightsbridge, St

11. P. Cross (1630?–1716?)
Mr. T. Carter. $3 \times 2\frac{13}{32}$ in.

12. William Wood (1769–1810)
An unknown man. $3\frac{1}{8} \times 2\frac{9}{16}$ in.

13. Andrew Plimer (1763–1837)
Mr. Thomas Pagan.
$3\frac{1}{8} \times 2\frac{1}{2}$ in.

14. Horace Hone, A.R.A. (1756–1825)
An unknown boy. Signed and dated 1793.
$3\frac{1}{4} \times 2\frac{3}{4}$ in.

James's Place, Cork Street and finally Golden Square, but he was in Bristol in 1791 and 1803, and in Gloucester in 1798. In 1803 he joined the Artists Volunteer Corps, and in 1807 was instrumental in founding the Society of Associated Artists in Water Colour, of which he was the first President, being succeeded after a year by David Cox. The Society, at whose premises Wood exhibited, lasted only a few years and was followed later by the Water Colour Society.

In 1808 he published *An Essay on National and Sepulchral Monuments*. His hobbies included landscape gardening, and towards the end of his life he took a great interest in making plans for laying out gardens and parks. He painted landscapes and was interested in and practised lithography. Wood made a careful study of the durability of the pigments used in miniature painting and noted those which, in his experience, deteriorated. His research was valuable in establishing which were the most stable colours for use on ivory.

His portraits showed Cosway's influence but were painted with a firmer touch and his draughtsmanship was considerably better. All his miniatures are dignified and one gains the impression that like Engleheart he strove after truth and achieved it, bringing out the salient points in his sitters' characters. His work can usually be recognized by the way in which he painted the background with separate dots and the shading on the faces is achieved by clearly defined brush strokes which are visible under a lens. In his portraits the men often have a slightly rubicund complexion; in many he used a patch of dark shading to the rear of the sitter and behind the head. He is known to have copied miniatures by Cosway, Engleheart and Smart.

Usually his signature is to be found on the back together with his name and address and a number corresponding to that in his manuscript. No miniatures have so far been recorded with a signature on the front. He died on 15th November, 1810, at his house in Golden Square, aged forty-one.

RICHARD CROSSE (1742–1810) was an artist about whom very little was known for many years and his works passed unnoticed and unrecognized in the sale rooms until Basil Long in the course of his researches obtained valuable information about his life and painting from a member of the artist's family. These details, together with a ledger of sitters and prices paid for portraits, were published by Long in the *Walpole Society*[1] and although the list may be incomplete it gives a very good idea of the quantity of miniatures he produced and who were his clients.

Coming of an old Devonshire family which had been resident in the parish of Knowle near Cullompton for many years, he took up miniature painting more as a hobby than as a way of earning a living. His parents owned and occupied an old manor house, subsequently burnt down through the carelessness of a servant in

[1] Vol. XVII.

setting fire to some straw in the stables where hounds were kept. It was here that Richard Crosse was born on 24th April, 1742. Unfortunately both he and his sister were deaf mutes and no doubt the frustration he must have endured from this affliction found some outlet in his painting. In 1758, when a boy of only 16, he was awarded a premium at the Society of Arts and as a result went to London and studied at Shipley's Drawing School and the Duke of Richmond's gallery. From 1760 he was an exhibitor at the Incorporated Society of Artists, becoming a member in 1763. He was exhibiting also at the Free Society of Artists from 1761–1766, and at the Royal Academy from 1770–96. Between the years 1776 and 1780, he painted as many as 100 miniatures a year but later his output lessened considerably, dropping to 7 in 1798. His health was always rather poor and, coupled with his physical disability, must have been a great trial to him. He had a distinguished clientèle and numbered among his sitters the Prince of Wales and the Dukes of Cumberland and Gloucester. Although her name does not appear in his list of sitters, he painted several miniatures of Mrs Siddons, and a fine one at the Victoria and Albert Museum is reproduced in colour as a frontispiece to Basil Long's *British Miniaturists*. In London he lived in Henrietta Street, Covent Garden, where many other artists had lived in the past.

The great tragedy of his life was unrequited love, for he fell in love with Miss Sarah Cobley, who was his cousin and whose brother was Prebendary Cobley of Wells, with whom he lived after his retirement in 1798. Miss Cobley refused his offer of marriage and chose instead a Mr Haydon by whom she had a son, B. R. Haydon the painter. Her refusal to marry him had left him an embittered man and he spent the rest of his life more or less a recluse. It was whilst he was living with Prebendary Cobley at Wells that his old love Mrs Haydon visited the house and they met for the first time since her marriage – a meeting which is described in her son's memoirs. Mrs Haydon had a premonition of her approaching death and insisted on her son escorting her to Wells. They arrived unexpectedly at the house before Crosse could be got out of the way and consequently, not knowing of her arrival, he entered the room where she was and the two met after thirty years. This meeting so affected all concerned that it caused great distress, and what must have been for Crosse years of pent-up emotion overflowed at this unexpected encounter, while he was quite unable to do more than utter unintelligible noises in his struggle to overcome his grief. Mrs Haydon passed away the next day and he lived only for a further three years, having returned to Knowle, his old home in Devonshire, where he died in 1810.

His charge for miniature portraits varied from 8 guineas for small ones to 15 and as much as 30 guineas for large ones. He succeeded in earning quite considerable sums by his art, and not being entirely dependent on his own exertions was able to make good investments which brought him in additional income. As well as miniatures in water colour and portraits in oils he executed miniatures in enamel – a particularly beautiful one of a man is illustrated in the *Walpole Society*.[1] He is said to have been appointed painter in enamel to George III in 1789, but if this is so he must have held the post conjointly with Richard Collins.

His style of painting is easy to distinguish once it has been thoroughly examined, for he used almost invariably a peculiar greenish blue tint which is visible in the shading of the face and often on the hair and in the background. In his earlier works he drew the hair rather in a mass but later emphasized the strands in definite lines, painting isolated curls. The style of the ladies' coiffure piled up on top of the head suited Crosse to perfection and all his miniatures are well drawn and refined. There is a softness about his technique which gives the impression of perfect modelling. As with so many artists, his flesh colours were fugitive so that where they have faded the portrait is left with a rather mask-like appearance. There is no evidence to support the theory put forward in the past that he signed his miniatures R.C. on the front, indeed, owing to the lack of a signature many have been attributed to other artists. Several exceptionally fine examples of this artist's work and a superb enamel have come into the sale rooms recently, including a few large oval miniatures.

JEREMIAH MEYER, R.A. (1735–89), a founder member of the Royal Academy where he exhibited miniatures, enamels and water colour portraits, was born in Tübingen in Germany in 1735 and came of an artistic family, his father being portrait painter to the Duke of Würtemberg.

Brought to England by his father when only fourteen years of age, he must have had some contact with Zincke, for this artist, although practically in retirement, taught Meyer the art of enamelling, and as a result much of his work was in this medium although he also painted in oils. Some of his finest works are to be found among his miniatures on ivory. He was an exhibitor at the Society of Artists from 1760–7 and in 1761 was awarded a gold medal for a profile of George III drawn from memory.[2] He became a naturalized Englishman in 1762, the year in which he was appointed miniature painter to the Queen, and received an appointment as painter in enamel and miniature to the King. In the following year he married a girl called Barbara Marsden who shared his love of art and was herself an accomplished artist and interested in music. She was a prizewinner at the Society of Arts when under 14 years of age, gaining fourth place on an occasion when Richard Cosway was first and John Smart second. In 1768 when the Royal Academy was founded he had the distinction of being the only miniature painter chosen as a member,

[1] Vol. XVII.
[2] Awarded by the Society of Arts.

and was a regular exhibitor there from its inception until 1783. (N. Hone, who afterwards painted miniatures, was at that time confining his interest mainly to oil paintings.) He numbered among his friends Engleheart, Hayley the poet and Romney, who painted his portrait. From start to finish Meyer's career seems to have been crowned with success, yet his character remained unspoilt and in an epitaph composed by Hayley we find these words . . . 'and ne'er shall sorrowing earth to heaven commend, a fonder parent or a truer friend'. He appears to have lived for most of his life in Covent Garden, but towards the end he retired to Kew, where he died in 1789.

In spite of his large output, Meyer's miniatures have until recently appeared less often in the sale room than one would expect, and as they are rarely signed, they may not always be recognized. An outstanding example of his work, in perfect condition, appeared in the sale room recently, of a young officer in a scarlet uniform with a blue collar and gold epaulets and facings. It had belonged to the late Mrs Budgen, a descendant of Sarah Siddons, and is thought to be of John Smith Budgen. I had the pleasure of seeing this miniature (together with many other family treasures) when Mrs Budgen lived in Edinburgh, and it is not surprising that it fetched £210 when sold on the 19th May, 1960. It was bought by the Victoria and Albert Museum and is now on view there.

His portraits can be detected by examining the treatment of the face. There is a slightly angular look about the drawing of the mouth, nose and eyes, the latter being rather sunk under the eyelids and often placed close together, the lips tending to protrude slightly and the hair to be drawn in distinct lines. The cravats and edging of the ladies' dresses are touched up with opaque white. Meyer imparted an elegance to his miniatures which Mr Winter likens to the fine porcelain of Meissen and Nymphenburg.

The miniatures are rarely signed. Some early ones have a cursive J.M. on the front and some are signed on the back. Her Majesty the Queen possesses some fine examples at Windsor Castle and there are examples of his work at the Victoria and Albert Museum. The Ashmolean Museum at Oxford possesses a number of his miniatures, some of them unfinished, which were presented by a descendant of the family.

SAMUEL SHELLEY (1750?–1808), an artist of considerable ability whose miniatures are easily distinguishable once his style and technique have been examined was a native of London born in Whitechapel in 1750. Of his education and early life nothing is known, and it has always been held that he was self-taught. He did not confine his art to miniatures alone, but painted figure subjects, in water colour and oil, as well as drawing book illustrations and engraving some of his own works. Bartolozzi and J. R. Smith also engraved some of his paintings. He did no

112. RICHARD CROSSE
(1742–1810)
An unknown lady.
Depth 7 in.

114. RICHARD CROSSE
Miss Barbara Bland (1764–83)

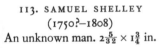

113. SAMUEL SHELLEY
(1750?–1808)
An unknown man. $2\frac{5}{32} \times 1\frac{3}{4}$ in.

115. SAMUEL SHELLEY
A family group. $3\frac{1}{4} \times 4\frac{1}{2}$ in.

116. WILLIAM GRIMALDI (1751–1830)
Admiral Lord Rodney (1719–92). $4\frac{5}{8} \times 3\frac{13}{16}$ in.

117. WILLIAM GRIMALDI
Mme Anna Storace (1766–1817).
Signed and dated 1795. $2\frac{25}{32} \times 2\frac{5}{16}$ in.

118. JOHN BARRY (worked 1784–1827)
Mr Inigo Thomas. $2\frac{27}{32} \times 2\frac{1}{4}$ in.

119. CHARLES SHIRREFF
(1750?; exhib.–1831)
Mr Henry Peirse. $3 \times 2\frac{3}{8}$ in.

appear as a miniaturist at such an early age as some artists, for when he won his first premium from the Society of Arts in 1770 he was in his twentieth year. From 1773 he was an exhibitor at the Society of Artists and from 1774 to 1804 at the Royal Academy. He also showed paintings at the British Institute and the Old Water Colour Society, being one of its original members in 1804. He was particularly fond of painting portrait groups and for these he frequently chose larger and longer ovals than those used by many artists, placing the oval on its side in order to accommodate the group more artistically.

As time went on he moved from Whitechapel to Soho, to Covent Garden, and to Henrietta Street, settling finally at No. 6 George Street, Hanover Square, where he remained until his death in 1808.

There appears to have been some difference of opinion between Shelley and the Royal Academy over the exclusion of water colour artists in general, and this led him and several other artists to form what was known as the Old Water Colour Society, of which he was elected the first Treasurer. After a disagreement over the proportion of his share of the profit of the exhibition held by the Society, he resigned as Treasurer, although his interest in the Society which he had helped to found did not cease. We are told by Dr Williamson that he was an attractive man with a kindly disposition and always willing to help his fellow artists. He had a good singing voice, excelled at telling a story, and was in great demand socially.

His miniatures, particularly those of young ladies, possess great charm and his draughtsmanship was good. All of them had the appearance of oil paintings owing to his practice of using rather more gum than usual with his paints, a method which made them more glossy than those normally used by other miniaturists. Characteristics of his work are a yellowish green flesh tint which sometimes appears in the background, and the enlargement of the pupil of the eye. At best his miniatures have a certain charm and are elegant and distinguished.

Signatures when found vary somewhat. Occasionally 'S.S.' appears in front with a date, but more frequently the signature is 'Sam Shelley' at the back, followed by his address. 'S. Shelley' in front is also found. He was a prolific artist and examples of his work may be seen in many public galleries and private collections.

HENRY EDRIDGE, A.R.A. (1769–1821), was another artist who was a native of London, being born at Paddington in August 1769, the son of a tradesman in St James's, Westminster. He began his career at the age of 14 as an apprentice to W. Pether the engraver, and a year later became a student at the Royal Academy Schools where, in 1781, he gained a silver medal. This brought him to the notice of Sir Joshua Reynolds, who allowed him to copy some of his pictures, and from then onwards he abandoned the art of engraving and took up portrait painting. He was still quite young when his father died and left him with the responsibility of helping to provide for the maintenance of his mother and her four other children. His work evidently met with success and he removed to 10 Dufour's Place, Golden Square, from which address he exhibited at the Royal Academy between 1786–1821. At first he painted his miniatures on ivory, but later frequently executed them on paper, drawing the portrait in black-lead or Indian ink, a method he subsequently abandoned in favour of a technique whereby he drew the figure in lightly first, and finished the face in water colour. Besides miniatures and water colour portraits, he was noted also for landscape paintings, and these and his portraits in pencil appear more frequently than do his miniatures.

His married life was full of tragedy. He had two children, a boy and girl, the latter said to have been very beautiful, and Edridge was devoted to her. Almost immediately after his wife's death she died of consumption at about the age of 17, and within a short time her brother succumbed to the same disease. The shock of these disasters had a serious affect upon Edridge, who had never been very robust himself, and he gave way mentally and physically. Even the honour of A.R.A., bestowed upon him in 1820, did nothing to restore his health. He died in his house in Margaret Street, Cavendish Square, on 23rd April, 1821, and was buried in Bushey churchyard.

Edridge was a good artist who was equally competent as miniaturist, landscape painter or in executing drawings or water colour sketches.

In his portraits it is often possible to discern a blue shading under the eyes and on the upper lip, and a distinct shadow may be found under the nose. He sometimes signed his miniatures with an H.E. in monogram in Roman capitals, and sometimes, as with his drawings, they were signed in full on the back with his address and the date on which they were painted.

CHAPTER XV

1. LESSER-KNOWN ARTISTS OF THE EIGHTEENTH CENTURY

*

It is impossible to do more than touch on many of the artists working in the eighteenth century. The immense popularity of the outstanding miniaturists meant that those who, for one reason or another were unable to attract the distinguished clientèle enjoyed by such men as Cosway, Engleheart and others had to content themselves with the patronage of those to whom they were fortunate enough to be recommended. More often than not no record has been kept of their lives or work and it is difficult if not impossible to discover much about them.

WILLIAM GRIMALDI (1751–1830) was the eighth Marquess Grimaldi (although he never as far as is known used the title) and was the son of Alexander Grimaldi, the seventh Marquess (1714–1800) of London, who had married twice, the first wife being Miss Mary Barton who died in 1744, and the second, Miss Esther Barton. She died in 1774 and her husband on 21st March, 1800. The family was of Genoese descent, their history dating back to the Merovingian Kings of France and being closely linked with the House of Monaco. One member of the family visited England as early as 1615 and several others came over during the French Revolution.

Many of them held important and influential posts in Genoa from early times, one, Luke Grimaldi, being sent as Ambassador Extraordinary to England on the marriage of Queen Mary and Philip. He was created a Marquess by the Emperor Charles V, who later bestowed further honours on other members of the family.

When Rubens visited Genoa, where he lived for a time, he found the Grimaldi family such generous patrons that he dedicated his views of the 'Palazzi di Genova' to them, and painted several of their portraits.

William, son of Alexander and Esther Grimaldi, was born on 26th August, 1751, in Middlesex and was an artist who at his best was able to produce extraordinarily good miniatures. He studied art under T. Worlidge and became great friends with John Wesley and his wife. He was married in 1783 at Maidstone in Kent to Frances, daughter of Robert Willis Esq. of that county. William and his wife had three sons and one daughter: William (1786–1835), Henry (1792–1806),

Louisa (1785–1873) and Stacey (1790–1863), who became the ninth Marquess.[1]

Grimaldi exhibited at the Free Society of Artists from 1768 to 1770 and at the Incorporated Society of Artists in 1772. He went to Paris for further study in 1777 and remained there until the year of his marriage. In 1786 he became an exhibitor at the Royal Academy and continued to exhibit there until 1830. He is believed to have practised at various towns in the provinces as well as in London, painting miniatures on ivory and in enamel, and, no doubt because of French influences while he was in Paris, his miniatures often have a continental look about them.[2]

He is known to have made many copies of the works of Reynolds, Hoppner, Beechey and others. He had the distinction of being appointed miniature painter to the Duke and Duchess of York, obtaining the same position under George III and, in 1804, George IV.

Characteristics of his work may be found by examining the shading on the face, the nostrils and the lower outline of the eyelids, which are usually picked out in a rather bright red. In portraits of men particularly, opaque white may be seen in the hair. The signature is frequently placed near the edge of the ivory, as 'Grimaldi', without the initials and written horizontally, or 'W. Grimaldi A.R.' in italics with the letters sometimes shaded. A.R. is supposed to indicate the Académie Royale but he was not in fact a member of that society. I have a miniature of Madam Storace the actress signed in this way. Other signatures include his name and address followed by a note of his appointment to the Duke and Duchess of York. The Wallace Collection possesses a good example of his work as an enamellist in a portrait of John Churchill, first Duke of Marlborough, inscribed on the back 'John, Duke of Marlborough by William Grimaldi, 1806'. Miniatures by him may be seen at the Victoria and Albert Museum, and the British Museum has some engravings of portraits executed by him.

He was living at 16 Upper Ebury Street, Chelsea, when he died on 27th May, 1830.

JOHN BOGLE (1746?–1803) was one of the comparatively few Scottish miniaturists. He is thought to have been born in 1746, the son of an excise officer and Mary Graham, whose brother was the 'Beggar Earl of Menteith'. The Earldom of Menteith had become dormant on the death of the 8th Earl on 12th September, 1694, and the right of succession was obscure. William Graham, younger son of William Graham of Edinburgh, assumed the title of 9th Earl and although he voted at the elections of Peers from 1744–61, his right to use the title was prohibited by order of the House of Lords on 2nd March, 1762, in spite of which he continued its use and was known as 'the Beggar Earl' as he had to subsist on charity. Mary,

---

[1] I am indebted to Miss Darlah Grimaldi, William's great grandchild, for supplying me with much of this information.

[2] A number of drawings of himself and his family came into the sale rooms on 9th February, 1960.

the wife of the excise officer, who died in May 1787, had three children, John (the artist), and two daughters. John was considered the heir presumptive through his maternal great-great-grandmother, but never made any claim to the title. After his death, his sister, who styled herself Lady Mary Bogle and died in 1821, became the next claimant. The earldom is now extinct.

Bogle studied art in Glasgow at the Drawing School which had been formed in 1753 by the brothers Robert and Andrew Foulis. He subsequently practised in both Edinburgh and London. There is an entry in the Edinburgh marriage register of his marriage in the New North Parish on 6th August, 1769, to Marion Wilson, daughter of one James Wilson, a merchant, deceased. His wife has been described as the beautiful May, or Mennie Wilson, whose family came from Spango, Uppermost Nithsdale.

From 1769–70 he exhibited at the Edinburgh Society of Arts, but after going to London in 1770 he entered works at the Royal Academy from 1772 to 1774. He is known to have accompanied Fanny Burney in May 1790 to Warren Hastings' trial which took place in the Great Hall of Westminster.

He returned to Edinburgh in 1800, and remained there until his death sometime in 1803. In a copy of his will, in the Records Office in Edinburgh, he is described as formerly of Panton, Middlesex, but late of the City of Edinburgh. Drawn up on 9th December, 1786, in the Parish of St James, Westminster, it left all his estate to 'my dear wife Mary', who was his sole executrix, and was witnessed by George Crozier and John Irving.

Allan Cunningham in his *The Lives of British Painters* considers him to be among the first rank of miniature painters, and particularly good at painting ladies. He describes him as 'a little lame man, very poor, very proud and very singular', but exactly what he meant by that we do not know.

His colouring was soft, and he painted with a minute stippling which, particularly in the treatment of hair, produces a curiously woolly effect when viewed under a lens. His miniatures have a certain charm without being spectacular. The majority of them are small in size, but a particularly fine one of Commodore Johnstone which was sold in London recently measured $3\frac{3}{4}$ in. He usually signed in one of the following ways: 'Bogle', 'J. Bogle' or 'J.B.', in neat Roman capitals followed by a date. The National Galleries of Scotland own one or two miniatures by him and examples of his work may be found also at the Victoria and Albert Museum and the National Gallery, Dublin.

EDWARD MILES (1752–1828), a native of Norfolk, was born at Yarmouth on 14th October, 1752. He began work there as errand boy to a surgeon who evidently took an interest in him and, discovering his aptitude for art, gave him every encouragement. In 1771 when he was nineteen years old he went to London, possibly to the Royal Academy Schools. B. S. Long tells us that he copied pictures by Reynolds, and that Beechey painted his portrait. From 1775–97 he exhibited at the Royal Academy but evidently did not remain in London, for in 1779 and again in 1782 he was working in Norwich.

Miles was given two Royal Appointments as miniature painter, firstly to the Duchess of York and later to Queen Charlotte. In 1797 he went to Russia, where he must have obtained recognition, for he was made Court Painter to the Czar. After having been resident in St Petersburg for about ten years he left Russia and settled in Philadelphia in 1807. There he continued painting portraits and took pupils. He appears to have made sufficient money to retire, for latterly he painted only for pleasure and for his chosen friends, who included Sir Thomas Lawrence and James Reid Lambden, an American artist who was his pupil and who painted a portrait of him in oils which was at one time in the possession of his descendants.

His work, although of high quality, is not so outstanding that it is immediately recognized. His treatment of the hair shows it as a mass rather than as individual strands, the drawing of the lips is often emphasized, and there is not infrequently a yellowish tone on the whole painting. His portraits are refined and elegant and those of older women particularly charming. There are some very good miniatures by Miles in the royal collection at Windsor and also in the collection of the Queen of Holland.

JOHN BARRY, who was active between 1784 and 1827, is an artist whose work is not widely known and he is therefore often unrecognized. He is however worthy of a much higher place in the ranks of miniaturists than has hitherto been accorded him, for miniatures by him that have come to light show him to have been an accomplished painter. Nothing is known about his life or education except that he exhibited at the Royal Academy from 1784–1827, was living at 83 Charlotte Street in London in June, 1788, and once visited Lisbon for health reasons.

A miniature by him of a lady called Mrs Hodges may be seen at the Victoria and Albert Museum; and one of a Mr Inigo Thomas of Ratton, Sussex, in my own collection, is a fine example of his work painted with bright clear colours which have retained their brilliance. Mr Thomas' second wife was the Hon. Frances Anne Brodrick and, according to an article in the *Journal of The Antiquary Society of Yorkshire* on Castle Howard, he was evidently a friend of Lord Hawkesbury, and mention is made of four portraits of him painted by Lord Hawkesbury. Characteristics of Barry's work are his method of painting eyebrows at an angle with the hair rather in a mass and slightly woolly, his bright flesh colouring, and his excellent draughtsmanship. His miniatures are strong and full of character. He also painted domestic subjects. I have seen miniatures by this artist where the flesh colouring has faded leaving a slightly green tinge which emphasized the grey shading on the features, and in the background.

JAMES NIXON, A.R.A. (1741?–1812) first appears in public as an exhibitor at the Incorporated Society of Artists in 1765, continuing to exhibit there until 1771. In 1772 he entered miniatures at the Royal Academy, where he exhibited until 1807, sending in addition works to the British Institution. In 1778 he was elected A.R.A. and appointed a limner to the Prince Regent and in 1792 he became miniature painter to the Duchess of York. Nixon spent most of his life working in London, but was in Scotland from 1795–98 and appears to have lived in Edinburgh, where in June 1797 he was residing at 9 St Andrews Square.

Whatever success he attained it was evidently not sufficiently lucrative to keep him, for he was unable to live on his earnings and had to apply to the Royal Academy for a pension. Little is known about his movements after he left Scotland, but he died at Tiverton in 1812. His miniatures are not all of the same quality, nor even painted in the same style, which makes them difficult to identify. Those that I have seen often resemble oil paintings rather than water colours. His portraits are often signed with a cursive 'N.' on the front. He did not confine his work to miniatures, but painted portraits in oil and water colour and executed historical subjects. He was noted for painting miniatures of actresses in character. A signed miniature 3⅜ in. high of Sir Joshua Reynolds after a self-portrait was sold recently for £50.

HORACE HONE, A.R.A. (1756–1825), was born in Frith Street, London, the second son of N. Hone, by whom he was taught to paint. When only sixteen years of age in 1772 he exhibited at the Royal Academy and continued to do so until 1822. He painted in both water colour and enamel, but his enamels are rare. He was married and had one daughter, Mary Sophia Matilda, who died a spinster.

In 1782 he went to Dublin, where his father had been born, and started a fashionable practice which proved so successful that he remained there for over 20 years. As with other artists practising in Ireland, after the Union with England he found there was a serious falling off of patrons and by 1804 he was back in London and is believed to have worked in Bath. Like his father, he was given to praising his own paintings, and after his return, a disappointed man, from Ireland, he became mentally and physically ill.

He had several distinguished clients, including the Duke of Rutland, Lord Albemarle and Mrs Siddons. Some of his miniatures were engraved.

Hone was a prolific painter and his works often appear in the sale rooms. He signed his miniatures either with the monogram 'HH.' formed by three sloping lines crossed by a horizontal one, or 'H. Hone', often followed by a date. The size varied from quite small miniatures to those measuring up to 3½ ins. The painting of the eyes is often dark and the colours are usually rich, more like those of oil paintings.

Examples of his work in enamel are rare, but an outstanding one of a Mrs Elizabeth Prentice came up for sale recently in London. It was of a large size, 4¼ in, and was inscribed on the back, 'Elizabeth/The wife of Thos. Prentice Esq./of Dublin, Horace Hone, A.R.A/Pinx. in London/1807', and signed on the front with the monogram '*HH*', followed by the date 1807.

PHILIP (OR PHILIPPE) JEAN (1755–1802), was born at St Ouen, Jersey, and began his career in the Navy, serving as a youth under Admiral Sir George Rodney. Nothing is known about his early training in art. His first appearance in the Royal Academy list was in 1787 and he continued to exhibit from then until 1802. Besides miniatures he painted oil portraits and both George III and Queen Charlotte sat to him, while the Duke and Duchess of Gloucester employed him to paint miniature portraits of themselves and their children. He was married and had five children.

He appears to have been well thought of, contemporary critics describing his work as 'spirited' and 'beautiful', and many of his miniatures are indeed very good and distinctive. From time to time he varied his style of painting and the attribution to him of unsigned works is consequently difficult. He signed 'P. Jean' in full, or with his initials only, and occasionally added the date. Examples of his work are to be found at the Victoria and Albert Museum and in the National Portrait Gallery, which possesses an outstanding example painted in 1788. It is of Dominic Serres (1722–93) a marine painter, sitting at an easel painting a seascape.

CHARLES SHIRREFF or Sheriff (b. 1750?), came from Edinburgh, where he is thought to have been born of wealthy parents. There is reason for thinking that his father may have been Charles Shirreff, a merchant at South Leith who married in 1730 Isobel Horsburgh, daughter of the Rev. Robert Horsburgh[1] (Sir William Foster, C.I.E. gives the father's name as Alexander) at one time the minister of Prestonpans.

After the failure of A. Fordyce's bank in 1772, Charles had to help to support his family, a task made doubly difficult by his being deaf and dumb. He was educated by a Thomas Brandwood, who succeeded in teaching him to write and even to articulate slightly, but it is not known who taught him to paint, and although there is no evidence of his having been instructed by John Bogle, who was working in Edinburgh at the time, he was a likely choice. In 1768 Shirreff went to London, became a student at the Royal Academy Schools and soon came to the notice of the public. He was in London at the same time as Anthony Stewart (1773–1846), another Scottish miniature painter, and in 1770 was sharing lodgings with Thomas

---

[1] *Walpole Soc.*, Vol. XIX, British Artists in India.

121. PATRICK JOHN
MCMORE(E)LAND
(b. 1741)
An unknown lady.
Signed. $1\frac{5}{8} \times 1\frac{1}{4}$ in.

120. ?DANIEL OF BATH
An unknown child. $2\frac{1}{16} \times 1\frac{21}{32}$ in.

122. HORACE HONE, A.R.A (1756–1825)
An unknown officer.
Signed H.H.A. 1789.
$2\frac{21}{32} \times 1\frac{5}{8}$ in.

124. JOHN BOGLE
Commodore Johnstone (1730–87).
4×3 in.

123.
JOHN BOGLE
(1746?–1803)
An unknown man.
Signed and dated 1788.
$1\frac{1}{4} \times 1$ in.

125.
JOHN BOGLE
An unknown man.
Signed and dated 1784.
$1\frac{3}{8} \times 1\frac{1}{8}$ in.

126. PHILIP JEAN (1755–1802)
An unknown officer. Signed.
$2 \times 1\frac{9}{16}$ in.

127. EDWARD MILES (1752–1828)
An unknown lady. $2\frac{23}{32} \times 2\frac{3}{16}$ in.

128.
SAMPSON TOWGOOD ROCH(E)
(1759–1847)
An unknown lady.
Dated 1806. $2\frac{7}{8} \times 2\frac{3}{8}$ in.

129. PHILIP JEAN
Dominic Serres (1722–93). $4\frac{1}{4} \times 3\frac{1}{4}$ in.

Burgess, a portrait painter and art teacher, and became acquainted with members of the theatrical profession including Garrick, Mrs Siddons and John Kemble, of the two latter of whom he painted miniatures. From 1770–3 he was an exhibitor at the Free Society of Artists and in 1771 he began to exhibit at the Royal Academy, continuing to do so intermittently until 1831. Shirreff drew in crayon and possibly painted in oils but is best known for his miniatures, both 'portrait' and 'subject', many of the latter being very successful.

He worked in Deptford, Brighton and Cambridge and according to Sir W. Foster was in Bath between 1791–5. In 1778 he had applied successfully for permission to go to India, with his father and a sister, but he delayed his departure for some years. His application was renewed in 1795 and sometime in the following year he sailed for Bengal. From miniatures of residents of Madras that have been discovered and are at the Victoria and Albert Museum, it is thought probable that he disembarked there and remained for a while. The New Oriental Register for 1800 names him as a resident, but by 1801 he also appears as residing in Calcutta and he apparently divided his time between the two places. In 1807 he announced that he was returning to England but did not actually leave India until 1809. On arriving in London he resumed his practice of showing at the Royal Academy and many of his exhibits had been painted in India. He is believed to have died at Bath, but this has not been established.

He employed a method of criss-cross hatching in shading the features as well as in the background and his miniatures tend to be plain and sometimes unflattering. One, which recently sold for £60, is $2\frac{3}{4}$ in. high and is inscribed on the back 'on the 23rd December, 1760, C. Shirreff, PINX 1798 27th Nov.'

ABRAHAM DANIEL (d. 1806), was the son of Nochaniah Daniel of Bridgwater in Somerset. He was one of a family of three brothers, of whom Joseph was a miniature painter in Bath, and Phineas a watchmaker, silversmith and engraver. Until recently all miniatures painted in a certain style have been attributed to him as 'Daniel of Bath', but Mr A. Rubens' researches have shown that Joseph was also a miniaturist and that both brothers worked at Bath.[1]

All three brothers are said to have received instruction from their mother, who is described as an 'ingenious woman'. Abraham removed to Plymouth, where he practised as a miniaturist, engraver and jeweller and had as a pupil Samuel Hart, apprenticed in 1779 to learn both miniature painting and engraving. There was evidently a certain amount of rivalry between the brothers and Abraham was in the habit of returning to Bath from time to time, both claiming to be 'Mr. Daniel'. Which was responsible for the advertisement in the *Bath Chronicle* of

---

[1] Mr Rubens has published the details of the Daniel family in an article in the *Transactions of the Jewish Historical Society of England*, Vol. XVII, and I am indebted to him for providing me with a copy of this publication.

11th January, 1787, is unknown. It reads as follows: 'Miniature Painting No. 3 Abbey Green. Mr. Daniel begs leave to inform the Nobility and Gentry, that he is returned to Bath for the season – Those who may not be acquainted with his terms etc. are respectfully informed that he will by no means accept payment for a picture which is not esteemed a striking likeness, and an approved Painting'. This advertisement was inserted for a second time on 12th April, 1787, and two further announcements add further confusion. On 5th September, 1799: 'Mr. Daniel, Miniature Painter, Begs to inform his Friends and the Public, that he is returned to No. 8 Alfred St. Bath.' And again on 26th September, 1799: 'Mr. Daniel Miniature Painter Begs leave to inform his Friends and the Public, that he is returned to No. 33 Milsom Street Bath.'

Abraham Daniel's death took place at Plymouth on 11th March, 1806. From his deathbed he dictated his will to Samuel Hart, disposing of an estate valued at £1,500 which he apportioned in the following manner: after legacies to his mistress and to two illegitimate sons, he left £20 to the charity of the Plymouth Synagogue and the residue to be divided between his two sisters Rachel Nathan and Rebecca Almon, who were both residents of Plymouth.

Little is heard of the third brother, Phineas, but he is known to have worked in Bristol as a watchmaker, silversmith and engraver, between 1785 and 1800. He died in Philadelphia in January 1805 but his widow, his son Abraham, and three daughters were then still living in Bristol.

JOSEPH DANIEL (worked 1777 d. 1803) who worked in crayons and oils and made pictures of hair, is therefore a new name to add to the list of miniature painters. From 1777 he was at Bristol living in Clare Street, from which address in 1783 he exhibited a miniature of a 'Jew Rabbi' at the Society of Arts. By 1785 his address was 'Mr. Baker's, Clare St., Bristol' and his next exhibits, five miniatures, were sent from 17 New Bond Street, London, in 1799 to the Royal Academy. His stay in London was evidently of short duration, for on 26th January, 1780, the *Bath Chronicle* mentioned his return to that city, where from 1786 onwards he appears to have remained.

He was highly esteemed for his painting and after he had been seriously ill a reference was made to his recovery in the *Bath Chronicle* of 11th April, 1796. His illness evidently caused some doubts as to his ability to continue painting and as a result he must have thought it necessary to publish the following notice in January 1802: 'Mr. Daniel Begs leave to inform his friends and the Public that he continues as usual to paint in Miniature; and the report of his having declined his profession is entirely unfounded and erroneous'. A tribute was paid to him by one of his patrons in a letter to the paper in which his ability as a painter is praised as well as the artist himself for having refused any extra payment from the grateful client.

His health did not improve and he died at Bath on 29th August, 1803, aged 43, after what was described as a painful and lingering illness of more than thirteen months' duration. He left a widow and one son, John, who were living at Exeter in 1806. He left also a number of illegitimate children at Bristol, where he had an address until 1792.

The problem of attribution of miniatures to either one of these two brothers is at present almost insoluble and will remain so until such time as a signed work appears to clarify the situation. All the miniatures attributed to 'Daniel of Bath' have definite characteristics which are more easily apparent to the viewer than possible to describe. They are usually on the small side, not exceeding $2\frac{1}{2}$ in., little or no stippling is to be seen, the hair is painted rather in a mass, the eyes are large and wide open, and the features clearly defined and clear-cut. The flesh colour is rather pinker than that used by most artists. Some miniatures show touches of opaque white on the costume, the background is more heavily painted, and a certain amount of stippling may be seen on the face. There is evidence of gum mixed with the pigments which tends to give the portrait the appearance of having been executed in thin oil. The portraits are often attractive. The one in my own collection of a small girl in a mob cap and broad blue sash is particularly charming.

CHAPTER XVI

2. LESSER-KNOWN ARTISTS OF THE EIGHTEENTH CENTURY

*

Among the numerous lesser-known eighteenth-century painters of miniatures appear the names of those whose main work was not executed in London, where the majority of the miniaturists congregated, but in Ireland, Scotland and parts of the provinces. Some came from the Continent and all of them were more or less successful in obtaining the patrons they required in order to be able to earn a living. Among these artists were ADAM and FREDERICK BUCK, both natives of Ireland born in Cork, Adam in 1759 and Frederick in 1771, the sons of a silversmith. Nothing is known about their education but they must have received some training in art, possibly at the Dublin Society's School. Adam (1759–1833) was the better painter of the two and a considerable number of his works were engraved. He painted in water colour as well as executing miniatures. He also drew fancy figure subjects, was noted for his book illustrations, and was the author of a book, *The Paintings of Greek Vases*. He started his professional career in Cork but in 1795 went to London, where he began to exhibit at the Royal Academy and continued to do so until his death in 1833 at No. 15 Upper Seymour Street, W.1.

His miniatures were frequently signed, the signatures varying; sometimes 'A. Buck' appears in full on the front, the 'A' being either roman or cursive and occasionally joined to the 'B'. At other times the letters are either in monogram followed perhaps by a date or simply 'A.B.' in block letters. The flesh colouring on the face of his sitters is often rather pink, but his technique varied and his work is not always easy to detect. His brother Frederick (1771?–1839/40) also practised in Cork, his address in 1830 being Buckingham Square. He painted a number of miniatures of soldiers and his draughtsmanship and modelling are not considered to be very good. The faces tend to have rather a red complexion. He died between 1839 and 1840.

FRANÇOIS FERRIÈRE (1752–1839), born in Geneva, was studying art in Paris by 1770 and afterwards returned to his native city, where he married and settled. With the outbreak of the French Revolution he fled the country and came to England, as did a number of other artists. He exhibited at the Royal Academy from 1793 until 1804, when he travelled to Russia, where he became a member of the

130. CHARLES ROBERTSON
(1760–1821)
An unknown lady. $2\frac{1}{2} \times 2\frac{1}{8}$ in.

131. FREDERICK BUCK
(1771?–1839/40)
An unknown lady.
$2\frac{3}{32} \times 1\frac{3}{4}$ in.

132.
JOHN DOWNMAN, A.R.A.
(1750–1824)
An unknown lady.

133. LOUIS AMI ARLAUD
(1751–1829)
Mr Bryan. Signed. $2\frac{3}{4} \times 2\frac{7}{32}$ in.

134.
THOMAS HAZELHURST
(worked 1760; d. 1821?)
An unknown man.
$1\frac{5}{8} \times 1\frac{5}{16}$ in.

135. JOHN DONALDSON
(1737–1801)
An unknown lady.
Signed and dated 1787.
$1\frac{5}{8} \times 1\frac{1}{4}$ in.

136. GEORGE PLACE (worked 1775; d. 1805)
Alexander, 4th Duke of Gordon (1743–1827).
$3\frac{3}{8} \times 2\frac{1}{2}$ in.

137. FRANÇOIS FERRIÈRE (1752–1839)
Major Gen. John Ramsay. $3 \times 2\frac{3}{8}$ in.

138. PETER PAILLOU (worked 1763?–1800)
An unknown lady. Depth 3 in.

139. PETER PAILLOU
Adam Crookes of Leven. Signed and dated 180●
$3 \times 2\frac{3}{8}$ in.

Russian Academy of Painting. In 1810 he went to Moscow, and during the French invasion of 1812 lost all his possessions there. After spending some time in St Petersburg, he came back to England in about 1817 and once more began exhibiting at the Royal Academy, continuing to do so until 1822, in spite of the fact that in 1821 he had again left England and gone home to Geneva. He continued painting until 1835, when he retired and went to live at Morges in Switzerland, where he died in 1839.

The National Galleries of Scotland possess several miniatures by Ferrière, a particularly fine example being that of James Wauchope after Raeburn. As his miniatures were painted in oils, they bear more resemblance to large paintings than do those of most other miniaturists. The ones I have seen are brilliantly executed.

SAMPSON TOWGOOD ROCH(E) (1759–1847) was another artist who began his career in Ireland, where he received his early training. He was born at Youghal in 1759, studied art in Dublin, and later practised there for some years. He is thought to have worked also in Cork, for in the *Dublin Chronicle* of 1788 reference is made to his marriage at Youghal to a Miss Roch, only daughter of a James Roch of County Waterford. In the same year he returned to Dublin and as far as is known remained there until 1792, when he went to Bath, residing first at No. 6 and afterwards at No. 12 Pierrepont Street. How long he remained in that city is uncertain, but it has been stated that he was there for thirty years. He is known to have gone to live in Ireland on his retirement. His earliest recorded miniature is dated 1779 and he was an exhibitor at the Royal Academy in 1817, while he was living in Bath. Characteristics of his style are an almost invariable smile or smirk that he gives to his sitters and the shading under the eyes and clearly defined outline to the features. Occasionally he painted opaque colours on the dresses.

His miniatures are usually signed either 'Roch' or 'Roche' without initials, although one is recorded as being signed 'S. Roch' and dated 1794. He favoured oval formats but a rectangular one of the Marquis of Salisbury exists, measuring $3\frac{1}{2} \times 2\frac{3}{4}$ in. He died at the age of eighty-eight at Woodbine Hill, Co. Waterford and was buried at Ardmore.

CHARLES ROBERTSON (1760–1821) was another native of Ireland to take up miniature painting. He was born in Dublin in or about 1760 and his work lay principally in that city. His earliest artistry was mainly in designing and making likenesses in hair but, owing no doubt to the scarcity of demand for such portraits, he turned his attention to miniatures, which he continued to paint from 1775 until his death. In 1785 he went to London, staying there until 1792, and made a second visit again in 1806. His miniatures can be distinguished by the rather slatey-grey that he employed in shading the face; he used a soft brush stroke and the features are painted with a delicate touch. Robertson was an exhibitor at the Royal Academy from 1790–1810. He married a Miss Christina Jaffray and they had four or more children.

His brother WALTER ROBERTSON (1765–1802) was also a miniaturist and although no portraits painted by him have come to light in Britain there are some in America which show him to have been a good artist whose work closely resembled that of his brother. The two men are thought to have been the sons of a Dublin jeweller and to have had their education in that city.

THOMAS HAZLEHURST (worked between 1760–1821) was another artist of this period who deserves our attention. He is known to have practised miniature painting between 1760 and 1818, but unfortunately little is known about his life or education. The scanty knowledge that is available suggests that he spent the whole of his life in Liverpool; in 1793 he was living at No. 9 Rodney Street. He exhibited at the Society for Promoting Painting and Design in Liverpool in 1787 and at the Liverpool Academy from 1810–12. His death is thought to have taken place in Liverpool in 1821. Those miniatures by him that I have seen are pleasing and well-executed. His method of painting involved the use of minute brush strokes on the features, while the hair is drawn with sweeping lines which are clearly visible. Occasionally these are interspersed with parallel straight lines and sometimes there is almost a halo of lighter background around the sitter's face. The whole effect of the portrait is soft and harmonious. Some of his works resemble those of J. Barry, while others have a distinct likeness to the paintings of C. Robertson. The size of his miniatures varies. Usually their shape is oval, but he is known to have painted at least one rectangular portrait. His signature is 'T.H.' in neat Roman capitals.

PETER PAILLOU (worked between 1763?–1800) was an artist of London origin who is known to have been in Islington in 1778. Nothing has been discovered so far about his early life and not a great deal about his work or training. I have seen a number of miniatures executed by him and all of them have had a certain charm and dignity. One can only hope that further knowledge about him will some day become available.

He evidently drew bird pictures at one time, although it has been suggested that these might have been the work of his father. Some were exhibited at the Free Society of Artists in 1763 and at the Incorporated Society of Artists in 1778. In 1786 he exhibited at the Royal Academy and continued to do so until 1800. His work is interesting as he appears to have had two totally different styles. Some of his miniatures show the influence of oil paintings and have objects such as bookcases and foliage placed in the background, others are painted in a softer manner and with a greenish hue. They differ so much in their execution that were it not for the signature, which is often 'P. Paillou' followed by a date and written along the edge, one would almost imagine that they were not by the same hand.

There are one or two miniatures by Paillou at the Scottish National Galleries. On these, as with others I have seen, the background is sometimes painted almost like a sunset and as it is certain that at some date he was in Scotland, his name being mentioned as working in Glasgow in 1820, he may well have had the beautiful Scottish sunsets impressed on his mind and used their colouring in his miniatures. In 1818 Robert Scott of Glasgow published a mezzotint of a portrait by Paillou.

JOHN DONALDSON (1737–1801) was a Scottish artist born in Edinburgh. The son of a glovemaker, his family were evidently poor and it was necessary for the boy to help to support himself. Fortunately from childhood onwards he enjoyed drawing and his father gave him every encouragement. At the age of twelve he is said to have been selling pen and ink drawings which were mostly copied from old engravings. In 1757 he won a premium of four guineas, given by the Edinburgh Society of Arts, for a drawing of a bust of Horace and in the following year he obtained a similar award. Soon afterwards he went to London and became an exhibitor at the Society of Artists from 1761 to 1774, being made a member in 1764. He lived for a time in Newcastle and while there was awarded a premium for an historical painting in enamel and later received two further awards for work in this medium. In 1775 and again in 1791 he was an exhibitor at the Royal Academy. Besides executing miniatures in water colour and enamel and drawings in black-lead, he did some etchings, painted on Worcester porcelain and was quite successful as a portrait painter. A man of many parts, he allowed himself to be led away from art into the world of chemistry and patented a method of preserving vegetables and meat. He also tried his hand at poetry and published an essay, *The Elements of Beauty*. He was not a worldly man but had an artistic temperament, being a dreamer, an idealist and totally unpractical. He remained extremely poor in spite of his gifts, apparently making no provision for his old age, and for the latter part of his life he was both blind and unhappy. But for the generosity of his friends he would have been destitute. He died in abject misery in lodgings in Islington.

The National Galleries of Scotland own a miniature of a lady by Donaldson which is signed in a neat hand on the front with a cursive 'J.D.' and dated 1787. The face is shaded with a bluish-grey round the eyes and elsewhere and a deeper bluish-grey is apparent on the hair, which is drawn in lines made partly by the use of a scraper and partly by painting with opaque white. The flesh colouring is rather pink and white and the red on the lips has retained its brilliance. Viewed at arm's length, the miniature bears a distinct resemblance to the work of J. Downman.

JOSEPH SAUNDERS (worked between 1772–1808), who lived in London, was an artist about whom little was known for many years and his work did not really come to the notice of the public until comparatively recently. Even now information about him is scant but those miniatures signed by him that have been discovered give him a much higher place among his fellow artists than has hitherto been the case. His miniatures of women are particularly attractive and it has been said that they formed the majority of his patrons. It is to be hoped that additional information will come to light to enable us to assess more fully the qualities of such an obviously excellent miniaturist.

GEORGE PLACE (worked 1775 d. 1805), has sometimes been described as the Irish Cosway, but although many of his miniatures are of excellent quality, it is doubtful if the assertion can really be justified.[1] He was the son of a linen draper in Dublin and received his training in art at the Dublin Society's School, which he entered in 1775. After his initial training he practised miniature painting in Dublin but went to London in or about 1791 and was an exhibitor at the Royal Academy from 1791–7. On leaving London he worked for a time in York before joining the throng of adventurous artists who were exploring the possibilities of making their fortunes in India. He applied successfully for permission to go to Bengal in 1797, but did not leave immediately, and in February, 1798, he was again given permission to sail for India, accompanied by his wife.

He appears to have established himself in Lucknow and to have obtained the patronage of many distinguished persons. According to Sir William Foster, C.I.E.,[2] it was proved before a committee of the House of Commons that up to the end of 1805 Place had received between five and six thousand pounds from the Nawab, and it was also asserted that he had painted pictures of that ruler and his court, but as most of his paintings were lost or probably destroyed during the Mutiny of 1857, it is impossible to verify any of these statements. One of his best-known works which perished was that depicting an incident which took place at the Battle of Laswari in 1803, when Lord Lake's son dismounted and handed over his horse to his father, whose own mount had been killed in the battle. Although this was not particularly good as a work of art, the subject was popular at the time and the painting was later engraved in England by R. Cooper in 1808. A portrait of Nawab Saadat Ali Khan by Place was also engraved in mezzotint by W. Say in 1806.

Although some earlier authors have stated that he died in England, it has been established that his death took place in Lucknow on 11th August, 1805. His works in miniature are usually good. Often a certain amount of blue shading is to be found on the faces of the sitters and long brush strokes are visible in modelling the eyelids. The fact that he did not usually sign his miniatures makes it difficult to attribute works to him.

[1] I have recently seen a pair of miniatures by Place which were in the manner of Cosway and superbly painted.

[2] *Walpole Soc.*, Vol. XIX, p. 63.

140. ANDREW ROBERTSON, M.A.
(1777–1845)
An unknown man. Signed and dated 1814.
$2\frac{7}{8} \times 2\frac{3}{8}$ in.

141. ANDREW ROBERTSON
An unknown lady. Signed and dated 1807.
$2\frac{7}{8} \times 2\frac{1}{4}$ in.

142. SAMUEL PAUL SMART
(exhib. 1774–87)
An unknown man. $3 \times 2\frac{3}{8}$ in.

143. WILLIAM NAISH (d. 1800)
An unknown man. Signed. $2\frac{23}{32} \times 2\frac{1}{8}$ in.

144. MRS MEE *née* FOLDSONE
(1770/75–1851)
Lady Lushington, *née* Lewis.
$3 \times 2\frac{17}{32}$ in.

145. SARAH BIFFIN
(1784–1850)
An unknown lady.
$3 \times 2\frac{1}{2}$ in.

146. Signature to No. 145

147. ANDREW DUNN (exhib. 1809–20)
Sir Joseph Banks (1743–1820).
Signed and dated 1809. $2\frac{23}{32} \times 2\frac{5}{32}$ in.

148. Artist unknown, after Dance
(1735–1811)
Captain James Cook (1728–79).
$2\frac{13}{32} \times 2$ in.

PATRICK JOHN MCMOR(E)LAND (b. 1741), a native of Scotland, practised in water colour, on ivory and in enamel and painted miniatures for rings, as well as executing tinted portrait sketches, drawings of landscapes, Italian views and sea pieces. His early painting is thought to have been done in Scotland but from 1774–1777 he was working in Manchester. From 1774–5 he was an exhibitor at the Incorporated Society of Artists and from 1776–82 at the Royal Academy. In 1777 he had an address in London but in about 1781 he was living in Liverpool, where he exhibited in 1784 and 1787 and gave lectures on art. From Liverpool he returned to Manchester, where he was living in 1793 and the last information so far available is that he was teaching there in 1809. According to Basil Long 'he was esteemed for blameless manners'. His miniatures are good, although his style varied somewhat. Specimens may be seen at the Victoria and Albert Museum. He signed with plain Roman capitals 'P.M.' or 'P.M.ᶜ' and examples also exist of 'P.M.ᶜ' in cursive writing.

JOHN DOWNMAN, A.R.A. (1750–1824) was the son of Francis and Charlotte Downman, his father being an attorney at St Neots, Huntingdonshire. His mother was the eldest daughter of Francis Goodsend, private secretary to George I. The family moved to Wales and lived in or near Ruabon, where John was educated, but by this time his parents were not very well off and his father was no longer in regular practice. Although his father no doubt hoped that his son might follow his own profession, John's obvious talents as an artist could not be denied and he was sent to learn drawing, first to Chester and later to Liverpool. By the age of eighteen he decided to go to London, where he was apprenticed to Benjamin West and was a pupil at the Royal Academy Schools.

Downman and West had interests in common other than art, for they had both come from Quaker families, and although it has never been established that Downman was an active Quaker, he is thought to have had every sympathy with 'the Friends'. He exhibited at the Free Society of Artists in 1768 and from 1770–1819 at the Royal Academy. He never settled in any one place for long and worked in Kent, London, Plymouth, Exeter, Chester and Cambridge, going to large private houses to paint the owners and their families, as in the case of the Duke of Northumberland, when he went to the Duke's beautiful home, Alnwick Castle, to paint his eldest son, Lord Percy. For anyone as artistic as Downman, his stay at Alnwick must have been very pleasant, for the Castle stands majestically on a hill overlooking a river from which its outline may be seen silhouetted against the sky.

While in Northumberland he executed portraits for other families in the north of England before settling in Chester. His only daughter married a solicitor, one Richard Benjamin of Wrexham, where they were then living. Unfortunately

Benjamin was a spendthrift and such money and possessions as they had were gradually frittered away. Downman lived with his daughter until his death in 1824, by which date she was herself a widow, her husband having died after a bout of drinking.

Downman is best known for his delightful water colour portraits and oil paintings, which are more frequently come by than his miniatures. Two of his miniatures, one of the Duchess of St Albans and the other of Lady Melbourne, were sold with the Dyson Perrins collection in February, 1960, one of them measuring 3 inches in height.

Louis Ami Arlaud (1751–1829), born in Geneva, was the grand-nephew of J. A. Arlaud, whose reputation as a miniaturist is well known, as is that of his relation Benjamin Arlaud. He studied painting under J. E. Liotard, a fellow Genevese, and later went to Paris and took lessons from Vivien, a historical painter, subsequently making a tour of Italy and returning to Geneva in 1778. Although he painted water-colour portraits and re-touched pictures besides painting in enamel, he is best known for his miniatures on ivory. He received from five to twenty-five louis for these works and was evidently a prolific artist, for he is known to have executed six hundred and forty-one portraits before 1792, when he left Geneva and went to London, where he painted a further two hundred and sixty-eight miniatures of Swiss and French subjects besides painting several portraits of Prince Edward, Duke of Kent (1767–1820), members of the English aristocracy, and well-known actresses. The miniatures painted by Arlaud are well executed, the colouring is pleasing and the portraits have a look of distinction, and although his work is rarely seen it is well worth including in any collection. I have one of a Mr Bryan which is a fine example and is signed on the front in full in a cursive handwriting. Arlaud was an exhibitor at the Royal Academy in 1792 or 1793 until 1800. In 1802, however, he returned to Geneva where he painted a further six hundred and forty-five portraits. In view of his output it is surprising that so few of his miniatures appear in the sale rooms, but no doubt many have remained in private collections on the Continent. He died on 8th August, 1829, at Pré-L'Evêque, a man of many interests, fond of fencing, riding and violin playing.

William Naish (d. 1800) was another artist about whom little is known. He was born at Axbridge in Somerset, but where he received his education or what led him to take up miniature painting is still obscure. He went to London, where he obtained many patrons and was an exhibitor at the Royal Academy from 1786–1800 and was employed by members of the theatrical profession. A miniature of a man in a black coat in my own collection is signed on the back 'Naish' in rather sloping writing. A bluish shading is evident round the mouth and chin and the eyelids are drawn with firm distinct lines; the hair shows the strands separately, some being painted in a deepish blue. He died at his house in Leicester Square towards the end of 1800.

SAMUEL PAUL SMART (exhibited 1774–87), was for some years thought to have been a relative of John Smart, but there is no evidence to support this theory. He appears to have worked in London and exhibited both portraits and miniatures at the Royal Academy from 1774–87 and at the Society of Artists from 1777–8. His address in 1777 was at Mr Boujonnar's, 15 Finch Lane, Cornhill, and he later had an address at Bethnal Green. The only known example of his work so far recorded is one in my possession of a gentleman in a brilliant red coat, which is well painted and the draughtsmanship is good. The complexion is painted in a brick-red, fine cross-hatching can be seen in the shading of the background on either side of the sitter, the shading round the mouth is bluish grey and the strands of hair are only lightly drawn. His technique closely resembles that of John Smart.

SARAH ADDINGTON (exhibited 1778) was another artist whose work was greatly influenced by John Smart and her miniatures all show characteristics of his painting. Many portraits have been attributed to her on account of the resemblance they bear to Smart's work. Her signature 'S.A.' is usually in cursive writing, often followed by a date. She occasionally signed with an 'S' formed rather differently. The hair of her sitters was painted more in a mass than in separate strands. She appears to have had a distinguished clientèle, but so far no information is available about her life and family.

Recent research and the appearance of certain signed miniatures has led Graham Reynolds to believe that the artist who signed S.A. was an Irishman called SAMUEL ANDREWS (1767?–1807), who worked mainly in India and also copied Smart's style, and not Sarah Addington as had hitherto been supposed.

CHAPTER XVII

NINETEENTH-CENTURY MINIATURISTS

*

As the eighteenth century drew to a close, many changes were taking place in Britain. This was particularly noticeable in fashion. The gay and attractive dresses of the Regency gave place to plainer and more classical designs for women, while in men's attire the brilliantly coloured coats and waistcoats that were so popular earlier in the century were put aside for those of a more sombre hue. These changes were soon apparent in art and portraits were forced to rely for their attractiveness more on the features or character in the faces of the sitters than on the clothing they wore.

There were still a large number of miniaturists working in Britain and elsewhere and even if great artists such as Cosway, Smart and Engleheart were nearing the end of their careers, others, although perhaps not of the same calibre, were coming forward to take their place.

Mrs Joseph Mee, née Anne Foldsone (1770/75–1851) was among those who came into prominence at this time. Her father John Foldsone earned a livelihood by copying pictures and the family lived at Little Castle Street, Oxford Market, London. Unfortunately, the father died when he was quite young and this seriously affected the family's position. Anne had been sent to a French ladies' school to be educated and from an early age had an aptitude for music, poetry and painting. She was the eldest daughter and on her father's death was obliged to leave school in order to earn a living and help to support her eight brothers and sisters. Fortunately her painting was admired, and she had no difficulty in obtaining patrons; it was said she had so many commissions that it was inadvisable to pay for a miniature in advance. With the support and patronage of a distinguished clientèle, she was eventually brought to the notice of George IV, who admired her work. From 1790 to 1791 she was working at Windsor and a number of her miniatures remain in the royal collection.

In 1804 she married Joseph Mee of Mount Anna, County Armagh, and it has been said that her husband would not allow men to sit for her. By the time she was thirty-three she was the mother of six children, and it is astonishing that she should have found time for her art. She exhibited at the Royal Academy from 1804–37, at least one exhibit being sent from Brighton, and her work was sufficiently good for some of it to be engraved. She died on the 28th May, 1851 at the advanced age of eighty-one.

Her miniatures vary a great deal: at their best they are good and have a certain charm, but all too often the draughtsmanship is careless and the general effect unsatisfactory. Though she was a protégée and pupil of Romney, there is a trace of Cosway's influence in her technique and her colour schemes are simple and subdued. The characteristics of her work are the drawing of the eyelids, which are outlined in red and frequently give the sitters the appearance of having been crying, and the faces, which are usually painted with both stippling and hatching, although I have seen portraits that are painted with stippling only. Many of her miniatures are rather large.

GEORGE CHINNERY, R.H.A. (1774–1852) is an artist whose work is more closely associated with large portraits and those drawings and paintings of Chinese scenes and people for which he is so noted. Nevertheless, he did paint miniatures, several of which have come into the sale room in recent years. There has been a renewal of interest in his work since the Chinnery Exhibition which was held under the auspices of the Scottish Arts Council in Edinburgh and London in 1957, and which gave a unique opportunity to those who had the good fortune to see it to study Chinnery's work in all its phases. Only fragments of information about his life are available and so far no biography has been possible. He was a prolific painter whose works are scattered through Britain, India, China, Japan and the United States of America. Many perished during the war or have been lost, and paintings of his may still be hidden in private collections.

He was born in London on 7th January, 1774, the fifth son of William Chinnery of 4 Gough Square, Fleet Street. His father was an amateur painter who exhibited at the Free Society of Artists. The family originated in East Anglia but as far back as 1620 a branch had become established in Ireland and it was from this Irish branch that the artist descended. It is not known who taught him to paint, but he would no doubt have had some help and encouragement from his father. In 1791, when only 17, he exhibited at the Royal Academy and his work was sufficiently good to be noticed and remarked upon by John Williams, alias Pasquin, a contemporary critic, who considered his paintings to be rather in the style and manner of Cosway. Chinnery was evidently of a restless disposition and in about 1794 or 1795 he went to Ireland, where a distant relative, Sir Broderick Chinnery, resided and where his father had numerous friends whom he may have hoped would assist him in his career. He managed to obtain accommodation at 27 College Green, Dublin, with James Vigne, a jeweller connected with the firm of Myre Vigne and Luard of Threadneedle Street, London, and it is possible that the two families were old acquaintances. At any rate in 1799 Chinnery married James Vigne's daughter, Marianne.

There were a number of miniaturists working in Ireland at this time, among them John Comerford, whose influence may have led Chinnery to paint miniatures and small portrait drawings in addition to portraits and landscapes in oil and gouache. Chinnery was connected with the drawing school of the Royal Dublin Society and was Secretary and Treasurer of an exhibition of painting, sculpture and architecture in November, 1799. He was an exhibitor at Dublin and also at the Royal Academy until 1846. He met with considerable success in Ireland, but his married life was apparently unsettled and in 1802 he left his wife and two small children and returned to London with the intention of sailing for India. His brother, John Terry Chinnery, was a civil servant in Madras and the family were connected with an old firm, Chase, Sewell and Chinnery, also of Madras, so he was not going into unknown territory. He sailed from England in the *Gillwell* on 11th June, 1802, reaching Madras on 21st December of that year. He had no difficulty in obtaining patrons and was fully occupied in executing portraits in oil, miniatures, portrait drawings on paper, pen and ink drawings and water colour landscapes. In June, 1807, he went to Bengal at the request of Sir Henry Russell, who had been appointed Chief Justice there and required his portrait to be painted for presentation to the Town Hall which was about to be erected in Calcutta.

Chinnery remained in India for twenty-four years and throughout the whole of this time he was kept busily employed. In 1817 his daughter, Matilda, joined her father and was followed by his wife and later by his son John. This family reunion was of short duration, for in 1825 he once more abandoned them and went to China, landing at the Port of Macao on 29th September, 1825. The residents and Chinese scenery appealed to him and he filled his sketch books with vivid and lively drawings of the life and occupations of the people. In spite of the amount of money that he must have made, he had spent so liberally in extravagant living that he left debts of some £40,000 when he quitted India. There is no evidence that he painted miniatures after leaving that country and he holds a unique place in British painting from the fact that no other artist spent so much of his life working in the East. His miniatures are forceful, even if their style varies somewhat, and show him to have been as competent a painter in miniature as he was in all other aspects of his work.

JOHN THOMAS BARBER BEAUMONT, F.S.A., F.G.S. (1774–1841), as he is known, began as 'J. T. Barber' but added the name of Beaumont in about 1820. He was born in Marylebone in London on 21st December, 1774, and entered the Royal Academy School at seventeen. He soon showed considerable talent, being awarded a medal by the Society of Arts in 1791, a silver palette in 1793–4, a silver medallion in

1794–5; and the Royal Academy awarded him three medals, two for academy figures and one for an historical subject. In 1794 he turned his attention to miniature painting and exhibited some of his work from that year until 1806. His miniatures found favour with members of the Royal Family. He was appointed Miniature Painter to the Duke of Kent and the Duke of York, and in the Royal Academy catalogue for 1799 is described as 'miniature painter to Prince Edward'. He was a versatile man, for in addition to painting he published in 1803 *A Tour Through South Wales* which he illustrated, wrote tracts advocating arming the people when Napoleon threatened invasion, and organized a rifle corps called the Duke of Cumberland's Sharp Shooters.

Not only was Beaumont a good organizer and well able to hold a commission as Captain Commandant of the corps he had founded, but he also possessed business acumen and in 1806 founded the Provident Institution, and later the County Fire Office, of which he was Chairman until his death, as well as the Provident Life Insurance Company. The responsibilities which must have come upon him as a result of his position in the business world meant that he was left little or no time to pursue his career as a painter. His style is not uniform and therefore difficult to describe, but his miniatures have depth and strength and he was a good draughtsman.

JOHN COMERFORD (1770?–1832) has already been mentioned in connection with George Chinnery. He was another artist who had his roots in Ireland, being born in Kilkenny in 1770, where his father was a flax dresser. He studied art at the Dublin Society's Academy in Grafton Street, Dublin. Comerford painted copies of pictures at Kilkenny Castle and executed portraits in oil at Kilkenny, Waterford and Carrick-on-Suir, among other places, but later abandoned the painting of oil portraits and concentrated on miniatures (which he occasionally signed with his full name), small chalk drawings and pencil portraits. He was in Dublin in 1793 and 1797, and in 1800 and 1801 he exhibited in Kilkenny. In the following year he returned to settle in Dublin. He exhibited at the Royal Academy in 1804 and again in 1809; in 1811 he was elected a member of the Dublin Society of Artists and became Vice-President.

Because of the amount of gum he mixed with his paints, his technique was that of a painter in oils rather than a miniaturist. He succeeded in drawing out the character in his sitters in spite of the fact that they were often, to the casual observer, not particularly good-looking. Comerford was without doubt one of the finest of the Irish miniaturists. He died at his house in Blessington Street, Dublin, on the 25th January, 1832.

THOMAS HARGREAVES (1775–1846) was born at Liverpool and his father is thought to have been a woollen draper. From an early age he practised miniature painting and in May 1793 was articled to Sir Thomas Lawrence, a position he retained for two years, during which time he must obviously have given satisfaction as Sir Thomas subsequently employed him for some time after that. His health failing, he gave up that work and returned to Liverpool, where he practised miniature painting. He was an exhibitor at the Royal Academy from 1798 and appears to have worked both in London and Liverpool. Hargreaves was a member of the Liverpool Academy from 1810 and exhibited there, and in 1824 he became one of the original members of the Society of British Artists. He died at Liverpool on 23rd December, 1846. The shape of his miniatures is usually rectangular and many of them show a resemblance to the work of Lawrence. His signatures were 'T.H.' in cursive capitals or 'T. Hargreaves' followed by the date, these being found on the back of the portrait. But 'T.H.' with the date, in cursive capitals, is occasionally found on the front. Some of his works were engraved.

Miss Sarah Biffin or Beffin (1784–1850), born at East Quantoxhead, near Bridgwater on 15th October, 1784, deserves our attention not only because of her skill as a miniaturist but because in order to paint at all she overcame the most overwhelming handicap: she possessed neither hands nor feet. The skill of modern surgery had not developed, nor were the many appliances now available to be obtained for any persons in such a condition, and yet in spite of this she succeeded in learning to paint by holding the brush in her mouth, and she was able also to do plain sewing and embroidery. Mr Basil Long describes how his grandfather once went to see Miss Biffin, whom he described as a handsome woman 'seated on a cushion while she deftly plied her needle with her mouth with which too she threaded it, her work resting on her shoulder stump'. The British Museum has an engraved self-portrait and a lithographed portrait of her.

She was taught painting by W. M. Craig and was cared for by a Mr Dukes, who took her on tours of the country and arranged exhibitions of her work. She practised at Birmingham, Brighton and Liverpool, and for a time she lived in the Strand, London. In 1821 she was awarded a medal by the Society of Arts and in the same year exhibited at the Royal Academy. Both William IV and Queen Victoria patronized her and there is a miniature of Edward, Duke of Kent, attributed to her in Her Majesty the Queen's Collection at Windsor Castle. She is said to have married a Mr Wright, and a miniaturist named Sarah Wright is recorded as living at 37 Paradise Street, Birmingham. In 1850 she again exhibited at the Royal Academy but in the same year was taken ill suddenly and died after a few days on 2nd October, 1850.

Andrew Robertson, M.A. (1777–1845), was one of the few Scottish miniature painters who attained any eminence. He was born at Aberdeen in 1777 and was the son of a cabinet-maker. The family consisted of three brothers, Archibald, born

149. JOHN THOMAS BARBER BEAUMONT,
F.S.A., F.G.S. (1774–1841)
An unknown lady. $2\frac{15}{16} \times 2\frac{7}{16}$ in.

150. JOHN COMERFORD (1770?–1832)
Possibly Charles Farran. $2\frac{13}{16} \times 2\frac{5}{16}$ in.

151. ANTHONY STEWART (1773–1846)
Major Edward Fanshaw. $3\frac{1}{8} \times 2\frac{1}{2}$ in.

152.
ANTHONY STEWART
Queen Victoria
(1819–1901).
$2\frac{1}{2}$ in. diam.

153. GEORGE CHINNERY, R.H.A. (1774–1852)
Mrs Sherson, *née* Taylor. $6\frac{1}{8} \times 4\frac{13}{16}$ in.

154. FRANÇOIS THEODORE ROCHARD
(1798–1858)
Miss Blood. Signed. $4\frac{17}{32} \times 3\frac{7}{16}$ in.

155. ALFRED EDWARD CHALON, R.A. (1780–1860)
An unknown lady. $3\frac{7}{8} \times 3\frac{1}{4}$ in.

156. THOMAS HARGREAVES (1775–1846)
Mrs Wager Allix. $3\frac{7}{8} \times 3$ in.

in 1765, Alexander, born in 1772, and Andrew, born in 1777. All three brothers became artists, Andrew remaining in Britain but Archibald and Alexander going to America, where they set up an Academy. The family were not affluent and from the age of fourteen Andrew was obliged to paint in order to earn a living. He studied under Alexander Nasmyth and Raeburn, and being a keen and able musician was asked to be the Director of Concerts in Aberdeen when only sixteen. He was allowed to copy Raeburn's work and this made a lasting impression on him and his own painting – its lighting and modelling were greatly influenced by Raeburn's technique. It was Robertson's intention to become a doctor and to this end he took a Master of Arts degree at Aberdeen in 1794 but, no doubt owing to the financial straits of his family, this idea was put aside and in 1801 he walked to London where he came to the notice of Benjamin West and was allowed to copy his portraits in miniature. He immediately began studying art at the Royal Academy Schools and exhibited from 1802 to 1842 both at the Royal Academy and at the Old Water Colour Society. Robertson's work met with great success in London, but fashions were changing and in place of the attractive but rather frivolous paintings of Cosway and the other eighteenth-century miniaturists, patrons were looking for more solid and richly painted portraits executed on a larger scale and more like the oil paintings and water colours that were becoming so popular at this period. Andrew Robertson came into prominence because his style of miniature painting was what was in demand. He felt that miniatures ought to be oil paintings on a small scale and by the time photography was invented it was only a short step to the large rectangular miniature which, standing side by side with the photograph, lost the personal appeal of portrait miniatures as they had been understood from the time of Holbein.

In 1805 Robertson had been appointed miniature painter to the Duke of Sussex and as his work commended itself to the Royal Family he was invited to go to Windsor in 1807 to paint portraits of the Princesses. His portrait of Princess Amelia has often been reproduced and after her death he was asked for several replicas of this work. He was a member of the Associated Artists in Water Colour, where he exhibited, but in 1817 he went to Paris. He married a daughter of Samuel Boxill of Barbados and they had a family. He never lost his interest in music, was a good violinist and wrote articles on art in the *Literary Gazette*.

The miniatures executed by Robertson are well-drawn and pleasing to look at. They are frequently sketched in brown monochrome and occasionally the background is in this colour. He placed his sitter in front of him rather than to the right and had his painting table in such a position that the light came down aslant from the rear of his left shoulder. Usually he signed his work 'A.R.' in monogram. In 1792 he charged 10s. 6d. a miniature but by 1807 the price had risen to twelve guineas for a small one. He taught F. Cruickshank, and Sir William Ross was for a time his assistant.

In spite of the fact that his work had such an affinity with large oil painting and that he much preferred large rectangular formats, he ranks among the best of the nineteenth-century miniaturists.

EDWARD NASH (1778–1821) was one of a group of artists who, having established themselves in Britain, went to India, where miniaturists were in great demand and money appeared to be plentiful. He was in all probability a Londoner, for in 1800 he exhibited at the Royal Academy from an address in Camberwell, continuing to show in 1811, 1812, 1814, 1818 and again in 1820. In 1800 Nash applied to the Court of Directors of the East India Company for permission to go to India as a miniaturist and, his application being successful, sailed from Portsmouth on the *Hercules* on 9th January, 1801, landing in Bombay in May. His work was well received and he is said to have made a considerable sum of money while in India, where he evidently took part in the affairs of the community, for he served as a member of the Grand Jury in Bombay. He left India in the *Dover Castle* in February, 1810, and landed at Deal in July. On arriving in London, he took up residence at 6 Hanover Square, and once more began exhibiting at the Royal Academy. It has always been held that he was a pupil, or possibly an assistant, of Samuel Shelley, who had resided at the same address in Hanover Square. Some of his work bore a strong resemblance to that of Shelley and he used a yellowish tint in the flesh colour.

Nash lived for a time in the Lake District and knew Coleridge, Wordsworth and Southey. He never married and died in London when only 43 years old in 1821. His signature when found is usually on the back, 'E. G. Nash, Bombay, November, 1801' being one known example.

Two other Scottish artists, although not in the first rank, deserve to be mentioned. ALEXANDER GALLAWAY (worked 1794–1812) is first heard of when, in the *Glasgow Courier* of May 1794, he inserted an advertisement announcing that he and a Mr Williams, who apparently executed views, had moved their drawing academy to Horn's Court, Argyll Street. He moved in 1801 to Smith's Land, Trongate, Glasgow, and from 1811–12 was residing at 6 James' Square, Edinburgh. He exhibited at the Edinburgh Society of Incorporated Artists in 1808. I have seen a miniature of a lady by Gallaway that was both pleasing and well painted. He used a minute stippling to achieve the modelling of the features. His signature varied: he used both cursive and Roman initials on the front and occasionally his full surname on the back.

ANTHONY STEWART (1773–1846) was born at Crieff in Perthshire. Having decided to take up art, he studied under Alexander Nasmyth at Edinburgh, where he painted landscapes and executed sketches of Scottish scenery. Later he was attracted to miniature painting and obtained patrons in Scotland and later in London. An exhibitor at the Royal Academy from 1807–20, he succeeded in obtaining the patronage of the Royal Family and was invited to paint portraits of Princess Charlotte and Princess Victoria, afterwards Queen Victoria. He was particularly noted for his paintings of children. There are examples of his work in the Royal Collection at Windsor and the National Galleries of Scotland possess several miniatures of the Dalrymple family by him, which incidentally vary considerably in their quality. He died in London in 1846.

ANDREW DUNN (worked 1809–20) was presumably an Irishman and studied at the Dublin Society's School under F. West. Having completed his training, he practised miniature painting at Waterford and Kilkenny and later worked in London, where he was an exhibitor at the Royal Academy from 1809–11. One of his exhibits was a portrait of Princess Charlotte of Wales. During 1808 he was again in Ireland and held an exhibition in Dublin, but his visit was of short duration for later in the year he returned to London, where he was living in 1820. A miniature in my possession painted by this artist is of historic interest as representing Sir Joseph Banks, who was President of the Royal Society from 1778 to 1820 and accompanied Captain Cook in his expedition round the world. It is signed 'A. Dunn' in cursive writing on the front and dated 1809. It is possible that this miniature once belonged to Sir Joseph Banks himself as it was purchased not far from his old home at Revesby Abbey in Lincolnshire, together with one of Captain Cook after the portrait by Dance, and inscribed on the back 'in ye possession of Sir Joseph Banks'. The painting is good, the modelling accurate and the colour soft, the background being a greenish-blue, and like most of Dunn's miniatures, it shows character and forcefulness. Another form of signature used by this artist was 'A. Dunn' in capitals.

ALFRED EDWARD CHALON, R.A. (1780–1860), was born in Geneva of French descent and just after the outbreak of the French Revolution was brought to England by his father, who became a French professor at the Royal Military College, Sandhurst in 1789. The family settled in Kensington. Alfred was destined for a commercial career but instead decided to take up art, and in 1797 entered the Royal Academy Schools, where he studied miniature painting under his fellow Genevese, L. A. Arlaud, who was then in London. His elder brother John James Chalon, R.A. (1778–1854), was also an artist of some repute, being noted for his paintings in oils and water colour. The two brothers remained bachelors and for some years kept house together. They were instrumental in founding in 1808 a sketching society which met with great success.

Besides painting miniatures Alfred Chalon also executed subject pictures in oil, and was reputed to be an able musician and a witty and entertaining companion. He died at Campden Hill, Kensington, on 3rd October, 1860.

His work varied. At its best it was of high quality, being well designed and composed, and imparting an air of distinction to his sitters. He was particularly successful with his portraits of ladies. His earlier works are simpler and more pleasing than those executed later in his life, when large quantities of thick white paint can be discerned on the draperies and lace.

His signature, A. E. Chalon in monogram, may be found in the upper right-hand corner of the painting, one rectangular miniature being thus signed in brown tones. The majority of his works are signed only in monogram.

From 1801 to 1860 he exhibited at the Royal Academy and amongst the portraits shown were those of Queen Victoria, Princess Charlotte and many of the aristocracy. In 1808 he became a member of the Associated Artists in Water Colour and was elected A.R.A. in 1812 and promoted to full membership in 1816.

It was said that his patronage dwindled considerably towards the middle of the century owing to a request he made to the Countess of Blessington for payment of sums owing to him for portraits which she had commissioned. This falling off of commissions may however have been due to other causes, for he was one of the first artists whose work had to compete with photography. Queen Victoria is reputed to have prophesied that this innovation would ruin his profession. Chalon maintained that photography could not flatter, but as time went on and the process was perfected this limitation was overcome, and the Queen's prophecy fulfilled.

157. JEAN PETITOT
(1607–91)
Sir Theodore Turquet de
Mayerne (1573–1655).
$1\frac{5}{8} \times 1\frac{3}{8}$ in.

158. CHARLES BOIT
(1662–1727)
An unknown man.

159.
PAUL PRIEUR (b. 1620?)
Frederick III of Denmark
(1609–70).
$1\frac{3}{16} \times 1$ in.

160.
ANDRÉ (or JEAN)
ROUQUET (1701–59)
An unknown lady.
$1\frac{3}{4} \times 1\frac{1}{2}$ in.

161.
CHRISTIAN FREDERICK
ZINCKE (1663/4–1767)
An unknown man.
$1\frac{5}{8} \times 1\frac{11}{32}$ in.

162. DENIS BROWNELL MURPHY (d. 1842)
Charles I, after Johnson. $3\frac{5}{8} \times 2\frac{15}{16}$ in.

163. WILLIAM PREWITT (worked 1735–50)
Mr and Mrs John Knight and Mr Newsham.
Signed and dated 1735. $4 \times 3\frac{5}{8}$ in.

164. JOSEPH LEE (1747–1859)
Frederick, Duke of York (1763–1827)
after J. Jackson. Signed. $3 \times 2\frac{7}{16}$ in.

165.
JOHANN HEINRICH HURTER (1734–99)
George III (1738–1820). Signed and dated 1781.
$2\frac{3}{16} \times 1\frac{25}{32}$ in.

166. RICHARD CROSSE (1742–1810)
James Crosse, brother of the artist.
Depth 4 in.

CHAPTER XVIII

ENAMEL MINIATURES

*

From the brief description of the art of enamelling in an earlier chapter it will be apparent that artists working in this medium were as clever as and in many ways more dexterous than those who painted portraits in water colour. Not only had the finely powdered colours to be applied to the prepared surface of the metal, but the portrait had to be submitted to the hazards of the kiln in which it was fired, where the slightest error or accident might result in the whole painting being destroyed. The finished article however had great advantages over miniatures painted in water colour. It did not fade, it could be hung in any position in a room and it could not be damaged unless dropped or roughly treated, when the surface of the enamel might crack.

JEAN FOUQUET (1420?–80?) was, as far as is known, the first to attempt to portray a living person in enamel and his self-portrait, which is signed in full on the front, may be seen in the Musée du Louvre, Paris. Although it is unlikely that this portrait had any real influence on the art of miniature painting it is of great interest as an isolated example of a portrait miniature dating from long before the art as we know it, came into being.

There is a long tradition of enamelling in France, and the art continues there to this day. In the fifteenth century there was a flourishing school of enamellers at Limoges which concentrated on painting religious subjects and used only a limited palette. This style continued until about 1632, when a French goldsmith named JEAN TOUTIN found that a variety of colours could be laid upon a thin ground of previously fired white enamel and that the portrait could be re-fired without any damage to the tints. This discovery allowed opaque colours to be applied upon an enamel ground in the same way that water colour could be laid upon ivory or vellum. Toutin, assisted by his son Henri, developed this method and a school of enamellers grew up under his tuition. Much of their work was devoted to the embellishment of the cases of elaborate watches during the period of Louis XIII.

A Swiss by the name of JEAN PETITOT (1607–91) very soon came to the fore as an expert in this medium. He was born in Geneva, the fourth son of a French sculptor who came of a Huguenot family which had fled from France, and was apprenticed to a goldsmith, JACQUES BORDIER (1616–84), who was almost his contemporary. Both Petitot and Bordier are thought to have been taught enamelling by Jean Royaume, who is believed to have been Petitot's uncle. A life-long friendship grew up between the two men who, after a time, became dissatisfied with their progress and in 1633 left Geneva for Paris, where they are thought to have been pupils of Jean and Henri Toutin in Blois. From Paris Petitot came to England and obtained employment under Charles I in about 1637. He had been presented to the King by Sir Theodore Turquet de Mayerne, the King's Physician, who gave him great encouragement and was his close friend, assisting him, by his chemical knowledge, in the technical process of enamelling. Thus it was Petitot who first introduced the art of painting enamel miniature portraits into Britain. He was no doubt encouraged to perfect this medium by seeing the works of the flourishing school of miniature painters in water colour who were already established. Charles I employed him to make rings and jewellery and to paint enamel portraits of most of the principal persons of the Court, a number of the portraits being copied from large paintings by Van Dyck.

Petitot seldom executed any portraits from life. Miniatures painted during his stay in England are usually signed and date from 1638 to 1643, which were in all probability the years he remained in Britain. He had certainly left England by 1650 and after his departure the art virtually ceased to exist until the latter part of the century, when another foreign artist re-introduced it. Some excellent examples of his work are in the Duke of Portland's collection at Welbeck, and another fine one of the Countess of Southampton belongs to the Duke of Devonshire.

At Charenton in 1651 Petitot and Bordier married sisters whose name was Cuper. It has been suggested that there may possibly have been some family connection with Samuel Cooper as Petitot sent his eldest son, Jean, to be taught by Cooper, but this might have been due to his high regard for the English school of painters. On his return to France Petitot was employed by Louis XIV to paint portraits of the Royal Family and many of the nobility of the Court. In 1686 he became a Protestant and was put into prison for heresy. After his release he went to Switzerland, where he continued to paint until his death at Vevey in 1691. He left a family of 17 children of whom the eldest, Jean, was a painter of miniatures in both water colour and enamel. In his enamels, which are of the highest quality and painted in harmonious colours, it is possible to distinguish a stippling touch when viewed under a lens. Miniatures painted in water colour by him are rare but the Victoria and Albert Museum possesses one attributed to him.

Petitot and Bordier collaborated in their work throughout their lives and Bordier is said to have painted the hair in many of Petitot's enamels. It is difficult consequently to know how much of a portrait may be the work of either individual. After Petitot left England, miniatures in enamel did not come into prominence again until 1687 with the arrival of CHARLES BOIT (baptized 1662, d. 1727). Boit was a Swede and the son of Charles Boit, a French salt manufacturer, silk merchant, and tennis instructor. His mother's maiden name was Marie Creveleur and her home was at Calais. He was apprenticed to the goldsmith's trade in Stockholm from 1677–82, but it is uncertain who taught him the art of enamelling. Signac, the court enameller to Queen Christina, died in 1684, and after his death only two enamellers remained in Sweden, Elias Brenner and Andreas Von Behn. It is therefore probable that Boit was taught enamelling by one of these two before he came to England, and not after, as is stated by Vertue. It has always been held that the earliest enamel by Boit is one in the National Museum in Stockholm dated 1694. But an example was sold at Sotheby's recently, signed C. Boit. PL | Coiventry | 1693.

In 1682 Boit went to Paris for three months and then to Gothenburg. He was married to a girl by the name of Flitzberg and in 1685 returned to Stockholm. He was introduced into England in 1687 by an Exeter merchant who had contacts in Sweden and had been instrumental in bringing Michael Dahl over to Britain a few years previously. Boit was married three times and is said to have been imprisoned in England for two years through having become engaged to a country gentleman's daughter.

He achieved great success in England and in 1696 was appointed court enameller to William III, but he seemed unable to settle for long and in 1699 went to Holland. In 1700 he obtained commissions at the Elector's Court in Düsseldorf and worked in Vienna, where he painted a large enamel of the Emperor's family. In 1703 he was back in London and Prince George of Denmark encouraged him to attempt a large enamel to depict the 'Battle of Blenheim', 1704, representing the Duke of Marlborough being led to Queen Anne and her Court by Victory. He obtained more than a thousand pounds from the Treasury as advance payment for this work, but in spite of the help of many assistants it proved too great an undertaking and was never completed. On the death of Queen Anne the project was no longer popular and in 1714 the Treasury demanded a repayment of their expenditure. As by this time Boit had got into debt, he left the country for France, where he obtained employment at the French Court and from Peter the Great of Russia. He died in Paris in 1727.

Boit showed great ability in his technique, which was smooth and executed with care. He favoured the use of pink and yellow in his colouring tints, which is a distinguishing characteristic of his work.

CHRISTIAN FRIEDRICH ZINCKE (1663/4–1767), sometimes spelt Zink, Zinks and Zincks, was a pupil of Boit and attained great prominence as an enameller, obtaining the patronage of both royalty and the aristocracy. Born in Dresden, he was the son of a goldsmith and was trained in his father's trade but studied painting in his spare time. In 1706 he came to England where, after studying under Boit, his work was soon in great demand, both portraits from life as well as copies of paintings after Lely, Kneller and others. Unfortunately his eyesight, which had been giving him trouble as early as 1725, grew steadily worse and after a visit to Germany in 1737 he was unable to practise his art to any great extent, although he is known to have taught J. Meyer some time after 1748. He lived for some years in Tavistock Row, Covent Garden, but in 1746 moved to South Lambeth. He was married twice and had a son called Christopher, a daughter by his first wife, who is reputed to have been a good looking woman, and a further three or four children by his second wife, Elizabeth. His enamels are not painted with quite the same smoothness as those of Boit and often a red stippling can be observed on the face, the dots of which are sometimes blended together. His works varied a great deal in their execution, not all of them being of equal quality and it is thought possible that he employed several assistants who may have painted a large proportion of his portraits.

PAUL PRIEUR (b. 1620?), the only son of a Parisian jeweller who appears to have been working in Geneva and to have died there, was apprenticed to another jeweller, J. Planchant. He later worked in Paris, Spain, England and Denmark, where he was employed by Frederick III and Christian V. His enamels are frequently signed and dated and an example of a portrait by him of Frederick III may be seen at the Victoria and Albert Museum.

JEAN ETIENNE LIOTARD (1702–89) was another native of Geneva and the son of a French Protestant jeweller. He studied art in his native town and later was a pupil of J. B. Massé in Paris. Fond of travel, he went to Italy and accompanied Sir W. Ponsonby, afterwards Lord Bessborough, to Constantinople, where he spent some years living in Turkish fashion. He exhibited in Paris between 1751 and 1753, and paid several visits to England, the first being in 1752, and in 1773–4 he exhibited at the Royal Academy. He was married at The Hague, but his wife's name remains unknown. He is most noted for his pastel portraits, but worked also in oil and crayon, besides painting miniatures on ivory and in enamel, many of his works being signed. He died at Geneva in 1789.

ANDRÉ or JEAN ROUQUET (1701–59), was born in Geneva and is believed to have been of French-Swiss extraction. He came to England when young and worked after the manner of Zincke, although details of his life and training are not known. His own assertion that he lived in England for thirty years places the year of his arrival as 1723 or even earlier, as he is known to have left for France in 1753. If, however, the statement that he came to England during the reign of George II is accurate, then his year of arrival is more likely to be about 1727. It has always been said that

167. WILLIAM ESSEX (1784–1869)
Princess Victoria, after Fowler.
Signed and dated 1858. $3\frac{3}{4} \times 3\frac{1}{32}$ in.

168. WILLIAM ESSEX
James V (1512–42), after an unknown artist.
$3 \times 2\frac{1}{4}$ in.

169. HORACE HONE, A.R.A. (1756–1825)
Thomas Bainbridge. Signed and dated 1805.
$2\frac{7}{8} \times 2\frac{7}{16}$ in.

170. JAMES ROUSE (1802–88)
Self-portrait on porcelain.
4×3 in.

171.
HENRY PIERCE BONE (1779–1855)
Lady Dorothy Sydney,
Countess of Sunderland (1617–1684),
after Van Dyck.
Signed and dated 1842. 4 × 3 in.

172. HENRY BONE, R.A.
(1755–1834)
Sir Ralph Abercromby, K.B.
(1734–1801), after Hoppner.
Signed. 5¼ × 4¼ in.

he numbered among his friends Hogarth, Garrick and other wits of the period.

He is not recorded by Vertue until 1739, when he is mentioned as 'imitating Mr. Zincke in enamel with some success'. In 1755 he published an essay entitled *L'Etat des Arts en Angleterre* and a further publication in French dealing with Hogarth's works. He exhibited at the Salon in Paris and became a member of the Académie Royale in 1753, at which time he had lodgings in the Louvre. He became insane before his death in 1759.

Rouquet was a good enamellist whose works, although somewhat similar to those of Zincke, were softer in effect. Miniatures by him are rare and it is possible that many of those which are unsigned are attributed to Zincke. His signature is a cursive R on the front of the portrait. Of those known to exist two are in the collection of Earl Beauchamp, who also has two unsigned works which may possibly be by him, one being dated 1745. The Victoria and Albert Museum possesses a miniature of William Pitt, Earl of Chatham, which is a typical example of his work and signature. His portraits are attractive. The costume of his sitters are painted with a delicate touch, the eyes are shown slightly protruding and moisture can be seen on the lower lips.

Another artist who painted enamel miniatures was GEORGE MICHAEL MOSER (1704–83). Like so many enamellers of this period, he came from the Continent, his birthplace being Schaffhausen in Switzerland, where his father was an engraver and metal worker. After an initial training in Geneva he came to England and practised as a medallist and enameller, decorating watches and bracelets. He had the distinction of having taught George III before his accession and numbered among his friends Oliver Goldsmith and Dr Johnson. In 1736 he became the manager of the St Martin's Lane Academy and was an original member of the Incorporated Society of Artists and the Royal Academy. His death took place at Somerset House in 1783 and he was buried in St Paul's, Covent Garden. His works do not appear very frequently.

WILLIAM PREWETT or Prewitt (worked 1735–50) was a pupil of Zincke but unfortunately no information has so far come to light about his life. Examples of his work may be found in the Victoria and Albert Museum and show him to have been a first-rate artist.

HENRY SPICER (1743–1804) was born at Reepham in Norfolk. He was taught art by G. Spencer and executed miniatures both on ivory and in enamel, the latter being better known. He exhibited enamels from 1765–83 at the Incorporated Society of Artists and was its Secretary in 1773. From 1774–1804 he sent portraits to the Royal Academy.

From about 1776 or 1778 he was in Dublin and was in great demand, but returned to London in 1782 and in 1790 was made portrait painter in enamel to the

Prince of Wales. Throughout his career he had a distinguished clientèle, but he must have spent his earnings liberally for when he died after some years of illness at 7 Great Newport Street, London, he left practically nothing. Ozias Humphry took a keen interest in Spicer and sat to him for his portrait.

JOHANN HEINRICH HURTER (1734–99) was another artist who was born at Schaffhausen. From 1768 to 1790 he worked at Berne. On the advice of Liotard, he then went to Versailles, but was not as successful as he had hoped and left for The Hague, where he became a member of the Painters' Guild in 1772. He copied a number of large paintings in the Mannheim and Düsseldorf Galleries and also executed pastels. In 1777 he came to London where he exhibited at the Royal Academy from 1779–1781, held an appointment as Court Painter and founded a factory for making mathematical and other instruments. In 1785 he visited the place of his birth, The Hague and Paris, returning to London in 1787. Having received an important commission from the Empress Catherine II, he lived afterwards partly in England and partly in Germany, where he died at Düsseldorf in 1799.

He was a good enameller and his work is pleasing and has a softer effect than that of many other artists. His miniatures are often signed on the back and one in my possession, a portrait of George III, has the following inscription: 'George III, King of Great Britain, J. H. Hurter, p. 1781'. Various other signatures exist: 'Hurter fecit,' 'J. Hurter pinx.', 'I. Hurter, pinxit', in the last signature the 'I' traversing the bar of the 'H'.

When HENRY BONE, R.A. (1755–1834) began his career a fresh impetus was given to enamel miniatures and he and his family were prolific artists, although most of their portraits were copies of other men's work. Bone's father was a wood carver and cabinet maker, and the son, who was born at Truro on 6th February, 1755, began by painting on china for Cookworthy at Plymouth and was apprenticed in 1772 to Richard Champion of the Bristol Porcelain Manufactory. In 1779 Bone came to London and lived at 6 Queens Row, New Road, Islington. In 1780 he married Elizabeth van der Meulen, by whom he had at least six children. (One of them, WILLIAM, also painted enamels, and a portrait by him of his father is illustrated by Hugh Owen in *The True Porcelain* published in 1873.) Henry Bone's wife was a descendant of a Philip van der Meulen, scene painter to William III. Bone was employed painting designs for lockets, watches and jewellery and is known to have executed miniature portraits on ivory, but none in enamel until 1780. He was an exhibitor at the Royal Academy from 1781–1834, his first exhibit being No. 328 the 'Miniature of a Lady', which was a portrait of his wife. He entered portraits at the Free Society of Artists in 1783 and exhibited at the British Institution and at the Society of British Artists. Whilst living in London he made tours, particularly in the west of England. He was elected an A.R.A. in 1801 and

R.A. in 1811, and received the patronage of George III, George IV and William IV. The miniatures he executed on ivory, which are rare, were usually painted from life, but his enamels are almost all copies, and although they are fine examples of enamelling, they do not have the same appeal to many people as do original portraits. In 1811 he obtained the sum of two hundred and twenty guineas for a framed 'Bacchus and Ariadne', after Titian, which measured 18 in. × 16 in. By 1832 his sight was failing and he died of paralysis on 17th December, 1834 in his seventy-ninth year at 6 Clarence Terrace, Somers Town.

He was described as a worthy, kind, liberal and affectionate man. Examples of his work are to be found in many private collections as well as in museums, and miniatures by him often appear in the sale rooms. He executed a series of historic portraits after the originals in the Royal Collection, 85 in number and varying in size from 5 in. × 4 in. to 13 in. × 8 in. They were dispersed by sale after his decease. He frequently signed his miniatures on ivory with conjoined Roman initials on the front. Occasionally the same method was adopted on his enamels, but more frequently they were signed in great detail on the back.

His eldest son, HENRY PIERCE BONE (1779–1855), was born at Islington and received his education at Tooting. His father taught him the art of enamelling and allowed him to assist him with his work. Like his father, he was a prolific artist and examples of his miniatures frequently appear and may be seen at the Victoria and Albert Museum and many other public galleries. He occasionally painted from life, but more often copied the work of artists in oil, notably those of Beechey, Collins, Northcote, Reynolds and Phillips as well as a number after Van Dyck. The one in my collection of Lady Dorothy Sydney, Countess of Sunderland, is from the original by Van Dyck owned by Earl Spencer at Althorp. It is fully inscribed on the back in red enamel and is a fine example.

His work is very like that of his father, but as he usually signed his miniatures on the back, we are left in no doubt which of the two was responsible for the portrait. He was an exhibitor at the Royal Academy and the British Institution from 1799 to 1855 and was a member of the Associated Artists in Water Colour from 1807 to 1808. In 1833 he was appointed enamel painter to the Queen, the Duchess of Kent and Princess Victoria and received the same appointment to Prince Albert in 1841. His death took place in London in 1855. He was married in 1805 and had at least five children, one of whom, William Bone Junior (exhibited 1827–51), painted enamels after Constable, Lawrence, Reynolds and Rubens.

DENIS BROWNELL MURPHY (d. 1842) painted somewhat in the manner of the Bone family. He was born in Dublin and studied at the Dublin Society's Schools, where he succeeded in winning a prize in 1763. He later practised in Dublin, where he exhibited miniatures in 1765 and 1768. In about the latter year he went to

London, but returned to Dublin in 1792. In England again, he worked at White-haven and Newcastle, in Scotland and in London and exhibited at the Royal Academy from 1800–27. He executed drawings as well as enamels, some of which were copies of oil paintings, and a number of his works were engraved. The Duke of Devonshire owns a good enamel of Charles I after Cornelius Johnson, signed 'D. B. Murphy, 42 Pall Mall, 1805'.

WILLIAM ESSEX (1784–1869) was the last artist of any note to paint enamel miniatures. Like the Bone family, his work lay mainly in copying oil paintings although he occasionally painted from life. He was noted for his portraits of dogs which were frequently set in tie-pins and other small articles of jewellery. He was appointed enamel painter in 1841 to Queen Victoria and the Prince Consort. A small enamel of Queen Victoria by him may be seen at the Ashmolean Museum at Oxford and one in my collection, a copy of a portrait by W. Fowler of Princess Victoria, afterwards Queen Victoria, at the age of five is particularly charming and is painted in brilliantly clear colours. The whereabouts of the original is at present unknown. Essex wrote a treatise on the art of enamelling and J. W. Bailey, W. B. Ford and his son, W. B. Essex, were his pupils. His signature and a full description is usually to be found on the back of his portraits.

JOSEPH LEE (1747–1859) was the second son of John Lee and his wife Rachel Oldroyd. It is uncertain where he acquired his knowledge of painting, but it is said that he did not begin to paint until he was more than thirty years of age. He studied the work of Zincke and modelled his own painting upon it. Although many of his enamels are from life, the majority were copied from the works of Van der Helst, Romney, Petitot, Boit, etc. There are two enamels by Lee in the Wallace Collection, London, a particularly fine one being that of Frederick, Duke of York. I have a miniature signed 'JO. Lee' which is said to be a portrait of his mother. His work is well executed and the colouring pleasing. He was appointed enamel painter to Princess Charlotte and to the Duke of Sussex.

Lee was married and had eight children. He died at 13 Victoria Place, Gravesend, on 26th December, 1859, his wife having pre-deceased him.

A number of other artists working in the eighteenth century painted in enamel as well as water colour and their works have already been discussed elsewhere. Among them are N. Hone, H. Hone, S. Cotes, G. Spencer, J. Scouler, C. Richter, J. Meyer and W. Grimaldi, to mention only a few.

CHAPTER XIX

ARTISTS WHO WORKED WITH PLUMBAGO, OILS AND ON PORCELAIN

*

In the early part of the sixteenth century a mine at Seathwaite in Borrowdale, Cumberland, was discovered which produced graphite, or plumbago, of the finest quality. Plumbago miniatures, or plumbago drawings as they are sometimes called, were popular from the early part of the seventeenth until about the middle of the eighteenth century and no book on the subject of miniatures is complete without some reference to them. While many painters have executed fine drawings either as sketches for portraits or as finished products, some artists have, as far as is known, confined their work to plumbago drawings on a background of vellum or paper. When the miniature was in monochrome the artists used graphite or pencil, indian ink or silver point but occasionally slight washes of grey or sepia were introduced into the shading and, in sketches for portraits, slightly more colouring was occasionally used. It is possible to include any portrait executed in this medium as a miniature provided that its size conforms to the accepted idea of a miniature.

In England there were several artists working in plumbago in the seventeenth century, the most notable being David Loggan, Thomas Forster and Robert White, and the miniatures they executed were exquisitely drawn and full of detail. They were particularly dexterous at drawing materials and lace, the latter being so well done that almost every stitch can be discerned. Artists abroad often worked in plumbago too but did not confine themselves to this medium, since they also executed portraits in water colour.

Although his main work lay in water colour portraits, the fine pencil drawings of Samuel Cooper must not be overlooked, especially the most outstanding of them, to which reference has been made in an earlier chapter, namely, the head of a boy called 'Henry Frederick, Prince of Wales', owned by the Duke of Buccleuch.

DAVID LOGGAN (1635–92) was probably the greatest exponent of plumbago. Of Scottish descent, he was born in Danzig, became a pupil of the engraver W. Hondius, and later studied under Crispin van der Pass in Amsterdam, where he remained for seven years. He is known to have visited Paris and to have lived for a time in London, where in 1663 he married Anna Jordan of Kencote, Oxfordshire.

During the Plague he left London and went to live at Nuffield, near Oxford, where he became friendly with Anthony Wood, who records occasions when they met in Oxford taverns.

By 1669 he was living in Oxford, where he received an appointment as Public Sculptor to the University, matriculated in 1672 and in 1675 became a natural-ized Englishman. Four years later he again had an address in London and in 1690 became engraver to the University of Cambridge. The most famous of his works are the splendid series of engravings in *Oxonia Illustrata*, which he produced in 1675, and *Cantabrigia Illustrata*, 1676–90, and he is also noted for his numerous plumbago and engraved portraits on vellum. Basil Long tells us that he is recorded as having executed a drawing on satin. He took pupils, among whom were Edward Le Davis (b. 1640), Robert Shepherd, Robert White and Michael Vander-gucht. His drawings show great skill, the character of the sitter being well expressed. The faces often have a buff or slightly orange tinge. Loggan usually signed his works either with cursive initials or sloping Roman capitals, but occasionally he signed 'D. Loggan'. Examples of his work are to be found at Christ Church, Oxford, and in the Ashmolean Museum, where a fine plumbago of Dr Thomas Willis is preserved. He died in London during the summer of 1692.

ROBERT WHITE (1645–1703), who was born in London, was one of Loggan's most notable pupils. His work was as carefully drawn as that of his master, and some consider his portraits to be even better than Loggan's. He was a prolific engraver and is known to have executed more than 400 portraits, some of them after his own drawings. He also engraved title pages for books and landscapes, as well as drawing buildings for Loggan. Among his finest works are three owned by the Duke of Portland: a self-portrait, a portrait of the Duke of Monmouth and a portrait of Charles II dated 1684. In this portrait, the details of the lace cravat, the robes and the Order of the Garter are truly superb. His signatures include, 'R. White, delin.', 'R. White, fec.' and 'R. White, fecit'. While travelling about the country in connection with his work he is said to have been quite well off, but when he died in Bloomsbury Market in November, 1703, he was a poor man.

THOMAS FORSTER (b. 1677?) has left scarcely a trace of information about him-self, but the examples of his work leave us in no doubt as to his ability. He evidently had a distinguished clientèle and a number of his works were engraved. The Victoria and Albert Museum has eight plumbagos by him and examples may also be found in the British Museum and the Holburne Museum, Bath. A miniature by him of William III is in the Duke of Portland's collection at Welbeck. His works are highly finished and he was able to portray the character of his sitters and to give his portraits an air of elegance. His signatures include the following examples: 'T. Forster, delin', 'Thos. Forster, delin.', 'T. Forster, del.' and 'Tho.fforster'.

DAVID PATON (worked 1660–95) was one of the few Scottish miniature painters in the seventeenth century. He was a good draughtsman and his portraits are to be found mainly in private collections. As far as is known, he practised only in Scotland and his miniatures, which were sometimes engraved, were usually copied from pictures, a well-known one being that of Sir James Dalrymple, which was engraved by his fellow-artist, R. White. He accompanied the Honourable William Tollemache, younger son of the Duchess of Lauderdale, on the Grand Tour and a manuscript relating to this journey is at Ham House, Richmond. According to a document dated 6th June, 1695, which is referred to by Sotheby's in a 1920 sale catalogue, at Oxenfoord Castle, Midlothian, the present home of the Countess of Eglinton and Lady Marjory Dalrymple, there is a receipt in which 'David Paton, limner, of Edinburgh, acknowledges having received from David McGill, Professor of Philosophy, in the name of Robert, Viscount Oxford, £186. 8s. as interest on £780 Scots money[1] from 20th May, 1690 to 20th May, 1695 as payment for a miniature portrait of the Prince of Wales set in silver and for two silver frames for other pictures'. Oxenfoord Castle still remains in the possession of the Dalrymple family. The castle is now a private school, but the family treasures still adorn the rooms.

Paton is known to have painted a few portraits in oil, but he is best remembered for his plumbago miniatures and copies. Particularly fine examples of his work are a miniature of Viscount Dundee now in the Scottish National Gallery and a rectangular one of Charles II, signed 'D. Paton fecit', which is in the possession of the Duke of Buccleuch.

CHARLES FORSTER (who was working from about 1709–17) is thought to have been the son of Thomas Forster, his style being somewhat similar, although the finished portraits have not quite the same quality in execution. The Victoria and Albert Museum possesses a miniature of a boy signed 'C. Forster'.

GEORGE WHITE (1671? or 1684?–1732) was, according to the *Dictionary of National Biography*, the son of Robert White and was his pupil. His miniatures on vellum closely resemble his father's work. He executed portraits in oil and crayons and was also an engraver, producing more than 60 portraits after Lely, Kneller and others, in both line and mezzotint. His signature was 'G. White', the cursive G. and W. forming a monogram. One portrait miniature in colour by him exists. He died in Bloomsbury, London, on 27th May, 1732.

Quite recently a new name has been added to the list of artists who worked in plumbago, for the National Portrait Gallery has purchased one ($4\frac{3}{8}$ in. × $3\frac{1}{2}$ in.) of John Locke, the eminent philosopher (1632–1704) by a man named SYLVESTER BROUNOWER, signed 'S.B. fecit'. Judging by this isolated example he must have

---

[1] £100 in Scots money was worth £8 . 6 . 8 Sterling in the seventeenth century.

had considerable talent as an artist and one can only hope that more miniatures by him will come to light. Brounower was apparently employed by Locke, possibly as his secretary.

JOHN FABER (1650 or 60–1721), a mezzotint portrait engraver, is best known for his pen and ink drawings in imitation of engravings. He was born at The Hague and did not come to England until about 1687, when he took up residence in Fountain Court, Strand, London. Examples of his work may be found at the Victoria and Albert Museum, one of them being a pen and ink miniature of Admiral Sir George Rooke which is signed and dated 1705. His son, John Faber Junior (1684–1756), was also an engraver.

WILLIAM FAITHORNE (1616–91) was born in London and studied the art of painting and engraving under Robert Peake the printseller, as well as having some instruction in engraving from John Payne. He was a more skilful draughtsman than many of his predecessors and whenever possible drew his subjects from life. He numbered among his friends Thomas Flatman.[1] During the Civil War he joined the Royalists and was taken prisoner at Basing House in 1645 and imprisoned at Aldersgate. Having been banished to France, he is said to have been taught by Philippe de Champaigne and Nanteuil. He returned to London in about 1650 and in 1662 published *The Art of Graveing and Etching*. It is for these works that he is best known, but although he is said to have executed many miniatures, original works by him are very rare.

The Duke of Buccleuch owns a large miniature after Lely of Barbara Villiers, Countess of Castlemaine which is attributed to Faithorne, and several drawings by him are known to exist. He died in Printing House Square in May 1691 and was buried in St Anne's Church, Blackfriars.

Portraits painted on porcelain have never been considered to be miniatures, but I have seen several that have been extremely well painted. Not all of them are signed so that it is almost impossible to attribute them. It would appear likely that miniatures in this medium, excluding amateurish attempts by potters on Delft during the seventeenth century, were all executed in the nineteenth century or later.

JOHN SIMPSON, who exhibited from 1831 to 1871, is known to have painted miniatures on porcelain and two of them were sold at Sotheby's on 14th May, 1959, from the Dyson Perrins collection. Simpson did not confine himself to porcelain but also painted enamel portraits, some of them being from life, while others were copies of pictures.

JAMES ROUSE or Rowse (1802–88), whose self-portrait on porcelain is at Derby Art Gallery, was an apprentice at the Derby China factory, where he was noted for

[1] See Chapter VII.

173. THOMAS FORSTER (b. 1677?)
Lady Anne Churchill (1660–1744).
Signed and dated 1700. $4\frac{3}{8} \times 3\frac{3}{8}$ in.

174. GEORGE WHITE (1671/84–1732)
William Popple. Signed and dated 1705.
$4\frac{1}{2} \times 3\frac{1}{2}$ in.

175. JOHN FABER (1650/60–1721)
Admiral Sir George Rooke (1650–1709).
Signed and dated 1705. $4\frac{5}{16} \times 3\frac{7}{16}$ in.

176. SYLVESTER BROUNOWER
(17th Century)
John Locke (1632–1704). Signed. $4\frac{3}{8} \times 3\frac{1}{2}$ in.

177. DAVID LOGGAN
(1635–92)
Dr Thomas Willis
(1621–75).
Signed and dated 1687.
$5\frac{7}{8} \times 5$ in.

178.
WILLIAM FAITHORNE
(1616–91)
John Aubrey (1626–97).
Dated 1666. 6 × 5 in.

his paintings of flowers and figure subjects. He also painted portraits in oil. John Haslem, who also painted on porcelain, writing of artists connected with the Derby works in his book *The Old Derby China Factory*, speaks of Rouse as having left the factory before 1830 and gone to work in the Potteries and later at Coalport. But at the time Haslem wrote Rouse was at Birmingham where he was employed in painting small enamels, mainly for jewellery. By 1875 he had returned to Derby and was employed by Mr Hancock at the China factory.

Some of the miniatures on porcelain compare very favourably with the work of enamellers and were obviously painted either from life or portraits and were distinct from the porcelain plaques, so frequently met with in brooches, which were copies from well-known paintings. It is more than likely that enamellers or artists who painted on porcelain were responsible for these miniatures.

Miniatures painted in oil have already been referred to briefly in an earlier chapter. Here again one is hampered in one's research by the fact that few, if any, bear a signature and it is therefore impossible to attribute them to any particular artist until some new information emerges. Such miniatures were executed as early as the sixteenth and seventeenth centuries and in many cases are beautiful portraits. I have a pair painted about the middle of the seventeenth century and still in their original carved wood frames which are fine examples and in every way as good as those executed in water colours. Another oil portrait in my possession, a gentleman in armour painted against a blue background, is clearly the work of one of the great masters. Cornelius Johnson and Mrs Rosse are known to have painted miniatures in oil during the seventeenth century and in the eighteenth century D. Heins, C. Barber, J. Collins, Mrs Denham, F. Ferrière, W. Jackson and others all executed oil miniatures, while in the nineteenth century, W. Bradley, J. Leakey, Passmore, Miss Weller, R. L. West and a few others also worked in this medium.

Nearly all oil miniatures were painted on copper, but wood, millboard and even slate were occasionally used and a few artists painted on ivory. I have in my collection a miniature painting of Augustus John painted in oil on hardboard.

CHAPTER XX

THE LATE NINETEENTH AND TWENTIETH CENTURIES AND THE DECLINE OF THE ART

*

It cannot be said that miniature painting took any decisive step forward during the nineteenth and twentieth centuries – rather the reverse. Andrew Robertson had developed what was at *that* time a new style of large-size miniatures which had more affinity to the oil paintings of the day than to the miniature portraits executed by earlier artists who had painted in water colour. This retrograde step had come to stay and the rectangular form became more usual than the oval which, although still in use, was less in evidence than in the past. With the introduction of photography in the mid-nineteenth century, miniature painting lost its popularity and there was a vast difference in cost. Only those who had a real love of art continued to commission artists to paint their portraits.

JOHN COX DILLMAN ENGLEHEART (1784–1862), a nephew of George Engleheart and the son of John Dillman Engleheart and his second wife Jane Parker, was taught painting by his uncle, whom he assisted and who allowed him to make copies of a number of his miniatures after Reynolds, Zincke, etc. By 1807 he is thought to have left his uncle and to have been taking his own commissions. He evidently worked for a time at Birmingham, giving as his address 'Miss Manton's, Birmingham;' and he married in 1811 a Miss Mary Barker of Edgbaston and had four daughters and one son who was later to become Sir John Gardner Engleheart, K.C.B. and live to be a centenarian. Engleheart exhibited twice at the British Institution and from 1801 to 1828 at the Royal Academy. When he was between forty and fifty years of age, his health, which had never been too good, broke down and he retired from active painting and left England in about 1830 to travel on the Continent, taking his family to Switzerland and southern Italy. They spent two winters on the shores of the Bay of Naples and two in Rome. On returning to England he lived first at East Acton. In 1852 he moved to Beechholme, Tunbridge Wells, remaining there until his death at the age of 78 in 1862.

He was a popular artist and had no difficulty in obtaining sitters. His work was not uniform in presentation, many of his earlier miniatures resembling those of his uncles, Thomas Richmond and George Engleheart, but as time went on he adopted a rather hotter colouring, following the example of other artists of the period. In the backgrounds of his portraits he painted a variety of objects, such as flowers, trees and vases. He usually signed his miniatures on the back, 'J. D. Engleheart' or 'J. C. Dillman Engleheart', followed by an address. Basil Long mentions one signed in front with a cursive E set in a gold heart.

SIR WILLIAM JOHN NEWTON (1785–1869) was born in London and came of an artistic family, being the son of James Newton, an engraver, and a nephew of William Newton, an architect who in 1803 joined the Artists' Volunteer Corps. He was trained in engraving but quite soon took to painting miniatures and became very popular, obtaining several royal patrons and a generally distinguished clientèle. He is thought to have been responsible for the innovation of joining together several pieces of ivory in order to accommodate the large portraits which he favoured. It was a most unsatisfactory method, for ivory is a treacherous material and changes of temperature have a disastrous effect upon it. His two largest works measuring 27 in. × 37 in. portrayed the 'Marriage of Queen Victoria' and the 'Christening of the Prince of Wales'. In 1822 he married Anne Faulder by whom he had a son, H. R. Newton, who became an architect. In 1833 he was appointed miniature-painter-in-ordinary to the King and Queen and in 1837, the year of Queen Victoria's accession, he was knighted.

His work is rather uneven in quality. The majority of his miniatures have a characteristic brown shading in the face, particularly in his early work. He used both rectangular and oval formats and his signature is usually to be found on the back, together with his address and the date.

SIR WILLIAM CHARLES ROSS, R.A. (1794–1860) was one of the most outstanding miniaturists of the nineteenth century. He was born in London on 6th March, 1794, into a family which originated in Ross-shire. His father, an artist who painted miniatures, portraits and groups which he exhibited at the Royal Academy, also taught drawing, his son being one of his pupils. The boy's talents showed themselves early and between the ages of 13 and 23 he had won at least ten prizes from the Society of Arts, one being for an original portrait of the Duke of Norfolk. In 1808 he entered the Royal Academy Schools and obtained several silver medals. From 1809 to 1859 he exhibited at the Academy, showing mostly portrait miniatures.

When in 1814 Andrew Robertson found that he had sufficient clients to warrant his employing an assistant he engaged Ross to help in painting the backgrounds of his miniatures. This was purely mechanical work and must have been frustrating to a young man with the ability to paint pictures of his own. Once he became known his popularity soon grew and as he was skilled in painting historical subjects and oil portraits he obtained a distinguished patronage, including members of the Royal Family. He was a prolific artist and soon became the leading miniaturist of the day. In 1837 he was appointed Miniature Painter to the Queen and commissioned by her to paint numerous portraits of the Royal Family. Elected an A.R.A. in 1838, he was advanced to full membership four years later and was knighted in the same year. He painted as many as 22,000 miniatures before a paralytic stroke brought his career to an end. He died in 1860 and was buried at Highgate.

His miniatures are well designed, show great accuracy of draughtsmanship and are painted in rich colours; they possess all the grace and charm of the Victorian Age at its best. A miniature illustrated by Mr Hand[1] in his book *Signed Miniatures* is of Napoleon III and measures $17\frac{3}{4}$ in. $\times$ $13\frac{1}{2}$ in., which is an exceptional size. While well painted, it is not, however, a typical example of Ross's work, which is usually more attractive. He frequently inscribed his work 'Sir W. C. Ross, R.A. miniature painter to the Queen' followed by the date.

JOHN LINNELL (1792–1882), born in Bloomsbury, London, was the son of a carver, gilder and picture dealer. He was taught painting by John Varley and in 1805 was a pupil at the Royal Academy Schools and was instructed in the art of miniature painting by James Holmes. In early life he was much influenced by William Blake, the poet, painter and engraver. Linnell is best known for his landscape paintings, which he much preferred to portraiture. Consequently, miniatures by him do not often appear, and the majority of them date from 1805–27. He exhibited at the Royal Academy, the British Institution and the Old Water Colour Society, and executed some engravings.

His miniatures are painted in a much more casual style than one is accustomed to see and he had a curious method of stippling, not easy to describe. The British Museum have a miniature by him of George Rennie, a civil engineer and son of John Rennie, famous for his construction of London Bridge, Waterloo Bridge and Southwark Bridge.

SIMON JACQUES ROCHARD (1788–1872), son of René Rochard who died while he was still a child, was born in Paris on 28th December, 1788. He showed an early aptitude for art and drew crayon portraits to help support his widowed mother and her twelve children. He studied engraving as well as miniature painting and is supposed to have been a pupil of Isabey and to have studied at the Académie du Louvre. Augustin employed him to copy some of his miniatures. In 1815 he came to England with introductions from the Duke of Richmond and Lady Caroline Lamb. His work met with such success that he became very popular and obtained a distinguished clientèle, including Princess Charlotte. He exhibited at the Royal Academy, the British Institution, the Society of British Artists and the New Water Colour Society. He is said to have been influenced by Reynolds and Lawrence, and his miniatures are indeed charming and brilliantly executed.

[1] *Signed Miniatures*, 1925, p. 3.

179. JOHN LINNELL (1792–1882)
George Rennie (1791–1866). $4\frac{1}{2} \times 3\frac{3}{8}$ in.

180. JOHN COX DILLMAN ENGLEHEART
(1784–1862)
An unknown man.

181. REGINALD EASTON (1807–93)
An unknown lady. $5\frac{9}{16} \times 4\frac{1}{2}$ in.

182. JOHN HASLEM (1808–84)
Prince Albert (1819–61). $5\frac{1}{4} \times 4\frac{1}{4}$ in.

183. MARIA CHALON
(Mrs Henry Mosley, 1800?–67)
Mr William Mellish. Signed and dated 1832.
$6\frac{5}{8} \times 5$ in.

184. ROBERT THORBURN, A.R.A. (1818–85)
Lady Munro. $5\frac{3}{4} \times 4\frac{1}{4}$ in.

185. ALFRED TIDEY (1808–92)
Sir John Conroy (1786–1854). Dated 1836.
$6\frac{5}{8} \times 4\frac{1}{2}$ in.

186. JOHN FAED, R.S.A. (1819–1902)
Mrs Mary Anne Jean Robertson, *née* Manson.
Dated 1854. $7\frac{1}{16} \times 5$ in.

187. SIR WILLIAM CHARLES ROSS, R.A. (1794–1860)
Prince Albert. $7\frac{7}{8} \times 5\frac{3}{16}$ in.

188. MURIEL SMITH
Helen Foskett (b. 1943).
Signed and dated 1954.
$2\frac{13}{32} \times 1\frac{15}{16}$ in.

189.
WINIFRED CECILE
DONGWORTH (b. 1893)
Daphne Kirk (b. 1911).
Signed and dated 1915.
$2\frac{1}{8} \times 1\frac{5}{8}$ in.

190.
SIR WILLIAM CHARLES ROSS, R.A.
The Hon. L. M. Portman. $2\frac{3}{4} \times 2\frac{3}{8}$ in.

191. FRANCES ELIZABETH WAY
(Mrs Thacker) (1871–1961)
King George V (1865–1936). Signed.
$3\frac{3}{8} \times 2\frac{21}{32}$ in.

Before leaving France he had married Henriette Petitjean but she did not accompany him to England and in 1846 he settled and exhibited in Brussels. At the age of eighty, he married a second time, the lady's name being Henriette Pilton. He died in Brussels in June 1872.

His brother, FRANÇOIS THÉODORE ROCHARD (1798–1858) was an equally gifted artist. He too was born in France and after studying art in Paris came over to England in 1820 to assist his brother who, by that time, was well established. He exhibited at the Royal Academy in 1820 and in 1823 was awarded the Silver Isis Medal from the Society of Arts for a water-colour copy of a portrait, and the same for an oil copy of an historical subject. Like his brother he soon became popular and his work was quite as well executed as that of Simon. He exhibited at the Society of British Artists and at the New Water Colour Society, of which he was made a member in 1835. On his marriage in 1850 he retired from painting. He must have been a prudent man for he was able to live on his savings. He went to live at Notting Hill where he remained until his death in 1858. Both brothers painted in a similar style and as the signature in either case is often just 'Rochard' without any initials, it is difficult to be sure to which brother a work belongs.

WILLIAM EGLEY (1798–1870) came from Yorkshire, being born in Doncaster. His early employment was in the house of a London publisher, but evidently he did not find the work congenial and in spite of lack of training pursued a career in art. He spent several difficult years before he succeeded in obtaining quite a distinguished clientèle. He exhibited from 1824–69, principally at the Royal Academy. A portrait of the artist by his son, William Maw Egley, is in the British Museum and the Victoria and Albert Museum possesses a miniature signed 'Painted by William Egley, 175 Connaught Terrace, Hyde Park, London'. He died in London in March, 1870. His miniatures bear a slight resemblance to the works of Sir William Ross but he never acquired such elegance in his composition and his painting was harder and occasionally rather careless.

REGINALD EASTON (1807–93) was another self-taught artist but in spite of this initial handicap he succeeded in becoming a fashionable painter both in water colour and in miniature and is particularly noted for his portraits of children. He was an exhibitor at the Royal Academy from 1835–87 and lived most of his life in London except during the year 1850, when he had an address at 4 Somers Place, Leamington. He was patronized by the Royal Family and examples of his work are in the Royal Collection at Windsor.

MRS HENRY MOSELEY, née MARIA A. CHALON (1800?–1867) was the daughter of Henry Barnard Chalon, who was noted for his paintings of animals. She is thought to have been born in London, and from an early age took a keen interest in music and painting and took lessons from her father and some of his friends, turning later to miniature painting. In 1813 and again in 1818 the Society of Arts made her an award and she exhibited at the British Institution and at the Royal Academy from 1819–66, among her exhibits being portraits of her father, James Ward, R.A., and J. Tenniel of *Punch*. In about 1823 she obtained an appointment as 'Portrait Paintress to the Duke of York'. Her work is of a high quality and like William Egley's resembles that of Sir William Ross. She is said to have painted miniatures in oil as well as water colour. Her husband, whom she married in about 1841, was Henry Moseley, a portrait painter. A miniature in my collection of W. Mellish of Nottinghamshire signed on the back 'Maria Chalon, pinxit, 1832' is full of character and shows good draughtsmanship. The features are painted with brush strokes rather than stippling and the shading round the mouth and sides of the head is grey. There are signs of the scraper being used in the hair and a fair amount of gum is apparent on the jacket and in the background.

ROBERT THORBURN, A.R.A., H.R.S.A. (1818–85) was a Scottish artist born at Dumfries in March, 1818. He developed a talent for drawing while quite a boy and at the age of fifteen was sent as a pupil to the Drawing Academy of the Royal Institution of Scotland in Edinburgh, where he received some tuition from Sir W. Allan and was successful in obtaining two first prizes. In about 1836 he went to London and studied at the Royal Academy Schools but finding that he was not becoming known as quickly as he would have liked, he took up miniature painting, a change made primarily in order to support not only himself but other members of his family. He exhibited at the Royal Academy from 1837 to 1884 and between 1835 and 1856 at the Royal Scottish Academy, of which he became an honorary member in 1857. He exhibited mostly from different addresses in London and in 1855 won a gold medal at the Paris Exhibition. For a time he worked in Edinburgh and the National Galleries of Scotland possess several very good miniatures by him, mostly rectangular, the sizes varying from $5\frac{3}{4}$ in. × $4\frac{1}{4}$ in. to 12 in. × $11\frac{1}{2}$ in. He lived for a time at Kelso but in 1884 went to Tunbridge Wells, where he remained until his death in November 1885. His painting was good and his composition attractive. He was commissioned by members of the Royal Family and many eminent people.

MISS ANNIE DIXON (worked 1844–1901) was born at Horncastle and appears to have executed her early works there, up to the year 1846. She worked in Hull in 1852 for a year and then went to St Lawrence, Isle of Wight and later to London, exhibiting at the Royal Academy between 1844 and 1893. Much of her work was done in private houses. She was also employed by the Royal Family and examples of her work are at Windsor Castle. The Victoria and Albert Museum has a miniature of a lady by her signed 'painted by A. Dixon, 1855'.

ALFRED TIDEY (1808–92) was the son of J. Tidey, proprietor of a private school at Worthing, where the artist was born. (His brother, Henry, also painted water colours.) It is not known when or by whom he was taught painting but soon after he went to London he became popular and obtained many notable sitters. He was an exhibitor at the Royal Academy from 1831 and also at the Society of British Artists. In 1834 he became a pupil of the Royal Academy Schools and later a member of the Dudley Gallery Art Society. He numbered among his sitters members of the Royal Family, the Empress Frederik, Crown Princess of Germany, Dr Arnold of Rugby, Miss Ellen Tree and other distinguished persons. He lived for most of his career in London, but was for a time in Jersey and at Twickenham and enjoyed travelling on the Continent. Tidey was considered a good artist and draughtsman. A manuscript list of his works is in the Victoria and Albert Museum, and there is a portrait by him of Sir John Conroy (1786–1854) at the National Portrait Gallery. He died at Glenelg, Springfield Park, Acton, on 2nd April, 1892.

JOHN HASLEM (1808–84) is more readily associated with the Derby China Works than with painting and although he had a great deal to do with porcelain-making he was at the same time an accomplished artist. Born at Carrington in Cheshire, where he began his education, he was later sent to Derby to be trained by an uncle. When fourteen years of age he became an apprentice at the Derby China Works and was taught flower painting by George Hancock, who had been employed at the factory since 1818. Haslem had a great love of art and in his spare time practised drawing and painting, executing enamels, portraits on china and in water colour, nearly all from life. He was patronized by members of the Royal Family including the Duke of Sussex and the Duchess of Gloucester. In 1835 he went to London and studied under E. T. Parris (1793–1873), a fashionable portrait painter. Miniatures by Haslem are not often seen, but the Derby Art Gallery possesses one of Prince Albert which is a good example of his work.

JOHN FAED, R.S.A. (1819–1902) was a native of Scotland, born near Gatehouse-of-Fleet, Kircudbrightshire, where his father was a mill-wright, farmer and engineer. He is reputed to have shown at an early age more than average talent as a miniature painter. For a time he was inclined to wander from place to place executing paintings, but in 1841 he went to Edinburgh and from 5 York Place began exhibiting at the Royal Scottish Academy, continuing to do so from various addresses until 1895. Not all his exhibits were miniatures and he is best known for figure subjects and outdoor scenes. He studied at the Trustees Academy and spent much of his time painting in oil. In Edinburgh he soon succeeded in obtaining patrons and had a very successful practice. In 1847 he was elected an Associate of the Royal Scottish Academy, being made a full member in 1851. He lived in London from about 1862 to 1880, during which time he exhibited at the

Royal Academy. When in his sixty-first year he returned to Scotland and spent his remaining years at Gatehouse-of-Fleet, where he died. He had a number of children, four of whom became artists. His painting is good and his technique somewhat resembles that of Sir W. C. Ross. A portrait in my collection of Mrs Robertson, née Mary Anne Manson, wife of Captain Robertson of the 8th King's Foot, painted in 1854 for her aunt, is one of the most attractive nineteenth-century miniatures that I have ever seen. The sitter is dressed in pale green silk, her bodice is edged with pale mauve ribbon with a deeper mauve border and there is a mauve shot silk shawl draped over the left corner of the chair on which she is placed. Every detail of the lace bodice and sleeves is shown to perfection, as is the brooch which is pinned to the collar. The features of an obviously beautiful woman are drawn and painted with a delicate touch.

As the nineteenth century drew to a close and photography became more and more popular, fewer miniatures of any quality were painted and the art remained in the hands of a small number of artists. The portraits produced were, on the whole, not to be compared with those executed by the miniaturists of the past and many took advantage of the possibilities of photography by having a faint photographic base placed on the ivory before the painting was started. This practice still continues and in many cases it has reduced miniature painting to a mechanical art rather than the execution of original portraits. The production of portrait miniatures on any large scale has never been revived although a limited number of artists have continued to paint miniatures for those patrons who required them.

Among the twentieth-century artists whose work I have seen are some who have maintained the standard of miniature painting at its best.

ALYN WILLIAMS, P.R.M.S. (b. 1865) was noted for his interest in guiding the destinies of the Royal Miniaturist Society, founded in 1894, of which he was President and which still holds annual Exhibitions in London each year. He was a popular painter and much of his work is in America.

FRANCES ELIZABETH WAY, afterwards MRS THACKER, (1871–1961), was an artist who obtained the patronage of the Royal Family. Two miniatures in my collection, one of the late King George V and the other of Queen Mary painted soon after their marriage when they were Duke and Duchess of York, are very good likenesses. The features are well painted, the flesh colouring has a slightly brick red hue, and the draughtsmanship is good. The background is painted in with numerous vertical brush strokes.

I am purposely illustrating a modern miniature in order to show that it is still possible to commission artists to paint portraits in this way. The artist, Miss MURIEL SMITH of Nottingham, is a most accomplished painter, not only in miniature but in oils, crayon and pencil. She has the gift of reading the character of her sitters and putting down what she sees so that her paintings are very lifelike and viewed from any angle the sitter is easily recognizable. The miniature of my daughter Helen at the age of eleven was exhibited at the Royal Miniaturist Society in 1954 and at the French Salon in 1956.

CHAPTER XXI

THE EYE OF THE COLLECTOR

*

It is impossible to do more than suggest ways in which the collector may train his eye to discern the factors which must be taken into consideration when purchasing miniatures for, as in any other field of collecting, knowledge can be acquired only gradually.

It is essential to study the art by visiting as frequently as possible galleries and museums and, where opportunity occurs, private collections, taking note of the mannerisms of the artists, the way in which they applied their paints, the type of background used and any other peculiarities, such as the use of vellum, card, ivory, etc. An acquaintance with the costume of different periods is necessary to establish a date with any degree of certainty and any information available about the subject or provenance of a miniature is of the utmost importance.

This basic knowledge is essential if a sound and independent judgment is to be brought to bear on a proposed acquisition, and I cannot emphasize too strongly the advantage to be gained from an examination of as many miniatures as possible of every quality and period, for without such experience a collector may easily acquire portraits of poor quality, or even fakes.

To examine a miniature adequately it is necessary to use a strong lens, if possible in daylight, so as to detect any touching up or repainting. Under magnification, fresh paint can usually be discerned, for when it is applied over old pigments it tends to be slightly more raised than the original surface, and a difference in colour is often apparent. Cracks in the ivory may also be revealed. It is advisable to avoid purchasing miniatures which have been damaged or restored, except of course for rarities.

A form of deception frequently practised is the placing of a false signature on the portrait, and miniatures with well-known names attached to them should be viewed with suspicion. Although the discovery of an important portrait in an unexpected place is not impossible, it is a piece of luck that may not happen more than once in a lifetime. Important portraits which appear on the market usually emanate from some old family in whose possession they have been since they were painted. When sold they tend to gravitate to the London sale rooms, and may with confidence be purchased from a reputable dealer.

Only recently I was offered a miniature copy on ivory of the painting of Oliver Cromwell by Robert Walker (d. 1658) which was said to be contemporary with the original. As ivory was not used for miniatures at that period it was an obvious imitation. Instances such as this are not infrequent. One is constantly being offered miniatures, supposedly by well-known artists, framed in square ivory frames made from old piano keys, or in frames of gilt metal with bows of metal ribbon decorating the top. Both these types are produced on the Continent, and more often than not the miniatures they contain are carelessly painted and have spurious signatures on the front which are quite unlike those of Cosway, Smart, Plimer and Engleheart, the favourite names. The painting is generally a thin wash of water colour, the details being often picked out in opaque white, over an almost invisible photographic base, the faint lines of which can be detected by careful examination, especially round the eyes and the outline of the face. Another form of deception is that of painting over prints and framing them in eighteenth-century frames. Here again a lens is invaluable, the best place to look for this imposture being where the colours are light and do not therefore conceal the printed line or stippled shading.

The value of portrait miniatures varies from year to year and one cannot do better than note the prices obtained in well-known sale rooms as a guide to current values, bearing in mind of course that miniatures of great historic or artistic interest are likely to command prices well beyond the normal range.

Whilst the beginner should endeavour to purchase items by using his own judgment, he would be wise at the outset to confine himself to modest sums. If he is tempted to buy expensive miniatures he should do so only from reputable dealers whose years of experience and reputation are the best guarantee of the authenticity of the goods they sell.

One cannot of course expect to buy from dealers at the prices they themselves have paid in the sale rooms, since they are entitled to a profit for their experience, their time, and their guarantee, but most of them are willing to advise the collector and to buy for him on commission any particular item which may appear at an auction. In spite of the upward trend of prices, it is still possible to buy a good portrait miniature for a modest sum.

When contemplating a purchase the quality and condition of the painting should first be considered and the probable date assessed from the general character and appearance and dress of the sitter. If no information is available about the portrait it is sometimes possible to identify the subject by examination of contemporary portrait prints, large collections of which are usually available to the serious student in the great public galleries. An attempt should be made to attribute the work to a particular artist and the collector's success in doing this will depend upon how closely he has studied authentic examples.

A signature, if not at once apparent, should be searched for. Signatures are sometimes found at the extreme edge of the background, or partly concealed in the hair, the draperies, or the shading. They are often visible only when the light falls at a certain angle, and the miniatures should be turned and tilted until the entire surface has been scrutinized.

When a miniature has been purchased the glass may require cleaning and although this is a delicate operation it can be done by wiping the surface gently with a camel hair paint brush, which should be dry. No moisture should be allowed on to the surface while it is exposed. The glass after cleaning must be perfectly dry before being replaced. Exceptionally fine portraits and those in valuable frames or lockets are best dealt with by a professional restorer or artist.

Any collection must be preserved with great care as the pigments, particularly those used on the face, are fugitive and if exposed to the direct sunlight will fade and ruin the portrait. Miniatures on ivory must be kept in an even temperature or the ivory may crack, and a form of mildew may appear on the painting as a result of condensation from the convex lenses often used to cover the portrait.

As a general rule it is a mistake to remove miniatures permanently from their original frames unless this is necessary because of damage. It is an open question whether or not they should be taken from the leather cases in which they were often kept, for although these are less attractive than open frames they have the advantage of preserving the colouring of the portrait.

An example of this may be seen at the Ashmolean Museum, where two identical miniatures of a young lady are shown as a warning. One has been kept away from the light and has retained its brilliance, while the other has been exposed to the sun and has consequently faded.

The best method is to house the miniatures in cabinets or frames to which a curtain is attached, or to hang them on a wall away from the light.

It is essential to catalogue even a small collection, not only because such data is interesting, but because it facilitates insurance. Any information available about each portrait should be noted, e.g. the names of the artist and the sitter, its previous history, its date and where it was acquired, and the price paid.

While there are those who confine their purchases to a particular century or to a group of artists, the majority will probably buy more generally and include in their collection a wide variety of artists of all periods. This method is often more rewarding, as miniatures purchased with care and knowledge will not only give lasting pleasure to their owners but may be the means of supplying new information about some artists and their work. The not too conservative collector will include good contemporary work and thus preserve in his collection examples of the skill of miniaturists of our own day side by side with others from the past.

BIBLIOGRAPHY

*

AUERBACH, ERNA, *Nicholas Hilliard*, 1961, London.

BOEHN, MAX V., *Miniaturen und Silhouetten*, 1917, Germany.

BOLTON, T., *Early American Portrait Painters in Miniature*, 1921, New York.

BOUCHOT, HENRI, *La Miniature Française*, 1907, Paris.

BOURGOING, J. DE, *Die Wiener Bildnisminiatur*, 1926, Vienna.

     Die Englische Bildnisminiatur, 1927, Vienna.

     Die Französische Bildnisminiatur, 1928, Vienna.

BRYAN, MICHAEL, *Dictionary of Painters and Engravers*. Revised and enlarged by Dr George C. Williamson, 1903–5, London.

BRYDALL, ROBERT, *History of Art in Scotland*, 1859, Edinburgh and London.

Burlington Fine Arts Club Exhibition, 1889. Two Editions, one without plates.

Burlington Magazine, London.

 November, 1943. *Holbein's Miniatures* by Carl Winter.

 March, 1947. *A Miniature Self-Portrait by Thomas Flatman* by Graham Reynolds.

 July, 1947. *Nicholas Hilliard, Some Unpublished Documents* by Noel Blaikiston.

 July, 1947. *Hilliard and Elizabethan Miniatures* by Carl Winter.

 April, 1948. *Nicholas Hilliard, and Queen Elizabeth's Third Great Seal* by Noel Blaikiston.

 June, 1949. *More Light on Nicholas Hilliard* by Erna Auerbach.

 June, 1949. *Nicholas Hilliard as a Traveller* by Noel Blaikiston.

 November, 1959. *Gerard and Lucas Horenbout* by Hugh Paget.

COLDING, T. H., *Danish Miniatures*, 1948, Copenhagen.

     Aspects of Miniature Painting, 1953, Copenhagen.

Connoisseur, March, 1953, *Mrs Mary Beale* by Elizabeth Walsh.

CUNNINGHAM, ALAN, *The Lives of the Most Eminent British Painters*, 1846, London.

Dictionary of National Biography, Oxford.

EDWARDS, E., *Anecdotes of Painters in England*, 1808.

FIELDING, M., *Dictionary of American Painters*, 1926.

FISHER, A., *Enamelling on Metal*, 1906, London.

FOSTER, J. J., *British Miniature Painters and their Works*, 1898, London.

    Miniature Painters British and Foreign, 2 vols, 1903. London and New York.

FOSTER, J. J., *Chats on Old Miniatures*, 1908, London.

Samuel Cooper and the English Miniature Painters of the Eighteenth Century, 1914–16, London.

Dictionary of Painters of Miniatures, 1926, London.

GOULDING, R. W., *The Welbeck Abbey Miniatures*, Walpole Soc. Vol. IV, 1916, Oxford.

GRAVES, ALGERNON A., *Dictionary of Artists*, 1901, London.

The Society of Artists of Great Britain, and the Free Society, 1907 London.

The British Institution, 1908, London.

The Royal Academy of Arts, 1905–6, London.

GANZ, PAUL, *Holbein*, 1949, London.

HAND, SIDNEY, *Signed Miniatures*, 1925, London.

HARDIE, MARTIN, *Miniatura, or the art of Limning*, 1919, London. Reprint of Norgate's *Treatis*.

HENNESSY, JOHN POPE, *A Lecture on Nicholas Hilliard*, 1949, London.

HOERSCHELMANN, VON B., *Rosalba Carriera*, 1908, Leipzig.

JAFFÉ, ALBERT, *Miniaturen Katalog*, 1900, Hamburg.

JAFFÉ, ARTHUR, Article on John Smart in the *Art Quarterly*, Autumn 1954.

Jewish Historical Society of England, Vol. XVIII, 1958, London.

JOSEPH, EDWARD, *Catalogue of a Collection of Miniatures*, 1883, privately printed.

KENNEDY, H. A., *Early English Portrait Miniatures in the Collection of the Duke of Buccleuch*, Studio, 1917, London.

LAMB, SIR WALTER R. M., *The Royal Academy*, 1951, London.

LISTER, RAYMOND, *The British Miniaturist*, 1951, London.

LONG, BASIL S., *The British Miniaturists*, 1924, London.

LUGIT, F., *Le Portrait Miniature*, 1917, Amsterdam.

LUND, E. F. S., *Danske Malede Portraeter*, 1912, Copenhagen.

MCKAY, W. D., *The Scottish School of Painting*, 1906, London, New York.

MORGAN, J. PIERPONT, *Illustrated Sale Cat.*, 1935, London.

NACHEMSOHN, JACOB, *Signed Enamel Miniatures*, 1926, London.

NORGATE, WILLIAM, *Miniatura*, c. 1648.

PEACHAM, HENRY, *The Gentlemans Exercise*, 1st Edit., 1607, London.

The Compleat Gentleman, 1st Edit., 1622, London.

PORCHER, JEAN, *French Miniatures*, Paris 1959, London 1960.

PROPERT, J. LUMSDEN, *A History of Miniature Art*, 1887, London and New York.

Cat. of his collection, 1880, privately printed.

REDGRAVE, SAMUEL, *A Dictionary of Artists of the English School*, 1878, London.

REYNOLDS, GRAHAM, *English Portrait Miniatures*, 1952, London.

Rijksmuseum Cat. of Pictures, 1910, Amsterdam.

ROBERTSON, EMILY, *Letters and Papers of Andrew Robertson*, 1895, London.

Royal Society of Arts, Derek Hudson and Kenneth W. Luckhurst, 1954, London.

SALMI, MARIO, *Italian Miniatures*, 1957, London.

SCHIDLOF, L., *Die Bildnisminiatur in Frankreich*, 1911, Leipzig.

SMITH, J. T., *Nollekens and his Times*, 1914, London.

South Kensington Museum, *Portrait Miniatures, and a series of photographs of them*, 1865, London.

STRICKLAND, W. G., *Dictionary of Irish Artists*, 1913, London.

USHER, WARD J. W., *An Art Collector's Treasures*, 1916, London.

Victoria and Albert Museum Publications.

    Pfungst Collection, 1915.

    Wellesley Collection, 1915.

    Nicholas Hilliard and Isaac Oliver, 1947.

    Portrait Miniatures, 1948, reprint 1959.

    Illustrated Hand List of Miniatures and Silhouettes, 1930.

Wallace Collection, W. P. Gibson, 1935, London.

Walpole Soc. Vol. I, 1911–12, Oxford.

          XVII, 1928–9.

          XIX, 1930–1.

          XXXII, 1946–8.

WALPOLE, HORACE, *Anecdotes of Painting in England*, 1st Edit., 1762–71, 3 vols., 1862, London.

WEHLE, HARRY B., *American Miniaturists*, 1948, New York.

WHEATLEY, H. B., *Historical Portraits*, 1847, London.

WHITTOCK, N., *The Miniature Painters Manual*, 1844, London.

WILLIAMSON, DR GEORGE C., *Portrait Miniatures*, 1897, London.

        Richard Cosway, R.A., 1897.

             1905.

      George Engleheart, 1902. Privately printed.

      Andrew and Nathaniel Plimer, 1903.

      The History of Portrait Miniatures, 2 vols., 1904.

      How to identify Portrait Miniatures, 1904.

      Miniatures at Belvoir Castle, 1904. Privately printed.

      Miniatures at Devonshire House, 1905. Privately printed.

      Miniatures at Castle Howard, 1905. Privately printed.

      Catalogue of the Collection, the property of J. Pierpont Morgan, 1906–8. Privately printed.

      John Downman, A.R.A., 1907.

WILLIAMSON, DR GEORGE C., *Portrait Miniatures English and Foreign*, Studio 1910, London, Paris, New York.

    Catalogue of the Duke of Cumberland's Collection, 1914. Privately printed.

    Ozias Humphry, R.A., 1918, London and New York.

    The Miniature Collector, 1921, London.

    Daniel Gardner, 1921, London, New York.

    Cat. of Lord Hothfield's Coll., 1916.

WILLIAMSON, DR GEORGE C., AND P. BUCKMAN, *The Art of the Miniature Painter*, 1926, London.

INDEX

*

References to the numbers of the monochrome plates are in **bold** type,
and those to the numbers of the colour plates are in **bold type within brackets**

189